Alan Stewart is a retired police inspector who specialised in poaching cases in the 1960s and 70s. Most of his service with Tayside Police from 1980 to 1993 was in CID in Perth and Drugs Branch at Force HQ. He was appointed Force Wildlife Liaison Officer in 1993. He lives in Perthshire with his wife Jan, two dogs and twenty domestic ducks. He is widely recognised as a pioneer in the area of wildlife crime detection and has promoted the cause of wildlife protection in books, magazines and on radio and tv.

Cover Photos:

(top left) A badger leaving a sett (Photo: Laurie Campbell)

(top middle) Typical police recovery after a search of an egg thief's car (Photo: author)

(top right) Goshawk seized during falconry raid (Photo: RSPB Investigations)

(bottom left) Using glass-bottomed buckets to look for freshwater pearl mussels in an Irish river (Photo: Padraigh Comerford, NPWS)

(bottom middle) The author with a Sulcata tortoise (Photo: Tayside Police)

(bottom right) A vet begins a post mortem examination of a seal, with notes being taken by Constable Bob Veighey, Shetland (Photo:Snr Insp Ron Patterson, Scottish SPC⅃

THE THIN GREEN LINE

ALAN STEWART

ARGYLL ✠ PUBLISHING

For my beloved daughters, Janet,
Andrea, Norma, and of course Leigh.

Argyll Publishing

Glendaruel

Argyll PA22 3AE

www.argyllpublishing.com

British Library Cataloguing-in-
Publication Data.

**A catalogue record for this book
is available from the Britis
Library.**

ISBN 978 1 906134 37 2

Printing

Bell & Bain Ltd, Glasgow

A North Wales police officer watches as an RSPB officer climbs to view into a goshawk nest – see North Wales chapter (Photo: RSPB)

Police and Customs officers searching a traditional Chinese medicine shop in South London

(above left) Elephant tusks seized during an operation against the illegal trade in ivory

(above right) Ivory shaving brushes seized

(left) The Metropolitan Police Wildlife Crime Unit display at an event in London

All four photos are by David Flint, MPS Wildlife Crime Unit – see chapter on London

Contents

The author with a Sulcata tortoise (Photo: Tayside Police)

ACKNOWLEDGEMENTS

This book would not have been possible without a huge amount of help from police colleagues, friends and some of the many people that I meet, speak with or communicate with by email on a regular basis. Detecting wildlife crime depends on a network of experts; writing a book about the subject is no different. Learning of these wildlife incidents has taken me – in most cases literally – to many parts of Britain and Ireland.

Most of those who have helped with or contributed text, ideas or photographs are mentioned in the chapter that relates to their particular adventures and I am indebted to you. For those who do not get a mention in the book I am equally grateful and will buy you a malt whisky the next time we meet. Remind me!

Special thanks must go to son-in-law and editor Sean Bradley, who worked tirelessly to advise on text and edit once it was committed to print. His literary flair has converted a chimera of chapters into a book.

Alan Stewart
May 2009

Typical police recovery after a search of an egg thief's car
– see North Wales chapter

FOREWORD

With a university education based on zoology and conservation
it is not altogether surprising that during thirty years' police
service I have maintained an interest in wildlife crime. In an
early stage of my career I became the first Wildlife Liaison Officer
in Sussex Police but it was not until 2002, when as Chief
Constable of North Wales I accepted the 'wildlife crime portfolio'
for the Association of Chief Police Officers (ACPO), that my
professional involvement became meaningful.

It is true to say that wildlife crime has never been seen as a
high priority for policing; it was not so when I accepted the
ACPO portfolio, and it will not be when shortly I retire and pass
it on. The Home Secretary, who sets our national objectives (in
England and Wales), will naturally always have bigger fish to fry.
However I think there is now a growing acceptance in
government and in the higher echelons of the police service that
wildlife crime is real police work. Parliament in London has
certainly made that point clear by repeatedly strengthening the
law, and the Scottish Parliament has also been unequivocal in its
support. As a result the law has changed much and for the better
in the last few years. I will not attempt to list the changes here,
save to draw attention to the introduction across the UK of
custodial sentences for some wildlife offences. This has had a
seminal effect, giving a much needed demonstration that our
parliaments see wildlife crime as a serious matter.

There is no place in the police service for a Wildlife Crime
Officer who wishes to pursue his or her own agenda. While it is
likely, even desirable, that a WCO will have a deep interest in
wildlife and environmental matters they must, in this as in all
other aspects of our work as officers of the law, maintain a strict
impartiality. If the police service as a whole is tasked with
addressing wildlife crime then we must approach the task in the
same professional and structured manner with which we
address any other area of work. The work of a WCO is a
professional task, not a hobby, and the investigation of wildlife
crime has recently developed rather dramatically as a
professional discipline within the police service in line with this
thinking.

The police service thrives on intelligence; it is one of the
primary drivers for our work. Wildlife crime, as is evidenced by

Alan Stewart, can involve serious and organised criminal activity that can only be addressed through the gathering and subsequent organised deliberate use of intelligence. In 2004, with the support of Home Office, Defra and ACPO, a small National Wildlife Crime Intelligence Unit (NWCIU) was established. This was a major step forward. It did much to raise the profile of wildlife crime as a 'real' subject and led quickly to the creation of government endorsed 'UK Wildlife Crime Priorities' for enforcers. For the very first time formal consideration was being given by government and the enforcement agencies to the threat posed by wildlife crime. Further developments have resulted in the present UK National Wildlife Crime Unit (NWCU) now based near Edinburgh. It is a now freestanding national unit under police command with overt government support. It is no longer just an intelligence unit – as well as intelligence and analytical capability it employs Investigations Support Officers whose job is to assist WCOs around the UK with the growing number of more complicated investigations. NWCU has already earned a national and international reputation for excellence, and its advice and assistance is in much demand. It is healthy, and its future looks rosy. I predict that it will grow in size and impact in the years to come.

The 'UK Wildlife Crime Priorities' are an essential part of the professional response. The UK government's statutory nature conservation advisor is the Joint Nature Conservation Committee (JNCC). We in the police are not competent to decide where the national conservation priorities lie, and without scientific help we will inevitably end up simply responding to those things reported to us, like badger baiting (a welfare crime, not one of conservation importance) rather than focusing our available resources where they can do the most good. An annual meeting now takes place each January chaired by JNCC at which the statutory nature conservation organisations, relevant non-governmental bodies and the enforcement agencies meet to decide the conservation priorities for enforcement. This process has become highly successful in, for instance, highlighting the need to concentrate our efforts to protect the freshwater pearl mussel, or the illegal trade in tortoises. Our enforcement work now has a strong scientific underpinning. This scientific base is not enough, however. The NWCU's analysis has clearly highlighted a need to respond to public demand for the police to deal with poaching and badger baiting as common crimes against wildlife even though there is usually little direct conservation need. As a result the UK's Wildlife Crime Priorities are now very firmly based in science *and* a wide range of public opinion, and can be firmly relied upon in deciding how to utilise our resources – a really significant development.

One further significant change has taken place in recent years – the advent of the seconded police officer into non-police conservation agencies. This started in 2001 with the attachment of a North Wales police sergeant to the Countryside Council for Wales (CCW), at shared cost. This concept has been a substantial success in ensuring a consistent and appropriate response across Wales to wildlife crime by the conservation agency and the police. CCW appointed a second police sergeant soon afterwards, heralding a revolution in the management of wildlife crime and allowing the development of specifically Welsh priorities for wildlife crime. This innovation has stood the test of time, with both police and CCW feeling that added value has been obtained, and the relationship has been highly influential in gaining police recognition of the importance of habitat, as opposed to species, crime – a development which has now manifested itself in several successful targeted prosecutions aimed at securing 'favourable conservation status' for the national network of Sites of Special Scientific Interest (SSSIs) – our most highly protected habitats. The idea of embedding seconded police officers is growing in its acceptance and has now spread to the Environment Agency, to the Forestry Commission, to Natural England and most recently to the Animal Health Agency. It is causing a quiet revolution in true partnership-working with real synergy arising from the merger of different perspectives, experiences and legal powers all working on a truly common agenda. Better value is clearly being obtained from the scarce resources that we are able to bring to bear, demonstrably in the public interest. The concept is still developing and I anticipate its further growth, including I hope, in Scotland in the near future.

The past seven years in particular has given me privileged contact with many people and organisations who are deeply engaged in combating wildlife crime. All of what I have said up to this point has related to a growing recognition of the absolute need for the police and other enforcement agencies to tackle these matters in an organised, professional and effective manner as part of our normal business. No better example of doing this can be found than the author of this book.

Alan Stewart's is undoubtedly one of the most readily recognised names amongst wildlife crime enforcers. 'Operation Easter' the national policing operation set up to tackle the taking of wild bird eggs was initiated and has been coordinated by Alan for many years. By any standard it has been hugely successful and has led to leading conservation agencies suggesting that this uniquely British problem has been reduced to an extent where it no longer impacts on the favourable conservation status of any native bird species – a situation almost impossible to envisage even ten years ago and a testament to what can be achieved by people working together, properly motivated, organised and led. My contact with Alan came about through work with the Partnership for Action against Wildlife Crime (PAW) and it soon became clear to me that his work was of enormous benefit to biodiversity not only in Tayside where he continues work as wildlife crime coordinator but also in Scotland and indeed the rest of the United Kingdom.

Devolved government in the UK has become a part of all our lives in recent years and I believe that it has greatly benefited biodiversity. The Scottish Government and Parliament have demonstrated the desire to enhance the protection afforded to Scottish wildlife over and above that offered in England and Wales by the introduction of their own modern legislation which those of us 'south of the border' now view with some envy – and I hope a determination to catch up!

Most recently the Scottish Government has made clear policy statements to the effect that wildlife crime is a heritage issue and will not be tolerated. This stance has won overwhelming support in the Scottish Parliament, and is now being put into practice in Scotland by a resurgent PAW Scotland under the leadership of the Scottish Environment Minister – a situation wholly unimaginable just a few years ago.

Alan has been personally instrumental in helping to bring this situation about. I commend him, and this his latest book, to you and I hope that he will remain active in the field, literally and figuratively, to cement the gains that he has helped to bring about.

Richard Brunstrom
Chief Constable
North Wales Police
February 2009

A brown long-eared bat (Photo: Bat Conservation Trust)
– see Lincolnshire chapter

Introduction

Wildlife crime is diverse in its range, often devastating to a species, usually complex to investigate, with perpetrators difficult to detect and with a low conviction rate. It is crime to which police forces, despite having the statutory responsibility for its investigation, paid little heed until relatively recently. Though crime committed against wildlife figures near the bottom of policing priorities, it captures the imagination, and the sympathy vote, of a large majority of the public.

My first book, *Wildlife Detective* (Argyll 2006), covering wildlife crimes I was involved in investigating in my home police force area of Tayside, was spawned from my involvement (and that of wildlife crime officers in other areas of Scotland) in a four-part 'fly-on-the-wall' television series entitled *Wildlife Detectives*. The interest both in the book and the television series was a revelation, possibly because of the unique amalgam of real-life crime and animals, each of which independently seems to have an irresistible fascination.

The demand led me to expand my horizons and start trawling a range of wildlife crimes, experiences and investigative methods from my colleagues in the rest of the UK and the Republic of Ireland. Over a period of a year and a half this information was gathered, and snowballed to include some animal welfare issues with which the police deal, often in conjunction with animal welfare charities.

The criminals described in the next three hundred or so pages are as heterogeneous as the crimes they commit, and are found to be the employed and unemployed working class, company directors, responsible representatives of councils and millionaire landowners.

The police officers featured are all extremely experienced investigators, while our partner organisations are experts in a variety of other skills, ranging from animal handling and welfare, species identification, species biology to veterinary forensic pathology. The range of characters is multifarious, relating fascinating stories that demonstrate the experience and dedication of a small, highly trained, group of police officers, police staff and specialist agencies. They are the backbone of the fight against criminals who seek to destroy not only our wildlife but our environment; our natural and national heritage. Truly they are the thin green line of policing.

Lurcher dog of the type used in coursing hares
– see chapter Wildlife Crime: A Prosecutor's Perspective

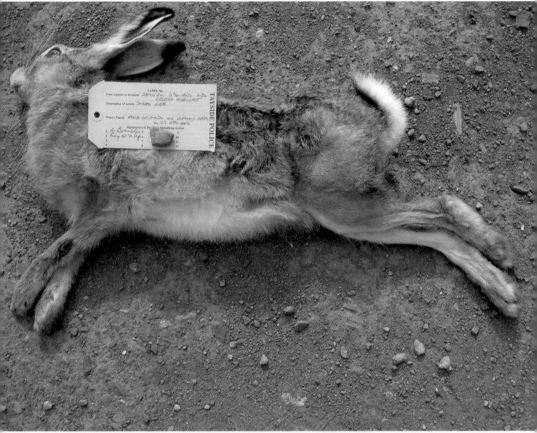

Evidence must be preserved. In hare coursing cases a post mortem examination is usually necessary to prove the means of death

Badger digging equipment, including dog collars and leads, locators for finding dogs underground and knife for killing the victim.

10 week-old badger killed at sett, now as a taxidermy specimen
(Photos: Neil Hughes, Leicestershire Police)

Slipper Orchid – see London chapter (Photo: Kew Gardens, London)

Two poisoned buzzards investigated by the Police Service of Northern Ireland – see Northern Ireland chapter (Photo: PSNI)

Osprey eggs taken in Scotland

Several drawers full of eggs recovered by Andy McWilliam during the search
of an Operation Easter target in Merseyside (Photo: Merseyside Police)
For details of the highly successful Operation Easter, see Note 3, p300

South Wales

Serving a population of 1.2 million, Sergeant Ian Guildford has the main responsibility for policing wildlife crime in South Wales. Of the 3,300 police officers whose help Ian can enlist, there are five trained as wildlife crime officers. Like most forces, they are part-time, fitting in wildlife crime investigation where they can amongst their other general policing responsibilities.

South Wales is a vibrant mix of rural and urban. Its two main cities are Cardiff, an important commercial centre and seat of Welsh Assembly Government, and Swansea, a maritime city with a rich and varied history. The once famous coal mining valleys have given way to light industry and the service sector, although remnants of the old mining industry can still be seen. More rural areas include the beautiful Gower Peninsula, in 1956 the first area in the UK to be designated as an Area of Outstanding Beauty, the Brecon Beacons national park and the Vale of Glamorgan.

South Wales has a first in innovative policing, in that their chief constable, Barbara Wildling QPM, CBE, CCML, has had the foresight to agree to a full time secondment of a wildlife crime officer to work with the Forestry Commission in the Neath area, investigating and advising on wildlife and environmental crime issues on Forestry Commission land.

The variety of wildlife crime with which Ian Guildford deals reflects the diversity of wildlife in the area. Red kites are relatively common, while there are rarities such as choughs, ring ouzels and honey buzzards nesting. Most species of bat can be found, plus good populations of dormice, otters and great-crested newts. In 1997 Ian was the inaugural, though joint, winner of the WWF Wildlife Enforcer of the Year award as a result of a large and successful operation investigating the laundering of wild birds of prey into the legal falconry market. Since 2003 he has been seconded to work with the Countryside Council for Wales (CCW) as a full-time wildlife and environmental crime officer.

Sammy the Sturgeon

One morning in June 2004 Ian Guildford got a phone call from Defra (Department for Environment, Food and Rural Affairs – see Note 5) who had been alerted by a member of the public about a sturgeon being offered for sale at the Plymouth fish market. Wildlife crime officers are never sure what to expect next: this was definitely a first for Ian.

The occurrence of sturgeon in UK coastal waters is quite rare though there have been reports of an increase in the discovery of sturgeon in inland waters. Rather surprisingly, this is believed to be due to the illegal release by fishermen who then catch them for sport. In this case, it appeared that a fisherman operating a small fishing vessel out of Swansea had caught a sturgeon in Swansea Bay, and had taken it to Plymouth fish market to sell it. Having obtained all the necessary details from Defra, Ian then contacted his wildlife crime colleague in Devon and Cornwall Constabulary, Inspector Nevin Hunter, who had just been made aware of the incident. Due to its listing under CITES (Convention on International Trade in Endangered Species – see Note 1) the sale of the sturgeon would have to be licensed by Defra and clearly there was no such licence in force. Nevin therefore quickly contacted the local police station at Plymouth and arranged for officers to attend at the fish market in order to seize it.

Officers with absolutely no background in the investigation of wildlife crime, and who would probably not be able to recognise a sturgeon if it jumped up and slapped them on the face, were duly dispatched and on their arrival they found the fish laid out on a slab ready to be auctioned. They advised the auctioneers at the market that the fish was a protected species and that they intended to seize it in relation to a police enquiry, but returned to their car in order to inform Nevin that the fish was there, and also collect some forms required for the seizure. Bad move. On returning into the fish market the red-faced officers discovered that the 264lb fish had mysteriously disappeared. Not a scale was left. They questioned various members of staff in the market but failed to shed any light on the whereabouts of the monster fish. It later transpired that while the officers were at their car the fish was seen disappearing out of the back door of the market under the arms of two men.

But this was not the end of the tale. After further enquiries by Devon and Cornwall Constabulary the fish turned up at a

The Law on Sturgeon

There are 15 species of sturgeon found across the world. Two of these, the short-nosed sturgeon (*Acipenser brevirostrum*) and the common or Atlantic sturgeon (*Acipenser sturio*), receive protection under both European and UK legislation, being listed under Annex A of CITES (Control on International Trade in Endangered Species of Fauna and Flora – see Notes 3). All other species of Sturgeon are listed under Appendix II and Annex B of CITES, this listing requiring the issue of import/export permits if they are obtained from outside the European Union. Illegal trade in endangered species is investigated by the UK Border Agency at points of entry to the UK under the Customs and Excise Management Act 1979. Once the species are into the UK the investigative responsibility lies with the police, under the Control of Trade in Endangered Species (Enforcement) Regulations 1997 (COTES – see Note 2).

The sturgeon is rarely seen in UK waters and it's a little known fact that the Queen has a claim on any sturgeon caught in British waters or washed up on British beaches as it's classified as a "royal" fish – a status granted by King Edward II. The law decreed that every sturgeon which was caught belonged to the Treasury and had to be offered to the monarch. This means that the Queen has to be consulted before anything is done with one. In recent years the Controller of Her Majesty's Household has rarely accepted the fish when offered. It appears the last time one was eaten at Buckingham Palace was in 1969 and in that same year the Queen gave a live one to an aquarium and a dead one to an orphanage. A sturgeon caught off Portland in March 1992 and taken to the Weymouth Sea Life Park was offered to the Queen, and the Master of the Queen's Household replied to say that the Queen very much appreciated the gesture; it was a tradition she greatly valued. She asked for it to be looked after at the Sea Life Centre.

Sturgeon are also listed under Schedule 5 of the Wildlife and Countryside Act 1981 and Schedule 2 of the Habitats Regulations 1994.

fishmonger's shop in Cornwall. The fishmonger was contacted and it was agreed that it would be transferred to the Natural History Museum in London in order to be identified. Although it was known the fish was a sturgeon it was necessary to identify the exact species in order to find out what offences, if any, had been committed.

Meanwhile back in South Wales, Ian had started his enquiries into the catching of the fish and arranged to interview the local fisherman in the company of his solicitor. He admitted catching the sturgeon while trawling out in Swansea Bay but said that it was a totally unintentional by-catch, in fact when he saw it in his nets he didn't even know what it was. He had even got onto the ship's radio and asked on an open channel whether anyone had any idea what he might have caught, this radio request later being confirmed by other fishermen who had been out in the bay that day.

One maritime advisor told the fisherman that the mystery fish was probably a sturgeon, which still meant relatively little to the fisherman. He decided to take it back to shore, but due to its size he couldn't pull it aboard and had to tow it, still in the net, to Swansea dock. Since, because of his radio broadcast, his catching of the sturgeon was common knowledge, he was greeted by an interested reception committee of local fishermen and coastguard officers.

So after posing for pictures our fisherman was duly informed that due to the fact the sturgeon was a 'Royal Fish' he was obliged to offer it to the Queen. A fax was duly sent to Buckingham Palace and a reply quickly returned thanking him for his offer but stating that the sturgeon could be disposed of by the fisherman 'as he saw fit'. Having received this fax he then set off with the sturgeon in the back of his van to Plymouth fish market, stopping en route at the local BBC studios to do an interview about his catch, the media quickly latching on to the name of Sammy the Sturgeon. On arrival at the fish market a price of £675.60 was agreed and the fisherman duly left Sammy at the market and headed back to Swansea.

At the end of the police interview the fisherman's solicitor asked Ian Guilford whether, as part of his enquiries he would be speaking to Her Majesty the Queen in relation to the fax she had sent giving the fisherman permission to dispose of the fish as he saw fit. He did initially consider this proposal but somehow doubted whether he would be following this line of enquiry.

It was quite apparent that the fisherman initially had no idea what he had caught. Having identified it he had dutifully offered it to the Queen and received permission to dispose of it. In view of this it was highly unlikely that a successful prosecution could be pursued against him.

Various lessons were learnt as a result of this enquiry and Defra subsequently sent a letter to Buckingham Palace asking them that when responding to future offers of sturgeon they include in their reply the fact that sturgeon are a protected species and require correct documentation from Defra if it they are to be subsequently sold.

THE PORT TALBOT PEREGRINE FALCON AND THE PIGEON FANCIERS

Pigeon fancying is a popular pastime in South Wales and it's clear that the hobbyists' predilection is in inverse proportion to their affection for peregrine falcons. Between 2000 and 2004 there were 11 confirmed poisonings of peregrines across the valleys; in addition to this a number of poisoned baits were also recovered. As well as poisoning, attacks on peregrines included disturbance of the birds in order to drive them off their eggs, shooting, rocks being dropped on the eggs and nets being thrown over the nest site in order to prevent them from returning to the eggs. Since the favoured prey of the peregrine is the pigeon, it was strongly suspected that those behind these illegal acts were involved in or connected to racing pigeon interests. Unfortunately, until the Port Talbot case, police officers were unable to confirm their suspicions due to the lack of direct evidence.

A Peregrine Watch scheme was set up in 1996 to help try and combat this problem. The group was made up of a number of enforcement agencies as well as interested members of the public who monitor nest sites across the South Wales valleys. The case at issue came to light when a member of the watch group discovered a dead pigeon set out below the nesting scrape of a peregrine (they don't build nests, simply make a scrape on the ground in which to lay their 2 to 5 eggs that make up the clutch.) The nest site was on the ledge of an old quarry located on the hillside overlooking the M4 as it passes Port Talbot. The quarry was very small and easily accessed, the only drawback for anyone trying to get to the nest being that it was easily visible from the surrounding area, including some local houses across the valley.

Having discovered the dead pigeon, the Peregrine Watch member contacted Ian who arranged for the recovery of the carcass. On examination Ian could clearly see that there were marks on the back of the pigeon's neck. This was a distinctive marking caused by someone coating a greasy type substance just behind the head of the bird and then applying whatever type of poison they had possession of. This had been a relatively common discovery on many of the previous pigeon baits recovered over the years.

It is suspected that pigeons used as baits are old birds, past their prime and of no further use to the owner. Usually the bird is killed before being placed close to the resident peregrine nesting scrape though Ian and his colleagues have come across carcasses which have been tethered by the leg. When the birds are discovered dead the police were never sure whether they were killed first or tethered live and died before they were found. The main indicator of pigeons being used as bait is the lack of particular primary wing feathers on the bird, the long feathers found on the end of the wing. The Racing Pigeon Association requires the telephone number of the owner to be stamped with an ink stamp on one of these feathers when the bird is flown in any competition; this aids the recovery of the bird if it ever gets lost when flying. When these stamped feathers are removed this is designed to cover the pigeon owner's tracks. The other common indicator of the bird as a bait is it being a one-legged racing pigeon; the purpose of the amputation is once again the removal of the identifying ring that would allow the police to track the bird back to its owner.

The bird Ian recovered had the distinctive missing leg but his hopes were raised when there was no indication that any of the primary wing feathers had been removed. With an air of hope he opened up the wings of the bird and thankfully, stamped on one of the feathers, was a telephone number. This was indeed a major breakthrough: in all the previous cases Ian has investigated the bird has had its leg ring removed and the primary wing feathers clipped.

The pigeon carcass was sent for analysis and Ian carried out a trace on the telephone number, which came back to an address in Port Talbot and a warrant was duly applied for. We'll call our suspect Columbo, near enough the generic Latin name for most species of pigeon, *Columbidae*.

On the day of the execution of the warrant a pre-operation briefing was held at the local police station. This involved a number of wildlife crime officers and a member of the RSPB investigations section assisting them. Unfortunately no member of the Technical Services Division from the Welsh Assembly Government based at Aberystwyth, who help deal with any poisons or pesticides that the police discover, was available on the morning of the search, although the team provided invaluable assistance during the subsequent investigation.

At Colombo's premises the police were met by his wife, who explained that her husband was seeing to his pigeons at his pigeons cots. She then explained the location of these cots which transpired to be directly below the quarry where the pigeon bait had been found. Nothing of interest was found during the search at his home address; in fact there was even very little evidence of any pigeon racing equipment. All the outside sheds were searched for the possible pesticide but the cupboard was bare.

When visited at his pigeon cots on a small allotment up the valley, Columbo explained that they were owned by him and his uncle. There was an old battered caravan that acted as a place for the people using the allotment to shelter as well as acting as a storage area. From the location of the pigeon cots the quarry where the peregrines had been nesting was clearly visible, in fact at certain times during the search the resident peregrines were seen and heard in the sky above the cots. When asked about the peregrines and whether they took any of his pigeons, Columbo was rather non-committal but did not show any great animosity toward the birds.

In searching the cots issues of health and safety became apparent; it was necessary to wear protective face masks due to the risks associated with zoonotic diseases passed from birds to humans, especially psittacosis where pigeons and parrots are particular vectors. The conditions were at times cramped and rather uncomfortable, but necessary in order to try to find evidence. Despite a thorough search of the cots the only pesticide – or at least rodenticide – found was a large pile of rat poison in one of the basements. Having completed the search and at that point feeling rather deflated, the police then turned their attentions to the old battered caravan which was used by Columba and Uncle as a place to make tea and shelter from the rain. By this time Uncle had turned up.

The first item of interest found was a .22 rifle which was tucked away in one of the cupboards, then some ammunition in a drawer. An initial explanation for the possession of this gun was that it was used for controlling rats which, looking at the state of the cots, was a plausible explanation. The main drawbacks were that it was kept in an unlocked caravan and of course neither of the two was in possession of a firearms certificate. The gun and the ammunition were seized and the search continued.

A short while later and bingo, the pesticide they were looking for was located tucked away in another cupboard in the caravan. The item in question was a packet of a pesticide called 'Ficam W'. On examination it was established that the ingredients included Bendiocarb, the same substance that had been identified as being present on the pigeon bait recovered below the peregrine nest. A first explanation by Columbo and Uncle was that they used it as a weed killer around the allotments.

Although the search team were not fully aware of the use of Ficam W at this stage they had their doubts about this explanation, and at this point both men were arrested and taken to the local police station for interview.

They were later interviewed in the presence of the duty solicitor, Columbo going first. He maintained that he had nothing to do with putting the poisoned bait out though he admitted the pigeon carcass did belong to him. He also agreed he was aware of peregrines in the area but said that they caused him no problem. His explanation about the possession of Ficam W was that a man – an unknown man – had come to the caravan and had offered the packet to him saying that it was a good weed killer. Naturally the details of this man were very sketchy to say the least, as was the time and date that he had appeared at the allotment. Despite this tall tale of pedlars in pesticide he was asked what he had done with the substance, and he went into a long explanation of how he had mixed it up with water and had applied it to the nettles growing around the caravan. This was thought to be a bit strange given that he had carried this out during the winter when everyone knows nettles have died back and are not growing. Despite these inconsistencies Columbo stuck to his story and denied having any involvement with the poisoned bait.

When Uncle was interviewed he was less expansive in his explanations but also denied having any part in the setting out of the poisoned bait. Further, he denied any knowledge of the packet of Ficam W recovered from the caravan.

At the end of the interview Ian was certainly not happy with the explanation provided by Columbo and Uncle though he was still not fully aware of the capabilities of Ficam W. Because of this he telephoned the manufacturers to find out more about the use of the chemical. They explained it was used as a pesticide by specialists but when asked if it would have any affect if used as a herbicide, in particular on nettles, they laughed and said that you could pour it on nettles all day and it would have no effect, unless you happened to drown the plant.

Armed with this information it was decided to charge Columbo and Uncle with various offences, including an attempt to kill a peregrine. Thankfully at this time there was a solicitor working for the Crown Prosecution Service locally who had a very keen interest in wildlife crime and was keen to take on the case.

After the usual legal processes, summonses were duly served

and after accepting not guilty pleas from both men a date was set for a trial at Neath Magistrates Court. Despite some very good probing questions by the CPS the defendants stuck to their original statements denying any involvement of setting out the poisoned pigeon bait. In due course, having heard all the evidence, the magistrates adjourned to consider their verdict.

Ian admitted that he wasn't overly confident that a guilty verdict would be returned; less so when the magistrates didn't take the bench again for an hour. His fears were unfounded and a guilty verdict was delivered against both defendants on all charges. After the defence and prosecution submissions in relation to sentencing each defendant was fined £240 in relation to the poisoned pigeon bait, Uncle was fined a further £40 for the illegal possession of the .22 rifle and costs of £250 were awarded.

Ian was pleased with the outcome as it was the first conviction of its kind in South Wales. The use of poisons to try to kill peregrines has been a long running problem in this area. Apart from killing one of our most beautiful and charismatic birds of prey, the use of poisons out in the open countryside presents a very serious threat not only to other wildlife and domestic animals but also to humans. It appears this conviction sent out the right message: since the court case, instances of poisoned baits being discovered has significantly reduced.

WWF Wildlife Enforcer of the Year Award

Since 1997 the Worldwide Fund for Nature (WWF) has sponsored a prestigious glass trophy presented annually to the police wildlife crime officer, either full or part-time, or the HM Revenue and Customs wildlife and endangered species officer who has the best record for wildlife crime prevention and investigation over the course of the year. Nominations for the award, open to the whole of the UK, are submitted by chief police or Customs officers and detail the year's work of the persons nominated. These are then considered by the High Level Group of the Partnership for Action against Wildlife crime – the group overseeing the strategy of wildlife prevention and investigation in the UK – and a worthy winner decided. The trophy is presented, usually to a very surprised winner, at the National Enforcers' Conference, and includes a scaled-down replica of the trophy for the winner to keep. And, of course, being a WWF award, a cuddly panda! Winners associated with chapters in this book, in addition to Ian Guildford in 1997, are Inspector Nevin Hunter of Devon and Cornwall Constabulary in 2001: Andy McWilliam, then constable in Merseyside Police, in 2002; and Constable Nigel Lound of Lincolnshire Police in 2007. (The trophy was won by the author in 1999).

The Case of the Cardiff Kangaroo

Sightings of strange and exotic animals in our countryside often result in a call to the local wildlife crime officer. A common sighting is of a 'big cat', usually a black panther, roaming the fields or woods. Like me, Ian had doubts about the validity of these reports, though both of us are in no doubt that in the majority of cases the person reporting the black panther or whatever large feline it may be genuinely believes in what they have seen. A professional police response to their call is the least they can expect to receive. To this end one of Ian's local wildlife crime officers, PC Mark Goulding, has done considerable research into the field of exotic animal sightings and has devised a standard questionnaire which is completed by officers and control room staff who are the first point of contact with the bemused panther-spotter. Not only does this provide some good quantified information which can be assessed and evaluated; it also provides the initial necessary professional response.

Over the years there have literally been hundreds of reports of strange mammalian sightings reported to the police. One of the more unusual ones reported to Ian was a call that came in of a kangaroo having been spotted in the suburbs of Cardiff. Not dismissing the sighting out of hand, Ian did have some serious doubts that the animal seen could have been a fully-grown kangaroo, but did consider the possibility of it being a smaller wallaby. Initial enquiries revealed that there was indeed a private collection, not far from the sighting, which included wallabies. Contact was duly made with the collection's owner but there were no missing marsupials. As often happens, by this time the media – even some of the national tabloids – had become very interested in the story and Ian carried out several interviews.

Local officers made enquiries and carried out searches. Ian also had a look around the area in the company of the local wildlife crime officer, but despite their best efforts the most unusual animal they saw was a three-legged dog hopping along beside its master. Because of the media interest the story had spread around the local area, prompting a rush of alleged sightings of the animal as well as a sighting of a 'big cat' in the back garden of a nearby house. Some of the calls sounded extremely unlikely but others appeared genuine.

Calls continued throughout the day without any further confirmed sightings and just as Ian was coming to the end of his shift he agreed to a BBC Wales request for an interview on the evening news programme. Just before entering the news room he was handed a grainy picture of what was alleged to be the 'Cardiff Kangaroo'. The photos had been taken by a local resident at a distance and were of pretty poor quality. The overall shape of the animal in the pictures was similar to that of a wallaby but there was something about them that was unconvincing and gave the definite hint that the subject was not what it purported to be. Despite this Ian carried out the interview but was non-committal about the identification of the animal.

The media interest showed no signs of abating, and by the next day the television company was keen that Ian accompany a film crew to try to find the mystery animal, an offer he politely refused. Further unconfirmed sightings came in although these appeared to have been driven by the media stories that were in plentiful supply. Despite the best efforts of the local police they drew a blank.

The answer came about a week later when a further sighting of the 'Cardiff Kangaroo' was reported. Local officers were dispatched, and were joined by an RSPCA inspector. The information this time was altogether better and they found the animal in the back garden of a house. Fully expecting the kangaroo to make its escape by bounding over the nearest hedge they were surprised to find that the 'kangaroo' was a fox. The poor beast had a serious case of mange and very obvious injuries to its front legs. It tried to escape by making strange hopping motions on its back legs. It then became clear that the animal was in so much pain that it had hunched itself up and was forced to hop around, giving a plausible impression of a small marsupial such as a wallaby. This was exacerbated by the mange from which it was suffering as this had changed its appearance from the normal bushy-tailed creature Reynard is meant to be.

The RSPCA duly set a trap and a short time later the fox was caught. Unsurprisingly, because of its poor state of health a local vet had to put the animal down. Suffice to say that after its capture, sightings of the 'Cardiff Kangaroo' dried up. And of course, as is expected in the police, Ian was continually mocked (in a friendly way) on his poor powers of identification: failing to be able to tell the difference between a fox and a kangaroo. His protestations that never at any stage did he either see the animal or verbally confirm that it was a kangaroo fell on deaf ears.

CASES OF ILLEGAL FALCONRY

In the mid nineties the laundering into falconry of particular species of birds of prey taken from the wild, either as eggs or chicks, was a UK-wide problem. Peregrines, and sometimes golden eagles, were the main target and those involved in this illegal trade invariably had criminal links with falconers in central Europe or the Middle East. The investigation of these cases was often complicated but success improved dramatically with the advent of DNA fingerprinting. DNA profiling had been used for some years in the prosecution of crime committed against humans and began to be, if not quite standard practice, much more commonly used in wildlife crime investigations.

In early 1996 information was received that a number of falconers in the South Wales area were suspected of being involved in illegal falconry, including taking birds from the wild. A meeting was organised, to which the police invited staff from Defra, the RSPB investigations team and PC Paul Beacroft, a Thames Valley police officer who, in addition to having an excellent knowledge of the world of falconry, was also an expert falconer.

At the meeting certain individuals were identified as suspects and enquiries began into the background and activities of these men. Good policing is about building up good quality intelligence on and a profile of suspects to give the best possible chance of finding evidence and gaining a conviction. Part of the intelligence-gathering process in this case involved building up a record of birds that each falconer allegedly owned and trying to establish their origins and provenance. To achieve this, Ian worked very closely with Defra, making use of the records they kept under the Bird Registration Scheme.

The law states that if you possess a bird listed under Schedule 4 of the Wildlife and Countryside Act you must register it with Defra. The normal process involves the fitting of a closed ring to the leg of the bird soon after hatching – normally within about 12 days – since at this stage it is still reasonably easy to slip a closed ring over its foot. If it is left any longer the bird's feet will have grown too large and the foot will not pass through the correct sized ring. This ring carries a unique number which is registered with Defra and the owner is issued with a registration document. If the bird is sold on a tear-off slip at the bottom of the document is completed by the seller and sent to Defra whilst the new owner completes a section on the original document in order to register it in his name. It is a system mirroring that of car registration and ensures that it is possible to keep track of the movements and locations of Schedule 4 birds, a factor that was critical to the success of this case.

Ian had the Defra registration system interrogated and started to build up details of what birds the falconers currently held, as well as tracking the history of movements of the birds. This in effect allowed Ian and the team to build up family trees of all the birds relevant to the investigation, identifying each species, who owned what bird, which falconer bred what bird, the bird's parentage and where each now was. Many of the birds were found to be in the possession of other falconers spread out across the UK. It was during this initial intelligence-gathering that the team started to see a lot of anomalies in the alleged breeding claims of their suspects. Early intelligence dictated that Ian should target three falconers living in the South Wales area since there was strong evidence of involvement in illegal activity.

After months of painstaking research, Ian and the team decided they were in a position to execute warrants on the homes of their three targets. A date was set in September to ensure that there were no birds still breeding within the aviaries, since the stress to breeding birds, if searches were carried out earlier in the year, may well have caused eggs to fail or chicks to die. The next operational issue was to ensure there was sufficient expertise not only to carry out the search of the aviaries in South Wales but also to obtain the support of twelve other forces across the UK to execute warrants on bird keepers who were in possession of either offspring, parent or grandparents of the birds which were central to the investigation. In total warrants were executed at fifteen addresses including the three within South Wales. This necessitated the co-ordinated involvement of the officers from the other forces together with vets who were required to take the necessary blood samples.

In South Wales Ian enlisted the services of two highly qualified vets, the RSPB Investigations team from RSPB headquarters in Sandy, Bedfordshire, a Defra wildlife inspector, an RSPCA inspector and, at one of the addresses, the services of PC Paul Beacroft. Warrants under the Wildlife and Countryside Act 1981 allow the use of officers from other police forces or staff from other named organisations. The use of all these agencies meant that they all had to be specified on the warrants to enable them to legally enter the premises with the police.

September, 1996 was a lovely warm and dry month – until the day of the operation when it decided to rain continuously for the whole day. Undeterred, the teams in South Wales arrived at the first of three addresses to be searched, two in the Rhondda Valley to be searched by Ian's team, and the other at Ponterdawe. Ian, in overall charge on the day, takes up the story.

'After a search of the first address we were directed to a nearby allotment where the bird keeper had his aviaries. We began the examination of the birds we were interested in, in this case goshawks. With the help of the falconer (it is quite common for suspects to help the police handle their birds since they know them best) the birds were caught up and blood samples taken for DNA testing.

'At blood sampling stage it was critical to have a vet who was confident in dealing with birds of prey. This became very apparent when the falconer suddenly started shouting at us saying we had killed one of his birds. Fearing the worst, the vet examined a sparrowhawk which had been found dead on the floor of the aviary. With its owner shouting all sorts of threats at us the vet calmly explained to him that bird was as stiff as a poker due to the effects of *rigor mortis*, and had died a considerable time before our arrival at the aviaries. Having heard this, the falconer went very quiet. I would guess that he knew fully well that the bird had died some time ago but I'm not sure whether he was just trying to discourage us from searching any further or trying to get a case together to sue us for the loss of his bird.

'In addition to the birds we also recovered four gin traps which we discovered set, completely uncovered, around the aviaries, and a .22 rifle which was in a shed on the allotment. Both of these, the falconer explained, were to deal with the problem of rats. We took possession of the traps and the rifle and arrested the falconer for possessing an unlicensed firearm. At this stage we had not taken possession of any birds but the keeper signed an undertaking not to dispose of any of the birds pending the outcome of the investigation.

'We then moved on to the next keeper who lived in the same valley. Again his aviaries were on allotments some distance from his house. By this time the rain was coming down in buckets. Crouched on the floor of the aviaries while the birds were being caught up and blood tested we began to look a very sorry and bedraggled group. Blood samples were taken from the target birds including red kites, peregrines, merlins, marsh and hen harriers and goshawks. Due to their poor condition, and certain anomalies in the paperwork, we took possession of three birds, boxing them up and putting them in a police vehicle before moving on to the next allotment.

'The boxes in which these birds were placed were cardboard carrying boxes and due to the heavy rain beginning to get a bit soggy. This we found to our cost: as we were driving from the first set of aviaries to the next, one of the cardboard boxes disintegrated expelling its contents of one rather upset and angry peregrine into the car. Dodging beak and talons we managed to recapture the bird without crashing and boxed it up in a dry, firm box.

'The process of blood-taking was again completed at the second allotment and a sparrowhawk which had had its wing feathers clipped by the falconer was seized. As well as breeding birds of prey, this falconer also had a number of 'wild disabled' birds in his possession. This is perfectly lawful although the bird must be returned back to the wild as soon as it becomes fit to be released. A number of alleged 'wild disabled' birds in the falconers possession were seized for examination by the vet who doubted their continuing injuries.'

While Ian and his team carried out a search of the aviaries of the two suspects in the Rhondda Valley, the third target in the Ponterdawe area was searched by other police officers, assisted by a vet and PC Paul Beacroft from Thames Valley. Ultimately no bird of prey-related offences were found there but there was a second prize: a barn on the farm hosted a large skunk cannabis plantation together with lights, heating and water supply. The falconer was arrested and in due course was jailed for a year for his entrepreneurial but illegal activity.

So far the operation had gone pretty much as planned, the only hiccup being that at the aviaries of the second falconer the officers discovered that a number of birds registered with Defra were in fact missing. These included ospreys and Montague's harriers. The keeper explained that earlier in the year a heavy snowfall had caused the collapse of an aviary and the birds had escaped. Ian and his team were highly suspicious that he had become aware he was under investigation and had tried to get rid of any birds that might incriminate him.

All the blood samples were sent to Nottingham University where they underwent DNA analysis. The results showed that the two falconers' breeding claims for a number of the birds were false. There was a problem unfortunately due to the 'loss' of a number of the second falconer's birds which meant there could be no comparison of DNA samples between siblings and parents in some of the families.

Unfortunately for the falconer he had sold on some of the offspring and grandparent birds. Some turned up during other searches and their blood samples ultimately showed that the alleged offspring did not originate from these birds as claimed. Under the Wildlife and Countryside Act the onus of proof lies with the keeper to show that the bird he has in his possession is not a wild bird. The falconer tried to do this by relying on the alleged breeding claims, but by the DNA conclusively disproving this, the police were able to charge him and in due course summonses were issued for offences of unlawfully possessing a wild bird.

Both men had a life-long interest in keeping birds of prey and were very knowledgeable on their subject. Despite their knowledge and expertise in breeding captive birds of prey they appeared to have been involved in the taking of wild birds or at best, possessing them. Ultimately they appeared at Ton Pentre Magistrates Court to answer a number of charges. After a three day trial each was found guilty. The first falconer was found guilty of the possession of three wild goshawks and fined £1900 plus £250 costs. The second man was found guilty of a number of offences including the possession of three red kites, two merlins, a peregrine, a sparrowhawk and also three registration offences. He was fined £3200 plus £300 costs. All the birds subject to the summonses had been taken by the police and were either re-homed or, where possible, released back into the wild.

Ian concluded:

'This was a complicated and expensive case to investigate. It did, however, show our commitment and ability to investigate the laundering of wild-taken birds of prey into the legal falconry market by the use of DNA forensic techniques and it effectively closed a loophole in the law.

'The discovery of the cannabis plantation also highlighted the connections that are regularly found to exist between wildlife crime and other forms of criminality.'

The Case of the Missing Feet

Wildlife crime officers do not just deal with live or dead creatures or plants. The role extends to investigating crime that involves parts or derivatives of once-living things. This might include elephant ivory, parts of tigers, bears and other animals that may be constituents of traditional medicines, or even wood from rare trees such as ramin. Since 2004, at least in Scotland, the police responsibility has also been extended to include the investigation of offences committed against specially protected areas, such as Sites of Special Scientific Interest (SSSI – see Notes 6) Ian's next case goes beyond even these more obscure and unusual investigations and, incredibly, takes us back many millions of years.

The case relates to 'third party' damage to a SSSI in the Barry area of South Wales. The site in question is called the Bendrick Rock, notified as a SSSI in 1996 due to its geological composition: the presence of three-toed dinosaur footprints in the bedrock on the shore. The footprints date back 200 million years when the land formed part of the shore of a large lake. The land is a pretty nondescript piece of coastline adjoining Barry Docks and until quite recently owned by Associated British Ports.

The police first became aware that something was amiss when the senior geologist for CCW was told that fossilised dinosaur footprints – allegedly from Bendrick rock – had appeared for sale at a Gem and Mineral Fair in Arizona. Alerted to the fact that some of the fossilised prints may have been removed a visit to the site confirmed that a large section of rock containing the prints was gone. At the same time, fossilised prints allegedly from this site began to appear for sale in other locations around the UK. One print was found advertised for sale on the internet by a dealer based in Hertfordshire. Enquiries by the local police revealed that this had been sold for £199, in good faith, to a gentleman living in Tennessee, USA. A number of fossils then appeared on display and for sale in a shop in Lyme Regis. These were being sold for £30 up to £80 for a matching pair.

A warrant under the Theft Act was therefore obtained by a local police wildlife crime officer and subsequently fifteen fossils were recovered from the shop, while the owner surrendered three more which were at his home address. These fossils varied in size from between 5 and 15 inches square.

A picture was starting to emerge of the route that these fossils had taken from the beach in South Wales to the various locations in which they were recovered. This appeared to implicate a local amateur fossil collector living in the Cardiff area.

Ian explains:

'The fossil that had been sold from the dealer in Hertfordshire subsequently made an appearance on the internet trading site, ebay. I managed to contact the seller, whose home was in Tennessee. When the origin of the fossil was explained to him and he was told that it had been taken illegally he promptly withdrew it from sale.

'Having located the source of the fossils we formally interviewed the suspect in Cardiff in the company of a duty solicitor. During the interview he admitted collecting the fossils but said that he had done this over a period of years rather than all at once. In fact he seemed to be obsessed by the site and described it as a 'haven he could escape to'. Having established that he was responsible for the taking of the fossils, I then asked him if he knew whether the site was a protected site fully expecting him to deny all knowledge of the site's protection, the usual reply to this question. I was flabbergasted when he admitted that he was fully aware that it was a SSSI and had known this for some considerable time.'

With the enquiries complete an unusual situation arose in that the collector from Cardiff had committed two different offences relating to the same set of circumstances, one reportable by CCW and the other by the police. These were the offence of 'third party' damage to an SSSI, and the other being theft, the latter due to the site (and its fossil contents) being owned by Associated British Ports.

Advice was sought from both CCW and the Crown Prosecution Service in relation to a course of action. After considering all aspects of the case including the personal background of the offender it was decided that CCW would take the lead in the case and they subsequently decided to issue him with a formal caution. In view of this the CPS advised that no further action should be taken by the police in relation to the offence of theft.

Having resolved the prosecution question relating to the person who took the fossils, Ian turned his thoughts to those who had been involved in trading them. He was unable to prove that the dealers involved in the case had any knowledge that the fossils had been stolen from an SSSI or that they were in fact stolen property. Due to this he was unable to take any action against these people. Thankfully the majority of the rocks were recovered. This meant that a lot of the dealers were ultimately out of pocket, a degree of punishment in itself.

Though there was no prosecution, the most important aspect of this case is that it sent a message out to those involved in the fossil trade that the police would rigorously investigate reports of offences and take action where necessary.

The Case of the Cat in the Trap

The illegal use of traps is still a common problem dealt with by wildlife crime officers in many police force areas. The majority of these relate to birds of prey which have been caught either deliberately in traps set specifically for them, or caught through a reckless act in traps which have been set illegally, most often with an entrance much too wide. There was, however, one case in South Wales that was slightly different and it provided the owner of the trap with a rather a nasty surprise when he ended up in court over its use. The case in question involved a domestic cat caught in a gin trap.

This case took place in the Cynon Valley. Ian was on duty at his local police station when he had a call to go to the reception desk. There he was met by a very distraught lady who explained that she had just found her cat hanging from her next door neighbour's fence, having been caught in a trap which was still attached to the fence. The cat had been taken to a nearby vet with its leg still caught in the teeth of the trap. The vet had released it but the damage to its front leg was so severe that she had been forced to amputate it. Ian found a very sorry-looking three-legged cat which was just recovering from the operation and the effects of the anaesthetic.

It was established that the trap appeared to have been placed on the wall between the neighbour and the cat owner. Ian went to the neighbour's house, accompanied by an RSPCA inspector and a local police officer. They were met by the son of the owner who was home from work, and who invited them in to have a look around. In a case like this the police wouldn't expect to find much in the house that was relevant to their enquiry but this one was different. The first things they saw were three stuffed and mounted birds in the living room. Bearing these in mind they extended their inspection into the back garden, where they found a Fenn trap set in the open in one of the flower beds. Setting it in an open flower bed is an illegal act which could well have resulted in another domestic pet or a bird being caught.

Having searched the outside of the house Ian then went to a shed, which he found to contain a chest freezer. A search of a freezer is often very revealing and on this occasion it resulted in the discovery of the frozen body of a peregrine. His attention then returned to the stuffed birds he had seen when they first entered the house. There was a goshawk, buzzard and a peregrine. In the absence of the owner of the house to give an explanation of his possession of these birds they were seized, along with the Fenn trap and the deep-frozen peregrine, pending further enquiries.

A few days later the owner of the house voluntarily attended at the police station in the company of his solicitor (with whom Ian had had previous dealings in relation to badger digging cases). An interview was carried out and on the instructions of his solicitor the defendant gave a 'no comment' interview.

If anyone is found in possession of a wild British bird the onus falls to them to prove that it had been obtained legally, for example, by being killed on the road or by some other accidental or natural cause of death. Due to the 'no comment' interview given by the defendant he had failed to give any explanation for his possession of the peregrine. Ian was therefore obliged to charge him with the illegal possession of the peregrine and the taxidermy specimens, and also the offences relating to the Fenn traps and the cruelty to the cat. It was not best advice from the solicitor.

The matter was heard at the local magistrate's court where the defendant produced a number of witnesses to prove that the taxidermy specimens had been acquired legally. Had he provided these details during his interview he would not have been summonsed to appear at court for these offences. It also transpired that the deep-frozen peregrine had died by natural causes, possibly a flying accident. Again if this had been raised in the interview no charge would have been made. As a result of this the offences relating to the possession of the frozen peregrine and the taxidermy birds were dismissed, the time of everyone involved in the proceedings having been wasted.

He continued with a plea of not guilty to the offences relating to the traps and after a day-long trial the court found him guilty. The magistrates then adjourned to consider sentence and much to the surprise of the defendant and his solicitor – as well as to Ian – they returned and sentenced him to one month's imprisonment. This was unusual due to the fact that it was his first offence and he was of previous good character. After his client was taken down to the court cells the defence solicitor appealed against the sentence and the matter was adjourned to the crown court. At a subsequent hearing at Merthyr Tydfil Crown Court the verdict was upheld although the sentence was reduced to a fine of £1000.

Ian comments:

   'Why the magistrates initially imposed a custodial

The Law on Traps

A gin trap is a particular nasty trap which became illegal for use against rabbits in the early 1950s and against foxes in the 1970s. Although their use is completely against the law, *possession* of gin traps is legal provided there is no intent to use them; in fact it is one of the types of trap sometimes seen hanging on the walls of 'rural' theme pubs. The gin trap is a leg-hold trap, in other words its purpose is to catch and hold the target animal by the leg until the person setting the trap comes along and dispatches it. To hold the leg of the animal in the trap and to stop it pulling it out, gin traps have serrated jaws.

Legal traps currently approved by the Government are often referred to as 'break-back' traps, and their design is such that if set properly they will catch an animal across the body and kill it outright. The most widely-used versions are sold under the trade names of Fenn or Springer. These and other approved traps are listed under a Spring Traps Approval Order and if used correctly are perfectly legitimate provided they are used in a covered tunnel or run and access to them is restricted to the target animal such as rats, stoats, weasels, grey squirrels, and in larger and more powerful versions, rabbits and mink. These traps must never be used in the open or set to catch birds. Unlike live-catch traps there is no legal requirement for a daily check.

sentence is not clear but I suspect they considered the defendant had deliberately set the traps for a cat. Whether this was the case only he will know but in any case the cat suffered considerably due to his actions. On a positive note, when I visited the cat owner a few weeks after the incident the cat was running around on three legs and appeared in good health and managing very well.'

North Wales

North Wales Police covers the six local authority areas and while it may be perceived as a predominantly rural patch, the eastern half contains heavily industrialised areas. Snowdonia National Park, which lies entirely within the force area, attracts many thousands of visitors each year who generally seek the enjoyment of the environment often by participation in outdoor sports. Other areas such as Anglesey and the Cambrian Mountains have been identified as Areas of Outstanding Natural Beauty, attracting many visitors in their own right.

The force receives in the region of 350 reports of wildlife crime annually. By far the greatest proportion of calls relate to incidents involving birds but the eastern side of the force holds important populations of great-crested newts, with a number of incidents each year revealing the problems associated with commercial development and protected species. The partnership between the force and the Countryside Council for Wales (CCW), the Welsh Assembly Government's statutory nature conservation agency, has resulted in a greater emphasis on habitat issues than in most other police areas.

The taking of wild bird eggs has long been a problem in North Wales although there are indications that the level of offending may be declining. Interestingly no major egg collectors have ever been identified as residing within the force area but it is annually visited by many of the UK's most active collectors.

North Wales Police takes its responsibilities to biodiversity very seriously and have installed a peregrine falcon nest box on the roof of its highest police station. Annually 3 or 4 chicks are successfully reared. Elsewhere in the grounds badgers and great-crested newts are in residence whilst a wild flower meadow has been created where lawns previously existed. Most recently the suite of protected species has been increased with the discovery of bats in one building.

Between 2000 and the end of 2007 Sergeant Pete Charleston considered himself very fortunate to have been carrying out the role of full time wildlife and environmental crime officer for North Wales Police. It is always interesting when new ground is broken in any form of policing and Pete's full-time appointment in 2000 was certainly that: uniquely he was seconded to work with the Countryside Council for Wales and became the first ever police officer in the UK seconded to a statutory nature conservation organisation, an approach that was later replicated with the appointment of Sgt Ian Guildford in a similar role in South Wales. (In 2008 this trend was continued in England, when wildlife crime officers were seconded to work in Defra and English Nature).

One early summer morning in 1993 a rather bedraggled visitor arrived at the Holyhead police station counter asking to see the town sergeant. Two or three customers were in the cells recovering from the previous night's exuberances and Sergeant Pete Charleston had a team of three officers, two of whom were very young in service, and a list of jobs to be attended to and investigated. Can you guess Pete's reaction when the caller introduced himself as an RSPB investigations officer seeking the assistance of police officers to attend at Cemlyn nature reserve in order to track down two men who had been seen taking birds eggs? Well, it was in no way typical of the unenlightened police attitude in the early 1990s when 'wildlife' was far more commonly used to describe Pete's customers in the cells.

Cemlyn nature reserve is situated on the beautiful, rugged coast on the North of Anglesey. It is a shingle beach that has been built up by decades of storms sweeping in from the Irish Sea. Behind the spit and protected from the sea is a shallow freshwater lagoon dotted with islands. The entire area is home to a range of bird species but the islands in particular are extensively used as a ternary, not only by common, Arctic and sandwich terns but at that time also by the rare roseate tern which has since sadly disappeared from the site. The reserve is managed by the North Wales Wildlife Trust, an organisation that employs seasonal wardens to monitor and protect the wildlife, their duties lying primarily with the terns.

From Pete's conversation with this unusual caller it appeared that the RSPB had earlier received information that two well-known egg collectors from the English Midlands had decided to visit Cemlyn with the intention of taking roseate tern eggs. The information was such that it had been decided that a number of wardens, RSPB staff and volunteers would carry out 24 hour surveillance of the site. That morning as dawn broke the two men appeared on a shingle ridge and waded across the expanse of water separating the nesting islands from the shingle bank. They were then seen walking around the island overturning shelters that had been provided for nesting terns, clearly seeking eggs.

The eggs of roseate terns are an obvious attraction for egg thieves because of their rarity. Egg thieves have no scruples and despite the real risk of making some of their rare targets locally extinct they are not deterred in their quest to have eggshells that few other like-minded plunderers have in their sorry collection. The roseate tern is a summer visitor to Britain, where only around 100 or so pairs nest annually. Their nesting distribution is mainly round the coast of Northern Ireland, the east coast of mainland Britain from the Forth estuary south to about the southern edge of the Northumbrian coast, the Wash and of course Anglesey in North Wales. Among the rarest of birds, like many of our summer visitors, they have flown from West Africa to nest on British shores. Often described as sea swallows because of their long pointed wings and forked tails, roseate terns must be among the most graceful and beautiful of sea birds.

Having spent some time on the island, causing mayhem from a tern perspective, the two men returned from the shingle beach to the car park, to be confronted by the RSPB staff carrying out the surveillance operation. Challenged as to what they were doing and who they were, neither spoke and, completely ignoring the nature reserve staff, continued walking through the car park and into the roads beyond.

The RSPB staff then had the less than easy task of contacting North Wales Police in an age when mobile phones, although they were in existence, were not available in North Wales. Indeed public telephones were in somewhat short supply and as a consequence one of the witnesses had to drive the twenty-odd miles from Cemlyn to report the matter directly to Pete Charleston at Holyhead Police Station.

It can safely be said that had many of Pete's colleagues been on duty that day the request to send half of the available constables 20 miles away from the main area of operations to search for two egg collectors may not have been met with the same degree of helpfulness that Pete was prepared to provide. Because of his custodial duties it was simply impossible for Pete to leave the police station but two very bemused officers were despatched to the area to see what could be done.

One feature of the Cemlyn area not previously mentioned is an industrial complex lying only a mile or so away, commonly known as Wylfa Power Station. This installation has been around for about thirty years and while in 2009 it is now coming to the end of its operational life, in 1993 it was contributing a significant proportion of the country's energy needs. As a consequence there was tight security and indeed the outer perimeter fence was being constantly monitored. It was perhaps not the best place to head for if you wanted to blend in to the countryside.

No sooner had the two officers left the Holyhead area when a phone call was received from Wylfa Power Station reporting that members of staff were monitoring a wet and bedraggled individual wandering around the perimeter fence apparently lost. The person in question was of course one of the egg collectors and he was soon traced by the officers and found to be in possession of birds' eggs. He admitted to having been into the tern nesting area earlier that morning but denied he'd had a companion with him. At that time because wildlife crime was seen to be a minor or summary offence, the officers only had a power of arrest if the offender refused to provide his name and address. The man, who probably knew the law that related to their egg-thieving activity better than the two police officers, had no hesitation in giving his name and address and it transpired that he was a well-known egg collector from the East Midlands. Since he had complied with the requirements of the law at that time – the Wildlife and Countryside Act 1981 – he could not be detained.

This situation was frustrating for the officers and certainly not in the public interest. It was anomalous that a person could be arrested for a minor salmon poaching offence, yet if he knew to give his name and address, could not be arrested for the taking of rare birds' eggs. It was to be 2000 in England and Wales (under the Countryside and Rights of Way Act) and 2003 in Scotland (under the Criminal Justice (Scotland) Act) before this ludicrous legal situation changed.

Pete commented, 'But there is always more than one way to skin a cat. Having been wandering around the Welsh country-side for some hours, wet and uncomfortable and without obvious means of transport back home, our egg thief was very happy to accept the offer by the police of a lift back to Holyhead. At the police station, having been supplied with the customary cup of tea, he was interviewed and admitted a number of charges relating to the intentional disturbance of nesting Schedule 1 birds and the taking and possession of Schedule 1 birds' eggs.'

It is not often that the opportunity arises for search warrants to be executed at the homes of known egg collectors and the legislation provided an opportunity to do so, not only at the home of the detained egg thief but also at the home of his companion, who by now had been identified although not traced. The searches took place during that afternoon with nothing being found at the home of the offender in custody at Holyhead.

Officers then went to the second person's house and were surprised at that time to find him at home. He denied having been in Anglesey or at Cemlyn, with the search of his house providing no evidence to the contrary. Fortunately the officers tasked with the searches thought to include a search of the vehicle, which produced clear evidence of fuel having been purchased in North Wales the previous day. This was a valuable piece of evidence, certainly sufficient to prosecute the man who had been arrested. Indeed he had admitted his intention to take eggs but refused to identify his companion in crime. There were witnesses available who were able to identify both egg thieves but only of course by sight, not by name. The only way in which Pete could hope to bring a prosecution of the second man was by placing him on an identification parade and hope that he would be formally identified by the witnesses. The question was how that could be done.

Many people believe that the police can arrest people pretty much as they wish. This is not the case. There are many offences for which there is no power of arrest and of course at the time no unconditional power of arrest was available for nearly all of the offences under wildlife legislation. This meant that the second man could not be compelled to stand in an identity parade in North Wales.

'Some discussion took place and kicked off quite possibly one of the most bizarre lines of enquiry I had ever undertaken,' Pete explained. 'I realised that the suspect would be unlikely to travel to North Wales on a voluntary basis for the identity parade but I thought that if the opportunity was provided for him to do so and he still refused this might provide the extra piece of evidence required for the jigsaw and allow a case against him to go ahead. However the offer had to be one that he could not reasonably refuse.'

On this basis further contact was made with the man and he was formally asked to attend an identity parade in Holyhead. He had no work commitments with the associated loss of earnings, so when the request was made the perhaps inevitable answer came that he would certainly like to attend such a parade but finances would not allow him to travel. 'That's OK,' was Pete's response, and the offer was made not just to pay for his travel but also to cover other reasonable expenditure that he might incur. This was an offer that could not reasonably be refused and sure enough our man indicated a willingness to attend.

The appointed day was set for several weeks hence and the witnesses for the identity parade duly arrived at Holyhead Police

Station. A travel warrant had earlier been posted to the suspect and a phone call to him the previous day had rather surprisingly confirmed his continued intention to attend. On the day of the parade the train on which he was scheduled to travel arrived on time. But no suspect alighted. A further phone call established that that the morning he had decided on his solicitor's advice not to stand in the identity parade.

It might seem that all the arrangements involved in organising the identity parade and troubling witnesses were all in vain. However the fact that the police had shown willingness to provide the opportunity for the suspect to take part in the identity parade, where he could either be identified as the second egg thief or indeed be cleared, was absolutely crucial. His refusal had provided the last link in the evidential chain and he was charged.

Many months after wreaking havoc at the tern breeding colony both men appeared before Magistrates in Holyhead in March 1994, where they each pleaded guilty to offences connected with the disturbance of nesting terns with the intention of taking eggs. Each received a fine of £400.

The partnership between North Wales Police and CCW has hopefully been of benefit for both organisations but specifically it was anticipated when Sergeant Pete Charleston was seconded to work there that he would bring investigative experience to dealing with criminal offences on Sites of Special Scientific Interest (SSSIs). His first such investigation was probably the first carried out by the police anywhere in the United Kingdom.

In Wales there are over 1000 SSSIs that have been designated to protect many different features, habitats and species. They extend to 12% of the land area and range in size from many thousands of hectares on upland moorland sites to a small outbuilding in a private yard that houses an important colony of bats.

One case in particular remains in Pete's memory because of the sheer audacity of the explanations being offered for carrying out work without CCW's consent. This involved the creation of a track several hundred metres long through a very sensitive area of upland bog. Despite the area in which the track had been scraped being very isolated, the damage had clearly been spotted by several people who were concerned about the ecological damage and reported the matter.

Pete said, 'I visited the scene and it was clear that the track had been made with no regard to the environment. It was six metres wide and 600 metres long and a very noticeable scar on the landscape, but the damage was exacerbated in that materials scraped away to form the track had been dumped at the sides effectively doubling the width of the damaged area. There appeared to be clear criminal offences involved.'

The owners of the land when interviewed were very amenable but seemed to have little understanding of the ecological issues involved. It was initially suggested that the track had been created in order that the sheep on the hill could be checked by quad bike. Quite why a track needed to be as wide as it was it was for a quad bike was not explained. It was then suggested that another reason for the track being created was to enable access to a remote forestry plantation. Further questioning revealed that the owners of the plantation had never indicated a need for such access and had certainly not made any approaches for the work to be done.

Feeling perhaps that the reasons offered so far were not overly convincing, a third reason – and possibly the most convincing –

was offered. The track had in fact been created, in part, as assistance to the emergency services in carrying out mountain rescues in the area, although once again there had been no consultation with those bodies as to whether this very considerate assistance might be required. Considering this work had been done at the philanthropic farmer's expense Pete felt the need to probe the explanation a little further and asked if such events occurred often. He was assured by Farmer Phil that these matters were regular occurrences; indeed on one occasion an aircraft had flown into the mountainside and great difficulty had been experienced in evacuating the casualties. That would not occur again thanks to the foresight displayed by the creation of the track. When had this rescue taken place? 1954 . . . of course the track may have required a lot of planning.

Farmer Phil appeared before Aberystwyth Magistrates Court. He was fined for carrying out operations on the SSSI without the consent of CCW and was ordered to restore the ground to its original condition. Obviously faced with such attitudes matters have to be dealt with formally, but in reality blatant and serious breaches of the law protecting habitats are uncommon.

THE ILLEGAL SALE OF TORTOISES

One area of the law that many police wildlife crime officers find particularly difficult to get to grips with is the illegal trade in endangered wildlife. The legislation is on the whole not overly difficult but the problems arise when it comes to species identification. For this, the assistance of experts is crucial. When Pete received reports of tortoises being illegally sold from premises in North Wales he was keen to look into the matter.

Broadly speaking in order to sell many species of endangered wildlife a licence known as an Article 10 (A10) is required from Defra. At the time of this incident the licence allowed for the single sale of a particular specimen of protected species by the named person with the transaction then being notified. Defra had received complaints from several people who had bought Hermann's tortoises that the seller did not appear to have A10s allowing him to trade in the animals. When asked by some of his customers to provide a copy of the tortoise's licence he had either lied or ignored the request.

Pete Charleston carried out an initial investigation that first involved visiting the tortoises' new owners to establish the facts. It transpired that the seller involved had been advertising Hermann's tortoises for sale through various outlets, including local classified advertisements, cards in local supermarkets and by word of mouth.

Hermann's tortoise is a species with a Southern European home range and has become endangered through habitat loss, although the collection of wild animals for trade purposes must have also had an impact. An adult animal grows to between 20 and 30 centimetres and is the most common tortoise in the trade. Many animals found on sale in the UK are in fact farmed or ranched animals bred in countries such as Croatia before being bought into the UK. European law provides no restriction on the movement of such animals between member states and of course Defra would not issue A10 certificates unless they were satisfied that the tortoises were captive bred rather than taken from the wild.

Pete's enquiry showed at the time that small Hermann's tortoises were being sold for £100 each, potentially a very lucrative trade. An application to magistrates resulted in a search warrant under the provisions of the Control of Trade in Endangered Species (Enforcement) Regulations (COTES) (see Note 2) being granted and Pete made preparations to execute the warrant at the home address and also the retail premises of the tortoise trader.

Pete said, 'He was known to live with his parents in a pretty ordinary three-bedroomed detached house on a typical suburban estate; however when we got in there it was anything but normal. The door was answered by the suspect's father who was surprised to find not only a number of police officers demanding to search his premises but also two wildlife inspectors from Defra. His son, not at home, was quickly summoned from his shop.'

The tour of the house started in the garage where instead of the anticipated Ford Mondeo or perhaps a collection of household goods Pete found that the whole area had been divided into compartments, each of which housed tortoises of differing varieties, some being warmed by heat lamps. Shelves on the walls held containers in which a number of spiders and young snakes were found. The officers next entered the rear garden of the house where more surprises were in store in the form of two wallabies. A couple of rheas (small ostrich-type birds) were wandering freely whilst an enclosure in one corner held a colony of prairie dogs.

In the main part of the house there was little evidence of exotic animals of any type and it became clear that other members of the family were hardly as enthused by wildlife as was the son. Eventually the search centred on the suspect's bedroom and any thoughts Pete had about tortoises being a quiet animal vanished. Against the walls of this room were stacked a number of vivarium type tanks all of which contained tortoises including one with over a hundred Hermann's. Pete explained, 'While I would hesitate to suggest that the noise generated by a couple of hundred tortoises was deafening, the noise levels resulting from their eating and movements was considerably more than I might ever have imagined and made me wonder how any occupant could possibly share the room and manage to get any sleep.'

Thanks to the assistance of the two Defra wildlife inspectors who had travelled from London to lend their expertise and assistance to this job all of the species of animals present in the house were identified, demonstrating the value of such experts in a police investigation. Aside from the Hermann's tortoise, none of the animals in question were listed as being endangered and their presence in the house, even though they were all intended for sale, was not of concern as no welfare offences were apparent.

Following on from the search, the police enquiry continued into the apparently illegal sale of the Hermann's tortoises. Documents showed that the suspect had quite legally brought 200 young animals into the country from Holland. The animals may have originally been farmed in one of the states of the former Yugoslavia but at the time those states were not members of the European Community. The movement into Holland may well have been illegal but there was nothing to show this, nor was there any evidence that the suspect had been involved at this early stage in the tiny tortoise's travels. Nevertheless he began to sell them without having obtained the required licences, which *was* illegal. Had this occurred in genuine ignorance of the legislation some sympathy could have been shown but in this particular case evidence of his knowledge of the legislation could be proved through his previous dealings with Defra.

In due course the tortoise trader was charged with three counts of illegally selling an endangered species (a total of six tortoises) without a licence and appeared before Denbigh Magistrates Court in November 2002. The fines, plus costs, amounted to nearly £1000. The fine in the case – the first of its kind in North Wales – didn't adequately reflect the level of offending since as many as forty tortoises remained unaccounted for as their new owners were unknown.

BLUEBELL BULBS BLUE MURDER

'One of the most unusual cases I have ever been involved with,' said Pete, 'drew more complaints to the Police than any other of the 2000-plus wildlife crimes I investigated. It did not involve any of the usual suspects: badger baiters, egg collectors or poisoning. It involved the digging up of bluebells.'

The isolated, sparsely populated, Llyn peninsula is a beautiful part of North Wales with a strong sense of community and a keen awareness of the natural environment which local people deem to be in their charge. Each Spring brings a wonderful display of bluebells that covers the hillsides in a misty blue haze, perhaps not widely publicised but highly cherished locally.

September is perhaps not the busiest time of year for phone calls relating to our native flora but that was when Pete Charleston started receiving calls complaining of a gang of people clearing bluebell bulbs from a hillside noted for its Spring display of flowering bluebells that could clearly be viewed from the main Caernarfon to Pwllheli road. It emerged that a couple of weeks previously a work gang from out of the area had arrived and began to clear bracken and remove bluebell bulbs with the consent of the landowner. This had caused resentment amongst the local community, concerned because of a perceived loss of local employment opportunity but equally through concern that the bluebells were being removed. Over a number of days local anger grew and issues of public disorder began to be reported. There were confrontations and challenges in the local pub and village shop, and graffiti and other criminal damage taking place. It was clear that the Police needed to intervene to restore order and ensure that the law was not being breached.

The Wildlife and Countryside Act 1981 is the primary piece of conservation legislation in the UK that not only protects a host of birds and other animals but also protects a substantial number of our native plants. Levels of protection differ according to the conservation status of particular plants and it is illegal to dig, destroy or pick our rarest species, those that are listed on Schedule 8 of the Act. In the UK a large proportion of bluebell populations are of the Spanish variety (*Hyancynthoides hispanica*), an introduced species which is afforded no legal protection. There is, however, a population of the native British bluebell (*Hyancythoides non-scripta*) which, although not rare, has limited legislative protection making it illegal to sell or advertise the plants or bulbs for sale.

None of the callers to the police had made any allegation or suggestion that the bluebell bulbs were being removed for sale but it was felt there had to be some commercial involvement and it was decided to make contact with the landowner to establish the facts. In due course he attended at the local police station accompanied by another man who identified himself as being the site foreman for the ongoing hillside work. In the conversation that followed assurances were given to the effect that the bluebell bulbs were not being sold. Instead arrangements had been made whereby the bulbs were being removed by an East Anglian horticultural company who *in exchange* were removing bracken from the hillside. The bracken had been preventing agricultural use of the hillside and its removal would allow the landowner to usefully graze the area. Whilst at the police station the site foreman handed the police sergeant a paper bag stamped *Produce of Holland,* containing a small number of the bulbs. The sergeant thought this a bit odd but assumed that he and the landowner were thinking that this would be seen as a helpful gesture and provide evidence of their work being legitimate.

On the face of it, there appeared to be no offences of sale of bluebells but in the course of the investigation Pete sought the advice of the Crown Prosecution Service (CPS). When he got their answer, Pete thought, 'Something new can be learned every day'. The CPS were of the view that under Section 27 of the Wildlife and Countryside Act, which deals with the definition of terms used in the Act, the definition of 'sale' also included any barter and exchange. This put a different perspective on the matter and a full investigation was initiated.

In due course the landowner was interviewed at a local police station where he again explained the terms of his contract with the horticultural company. As far as he was concerned no sale had taken place. He had seen an advert in a farming publication from the horticultural company to the effect that they were prepared to purchase bluebells and had made contact with them. They had visited the area and an agreement had been reached that the bulbs could be removed in exchange for uprooting and clearing bracken from the area. He was adamant that he had not been paid any money. The gentleman concerned was clearly unaware of what the term 'sale' meant in the legislation and, in the interests of the investigation, this was not the right time to enlighten him.

Later, the man who claimed to be the director of the horticultural company was interviewed and reiterated the landowner's explanation that no sale had taken place. He explained that the bulbs had been removed with a view to planting them in East Anglia, allowing them to mature, then collecting the seeds and cultivating the bulbs that would form from them. These could then be legally sold as they would no longer be considered to be wild. He had had a gang of 10-12 workers on site uprooting bracken and removing bluebell bulbs for six weeks and although he could not say how many bulbs had been removed, 200,000 was felt to be a reasonable estimate.

The horticultural company involved ran an internet site on which bluebell bulbs were being sold for £14 a hundred so if the bulbs removed were sold they would realise £28,000. The company also sells a large range of other bulbs and it was indicated in interview with the representative that annually it imports millions of bulbs from Holland. The supply of the bulbs to the police in that paper bag bearing the claim *Produce of Holland* became rather more interesting.

It was clear that both parties were accepting that an exchange had taken place when they agreed that bracken could be cleared and at the same time the bluebell bulbs taken away. A need to evidence that these plants were of the protected British bluebell rather than the Spanish variety remained and the value of good working relationships with the conservation sector was demonstrated when Pete later visited the site with an expert from the charity Plantlife. Examination of plant remains from the previous season and measurement of the vegetation that was by that time beginning to emerge once again proved beyond all doubt that these were British bluebells they were dealing with.

From the evidence available it was clear that the lead offender in this case was the man who had claimed to be a director of the horticultural company (but who enquiries revealed was not in fact a company director and therefore had to be dealt with by the courts as a private individual). The view was taken that the landowner would not have been in a position to commit the offence had he not seen the advertisement in the agricultural press. However the legislators when framing the Wildlife and Countryside Act had clearly not envisaged the sort of circumst- ances North Wales Police were faced with, because although selling wild bluebell bulbs amounts to an offence the purchase of them doesn't. Undoubtedly the way in which the legislation was framed was intentional in order that innocent purchasers of such bulbs from dodgy traders were not criminalised but this did present further issues for the Crown Prosecution Service to consider. After much consideration they were of the view that the offence of selling wild bluebell bulbs by the landowner could not have been committed without the assistance of the other party, the horticultural businessman. The landowner was therefore charged with the sale of the bulbs and the horticultural trader for aiding and abetting the sale.

Almost a year after the first telephone calls were received on this subject both men appeared before local magistrates. Having received legal advice on their position they pleaded guilty to an offence of selling 200,000 bluebells bulbs. The landowner was fined £1000 plus costs whilst the trader was fined £5000. The magistrates were demonstrating very clearly who they considered to be the primary offender.

The penalties for the landowner did not end there. As a farmer he was in receipt of agricultural subsidies which in recent years have very helpfully been linked to compliance with legislation, aptly referred to as cross-compliance. A breach of conservation legislation leads to the withholding of some or all of the subsidies in subsequent years and in this case that is exactly what occurred.

Maximum penalties under the legislation for selling wild protected bulbs are exactly the same as for stealing bird's eggs, or destroying bat roosts: a fine of £5000 and/or six months imprisonment. The trader in this case faced one charge of selling wild bluebell bulbs but the legislation is clear in stating that this penalty can be imposed in respect of each bulb, so in theory potential penalties imposed could have amounted to ten billion pounds.

Pete observes, 'In this context the fine of five thousand pounds imposed on the trader was a mere fraction of that which could have been imposed. This is not a criticism of the justice system because on the day I considered that the magistrates did a good job. Indeed this was by far the highest fine that had ever been imposed in relation to one of my cases and I believe one of the highest fines imposed anywhere for a wildlife case. This was also the first recorded case of this nature and as such the magistrates had little guidance as to an appropriate penalty.'

After the case there was some question as to whether the imposition of a £5000 fine would have been be a great deterrent. For technical reasons the bulbs could not be recovered and calculation on the likely value of the 200,000 bulbs agreed in the charge suggest that even having paid the fine the trader may still have made a profit from his venture. The fact that the landowner asked that he be allowed time to pay his fine in instalments and the trader was content to immediately write a cheque for his fine suggests that the latter was not severely inconvenienced.

It seems ironic that during the investigation it was noted that the website of the trader involved made the claim that they abhorred those who collected bulbs from the wild. That claim remained on the website for some time after the findings of guilt!

The Case of the Disturbed Goshawk

One of the duties of a wildlife and environmental crime officer, under the heading of education and of general awareness-raising, involves giving presentations to a wide range of clubs and societies. This suited Pete Charleston fine:

'This is an area of work that I particularly enjoy as many a good discussion takes place and they are well worth doing, though in many instances there is an element of preaching to the converted. Sometimes, however, you get rather more than might be anticipated.

'One particular talk took me to a country pub and a very well-attended meeting with an obviously well-informed audience. Things were going well and I got onto the subject of the national police operation, Operation Easter, directed against the collectors of wild bird eggs. I was illustrating how obsessive many collectors are and how far they travel to take eggs. In particular I related a tale as to how a known egg collector had been seen acting suspiciously around a lake on Anglesey and only a few days later had been seen acting suspiciously around a Scottish golden eagle nest.

'At the end of the account a hand arose at the rear of the room and, having always tried to encourage questions, I paused only to be told that I could not recount the tale because the person had not been convicted of any offences in relation to either incident. I think that that was the only time I had ever spoken to an audience that included a known egg collector and this just went to demonstrate that care needs to be taken not to identify or slander individuals. On that occasion I had not identified the man in question and had he not identified himself nobody present would have been any the wiser as to who had been involved. Quite bizarrely the individual in question, who I will refer to as Mr Brown, did write to me after the meeting demanding a written apology or legal proceedings would follow. He did not get his apology and I never received a summons. Thereafter I received quite regular correspondence from him where I was assured that he had ceased associating with known egg collectors and was now working against them and in the furtherance of conservation. As such he sought a licence allowing him to disturb rare birds for the purposes of photography. Perhaps not the ideal applicant!'

Some years later, in May 2006, local police officers were investigating a break-in to a sailing club at Llyn Brenig, an upland reservoir and country park. As part of their investigations they made a number of checks of vehicles parked in the area and came up with one that was thought to be of interest to Operation Easter.

Without giving away too much of the operational procedures of Operation Easter, the next step for the officers was to contact the author, who administers the operation nationally, in Tayside. I was quickly able to tell the North Wales officers about the owner of the car, his associates, and what to look for if they decided to search the car. Few beat officers are aware of the significance of some of the paraphernalia used by wild bird egg thieves. I advised them of the relevance of small drills and small glass tubes in the blowing of the egg contents, of the relevance of maps, especially with any markings on them that might indicate nest sites, of items that might be innocuous in other circumstances, such as cotton wool or toilet paper, or of climbing or abseiling equipment, cameras and film or memory cards. Most importantly I advised them of their police powers available to search the car and the occupant, to seize any items that they thought were of evidential value, and of the fact that the Wildlife and Countryside Act 1981 gave them a power of arrest if that was required. From my knowledge of Mr Brown I advised the officers that they should contact Pete Charleston without delay and if possible have him join them.

From the officers checking the car registration number in North Wales to contacting me in Tayside and getting the information that would help their on-the-spot investigation took no more than five minutes. Very quickly the North Wales officers learned that the car was owned by the man who had interrupted the flow of Pete's country pub presentation! Once they had learned this information they approached the car and found that the man sitting in it was not Mr Brown but another man who was a known egg collector who we'll call Mr Black. A search of Mr Black and his car produced nothing of interest, but when questioned, Mr Black told the officers that Mr Brown was with him but had gone off into the adjacent forest to take photographs.

Pete was immediately informed of the contact and from 40 miles away made a dash for Llyn Brenig and the forest. En route he was able to make contact with a good friend and raptor study group member who monitors the population of birds of prey in the area. Not only was he prepared to provide assistance to Pete but he downed tools at once and made a similar dash for Llyn Brenig.

When the two arrived they found an empty car, and faced the daunting task of trying to find two people in a forest of some 40,000 hectares. They set out into the forest more in hope than in confidence but soon found a Forestry Commission gang who told them that they had seen two people who were probably the suspects walking along one of the forest tracks. With that piece of information Pete and his friend were able to guess that a goshawk nest in the forest that had been the subject of nest robberies in previous years might be the target yet again.

Making their way to the area where they knew the goshawk nest to be, they continued through the dense larch forest until in a glade they saw two men, their two suspects, standing together gathering up equipment and not more than twenty metres away from a large nest. They approached Mr Brown and Mr Black and Pete made it clear to them that he wanted to know what they were about. Pete recounts, 'It was pretty much at this time that I began to regret the quick exit from the office as here I was somewhere in a very large forest, with two males whose temperament was not known, without the personal equipment I normally carried: truncheon, handcuffs etc. I don't know if it ever occurred to the individuals quite how vulnerable I was but in the event they were both gentlemen. Brown said that he had been walking in the forest and had spotted a buzzard nest. He had decided to set up a hide and take photographs of the buzzard when it returned to the nest. Black said that having been spoken to by the Police he had decided to find his friend and make him aware of the Police interest. He had been able to do so as each of them had a two-way radio.

Both men and their equipment were searched and Pete found a camera with a remote control and some camouflage netting. However, hidden in the leaf litter beside the men were two rolls of film, which when eventually developed showed pictures of three eggs and a Goshawk sitting on a nest. On the basis of the film having been hidden both men were arrested and taken to the local Police station. When he was interviewed, Brown maintained that he had stumbled across a buzzard nest and had decided to take photographs. Black's account was that he had only gone to tell his mate of the police interest.

The knowledge of the law shown by such people is impressive. Clearly Brown was prepared to admit to taking photographs of a buzzard on its nest in the knowledge that the species, being a common bird, is not as heavily protected by law as is a goshawk, a much rarer bird. It is not therefore an offence to disturb a buzzard on a nest through photography but it is an offence to disturb a nesting goshawk.

When asked about the species of bird that had returned to the nest they had been watching, Brown said that his vision had been obscured by other trees. He had been hidden and had heard a bird coming to the nest, so using his remote control had taken photographs with a camera that he had located in a tree adjacent to the nest tree.

To try to ensure that the birds were not disturbed at the nest, which could easily result in their abandonment of the nest after all of this activity, it was not revisited for two weeks.

Pete in the meantime contacted the RSPB. Their database showed a goshawk nest in this area had been raided by a notorious Liverpudlian egg collector in 1999. He had been convicted a few years later when a large collection of eggs and his egg collecting records, going back many years, had been recovered during a raid at his home. Checking their files the RSPB found they even had the photographs taken in 1999 at the time of the raid by the egg collector. These showed it was the very same nest! Also of significance was that during a police search under warrant on the home of Mr Black earlier in 2006, a mobile phone had been recovered which was sent off for analysis. This showed Mr Black had been in recent contact with the Liverpudlian egg collector and exchanged some very interesting text messages about breeding birds. It seemed a very strange coincidence that Mr Brown and Mr Black should be found at the same nest in a remote forest a few weeks later. The RSPB database also provided the previous convictions of both men for egg collecting and disturbance of rare breeding birds, which was introduced as 'bad character evidence' at the subsequent trial.

Two weeks later Pete returned along with members of RSPB's investigations unit, who were to provide invaluable assistance to the investigation. The crime scene was measured and photo-graphed, exactly as is done in any other investigation where accurate data are likely to be required by a court. Unfortunately it was found that the nest had been abandoned so the tree was climbed by one of the RSPB officers (hardly any wildlife crime officers would be capable of this) and the infertile eggs collected and sent away for further scientific examination. Examination of the embryos in the eggs showed that their state of development was such that abandonment of the nest had occurred on the day of the disturbance.

So was it pure chance that led Mr Brown to find one of very few goshawk nests in a very large forest; that the nest in question had been robbed in previous years; that a person from the same English city as these two men had been convicted in an earlier year of taking eggs from that nest and that all three men were known to associate with each other? Pete was being asked to believe that it was all pure chance, but wisely decided not to do so and charged both with intentional or reckless disturbance of a nesting goshawk.

During interview Mr Brown also admitted knowing the Liverpudlian egg collector and even admitted tracking him down having seen his conviction on TV. He admitted speaking to him very recently about rare breeding birds but denied ever being given details of actual nest sites. When it was put to him that the 'buzzard' nest he had 'accidentally' found in the huge Clocaenog forest was the very goshawk nest raided by the Liverpudlian egg collector back in 1999 he replied, 'It's a small world.'

When Mr Black appeared at Llandudno Magistrates' Court on 30 April 2007 he continued to maintain that he had not known what Mr Brown was doing and was eventually found not guilty. Brown pleaded not guilty and tried unsuccessfully to persuade the court of his bird misidentification story. He was found guilty and was sentenced to 4 months imprisonment, suspended for a year, plus £800 costs. In an innovative approach by the court he was also banned from entering nature reserves for a period of twelve months.

MERSEYSIDE

From *Andy McWilliam*'s Notebook:

An abundance of wildlife crime is not something that most people would associate with Merseyside. However, it is home to a wide range of wildlife and habitats and has some internationally important sites, most notably its estuaries, which are vital to birdlife. It has many nature reserves and several Sites of Special Scientific Interest (SSSIs).

Merseyside is home to numerous specially protected species, including bats, red squirrel, natterjack toad and sand lizard, along with water voles, badgers and 100 species of breeding birds. Unfortunately it also has its share of wildlife criminals and along with Coventry is one of the hotspots for egg collectors. In my seven years as the dedicated Wildlife Crime Officer we had a fair degree of success in targeting offenders, who would travel the length and breadth of the UK in pursuit of birds' eggs. This success resulted in numerous convictions and four Merseyside offenders being imprisoned for their transgressions. Another man was jailed for attempting to pervert the course of justice during an investigation into his possession of wild birds' eggs.

Over an eight year period Merseyside Police has seized in the region of 8,000 illegally-taken wild birds' eggs and hundreds of pieces of intelligence, which has led to successful Police Operations across the UK. The force certainly made a significant contribution to the success of Operation Easter (see Note 3), which is a national operation co-ordinated by Alan Stewart in Tayside, targeting the UK's most prolific egg collectors. Operation Easter is in my view one of the most successful police operations and has undoubtedly made a significant impact on the exploits of a few selfish individuals.

The Doorstep Goshawk

Merseyside has a large number of bird of prey keepers, the majority of whom are completely responsible and law abiding and treat their birds well – in some cases like royalty. Unfortunately some people keep birds of prey because they feel it is a macho thing to do and their birds end up being neglected and ultimately suffer. Interestingly, these keepers lose a great deal of credibility with those they are trying to impress. I know of one man whose first bird was a golden eagle. He had no background in handling any birds and soon had to get rid of it because he hadn't a clue how to deal with it.

I would regularly get information about bird-keepers, often well meaning, which would turn out to be false and actually refer to a totally legitimate keeper. One such example was from a lady who phoned me early one morning. Not unusually for Liverpool she had a pronounced scouse accent. She said, 'Is that the wildlife busy?', 'busy' being a colloquialism in Merseyside for police officer. I told her that it was. She then told me that she wanted to report her neighbour for abusing his bird of prey, which she described as 'brown and bloody big'. At this stage I was unable to accurately identify the species and enquired about the nature of the abuse.

She told me, 'He keeps it on an 'oop in the garden', which I took it to mean a bow perch (hoop) used regularly by keepers. She continued, 'It keeps falling pregnant and the babies are dying.' I was intrigued and asked her to explain what she meant. She said, 'I look out every day and the little yellow fluffy babies are dead on the grass.'

At this point I found it difficult to stifle my laughter, realising that what she was referring to was the bird's food that its was owner was supplying. I knew this lady had phoned up with the best of intentions and I tried to explain what she had seen was entirely innocent, but she was having none of it. I explained that in my experience birds of prey laid eggs, which they then incubated for several weeks before they hatched, to which she replied, 'Not this one love!'

Every now and again I would get information that I knew was credible and accurate. On one such occasion I had a wildlife crime display at a bird fair when I was approached by a man, who I took to be a keeper but he did not want to give his details. He told me about a man from a particular housing estate who he said was travelling to the Sheffield area with others and stealing goshawks from the wild.

I was aware that Merseysiders had been responsible for nest robberies in the past and I suspected some were still actively involved. Although my informant wanted to remain anonymous, I thought he was genuine and he wasn't trying to elaborate and fill in the blanks which some informants do. He did not know the goshawk thief's full address or surname, but gave me enough to be going on with.

A few months later one of Defra's staff contacted me about a man, let's call him Freddy, who had an address on the same housing estate as the unknown goshawk thief and was most likely the same person. Freddy had contacted Defra in an attempt to register a goshawk. Goshawks are included on Schedule 4 of the Wildlife and Countryside Act 1981 and there is a requirement for any keeper to register those listed species. It works very much like car registration: birds are fitted with a unique numbered ring, which marries up to a registration document.

Freddy's story was that he had gone to the shops and when he came home he found a cardboard box on his step, in which was a live goshawk. Not what most people would expect on their doorstep, nevertheless that was his claim and no matter how far-fetched it sounded there was always a possibility it could have been true. Defra sent a wildlife inspector to the address to fit a ring to the bird in order that the bird could be registered. This was only three days after the bird had been allegedly abandoned on his doorstep.

A ring was duly fitted and the bird was subsequently registered. The fact that a bird is registered is not recognition that a bird is legally held or acquired, but merely recognition that it is in that keeper's possession. Freddy was particularly familiar with the bird, which appeared used to being handled by him and was happy to fly to his glove. This was suspicious considering the keeper and bird had only met up few days earlier.

Defra staff contacted me and expressed their concerns about Freddy's possession of this bird. I had enough suspicion to apply for a search warrant for his address and thought this was the best course to take. If I had made a cold call he may have refused access. I may have had to walk away with my tail between my legs, and by the time I could obtain a warrant any evidence would most likely be gone. Magistrates accepted my application and were happy to issue the search warrant. A couple of days later I called on Freddy along with my colleague Steve Harris (Steve would later take over as force wildlife crime officer when I retired) and an expert bird handler Mal Ingham. Although it is always preferable for keepers to handle their own birds, it is necessary to cater for the possibility of them refusing. A good friend of mine, Mal is highly skilled in handling birds of prey and had successfully rehabilitated numerous birds back to the wild; he is also an expert on badgers and has often given evidence in badger trials.

We paid Freddy an early morning call and he was not very receptive to our visit. If I had carried out his suggestion as to what I could do with the search warrant, I would certainly have required surgery. He did not seem to be particularly fond of the police. Once we entered his house he kindly turned his television on at full volume. I told him we wanted to examine the goshawk, which was being kept in an aviary in his garden, and asked him to explain how he had come by the bird, but he refused to answer.

Under the Wildlife and Countryside Act 1981, the onus is on him to show that his possession is lawful and that the bird hadn't been taken from the wild. I pointed this out to him and was again given short shrift. It was apparent that Freddy had something to hide and from my experience keepers who are lawfully in possession of birds are more than happy to be helpful. In fact they don't like people who give them a bad name.

I gave him the opportunity to catch up the bird himself and again he refused. This vindicated the decision to take an expert handler on any such operation and Mal Ingham was called into action, expertly catching up the goshawk with a minimum of stress to the bird. Satisfied that we had the right bird and in view of Freddy's reluctance to explain to us how he had come by it, I took the decision to seize the bird, which was then removed to a pre-arranged location.

Returning to the house I told Freddy that I had seized the bird, news which was greeted by a series of unprintable expletives. The search warrant also gave us power to search his house and allowed us to look for relevant documents or items that may be used to take or possess wild birds. We conducted a search looking for the likes of climbing equipment and maps showing nest sites.

On several occasions during wildlife searches we have recovered evidence of other criminal activity including drugs, firearms and stolen property, which illustrates the link between wildlife and core crime. During this search I picked up an A4 size diary, which Freddy seemed to be concerned about. I opened the first page and found written across the year planner 'FIRST YEAR IN CHARGE OF A GOSHAWK', which was interesting because it pre-dated the date he allegedly acquired the goshawk and from checking with Defra I knew he hadn't previously had any goshawks registered to him.

Further down the page on the year planner the 6th May was circled and the words 'BIRDS TAKEN' written above it. I turned to the page for this date and was staggered to find a full account of how Freddy and others had been to several nest sites in Derbyshire and Yorkshire in an attempt to take wild birds. At one site they were unsuccessful because 'the nest had already been robbed' and at another they had been thwarted by the presence of Forestry Commission workers. But at a third site in the Derwent Valley they climbed to a nest and had taken two goshawk chicks, leaving an un-hatched egg and a single chick.

The diary continued giving a day-to-day account of keeping 'his' bird, day-to-day weights and significant developments, right up to its first hunting trips and kills. The second chick had been taken by one of his associates who we were unable to positively identify, although we had our suspicions. The diary indicated that the second bird died some months later.

Freddy was arrested and interviewed and in keeping with his previous non-compliance, he gave a 'no comment' interview. This again didn't really help his cause, because this was his opportunity to give an explanation. Although we already seemed to have a very strong case against Freddy, we still had some work to do and it was going to be useful to tie the diary account in with a confirmed nest robbery.

I contacted the local Raptor Group in the Derwent Valley, whose members monitor the goshawk nests in their area. Goshawks have been heavily persecuted over the years and there were relatively few successful breeding attempts. Because of the detail in Freddy's diary about an 'un-hatched egg' and the 'single chick' the raptor group were able to identify a nest site near to Lady Bower Reservoir that they suspected had been interfered with around the same date of Freddy's diary entry. They had noted a tree in which goshawks had nested that showed signs of having been climbed but because there was still a live chick in the nest, at the time they could not be 100% sure it had been interfered with. With the diary evidence we had found, their suspicions were confirmed.

Freddy was charged with taking two goshawks, possessing a goshawk and making a false declaration to Defra to obtain registration. Initially he pleaded not guilty, but after several months of court hearings and in the face of overwhelming evidence, changed his plea. He was jailed for four months, although this was later reduced to two on appeal.

Freddy was only jailed for the possession and registration offence and not for taking the birds. Despite being convicted of the taking offence, it had actually occurred prior to the Wildlife and Countryside Act 1981 being amended. Before this the courts did not have power to impose custodial sentences and their powers were not retrospective.

The case against Freddy came at a time when the government was reviewing the bird registration scheme and it showed its importance as an enforcement tool. I am sure that without it his crimes would have gone undetected.

Badgers, Three Daves and a Dog Called Brick

Merseyside has a small number of badger setts compared with some areas, but unfortunately it does have plenty of badger diggers and baiters, many of whom travel to other parts of the country to carry out the crimes. Merseyside's badgers are mainly on the Wirral Peninsula; setts on the Liverpool side of the Mersey have more or less disappeared mainly because of development, but also through human persecution.

Wirral has a very active Badger Group and the location of most setts is well-known to the members and to and local residents, who take a great pride in their badgers. As a result, attacks on these setts rarely go unnoticed, but nevertheless attacks on badgers and their setts do still occur.

One morning in October 2003 a school teacher and his assistant were taking a science class when they looked out over farmland next to the school to see three men with a couple of dogs acting suspiciously in a hedgerow. A white van was parked on a main road about 100 yards from the men. The witnesses innovatively dismantled a microscope in the classroom and used it as a pair of binoculars to get a better look. They were then able to see the men more clearly and observed the fact that they were digging. Initially they thought the men were hiding stolen property and called the police who arrived a short time later.

When the police approached them the men said they were just out ratting. They admitted they didn't have permission to be on the land and, having given the officers their details, they were asked to leave. Importantly, the officers, despite their lack of knowledge of wildlife or the appropriate legislation, established from the men that there were no dogs still underground.

The men, who I will call the three Daves, left the scene in the white van followed by the police, and all under the watchful gaze of our two teacher witnesses and 28 intrigued boys who had by now abandoned their studies.

Twenty minutes later the men returned to the same location, but from a different direction. They started digging frantically. The police were phoned again but this time one of the Daves was acting as a lookout and they ran off before the police could get to them.

During the dinner break curiosity got the better of one on our witnesses and he went to have a look for himself at where the men had been digging. He found several holes and heard a snuffling sound from one and further investigation revealed a black and tan Jack Russell terrier, which was fitted with a locator collar. Locator collars are commonly used on dogs that are put underground and the handler can keep track of the animal with a small receiver. The witness managed to pull the dog out of the hole and called the local dog warden. The terrier was taken to the local dog pound and I was informed of this highly suspicious development. Even after the dog had been removed the witnesses saw the three Daves return on several occasions, obviously in search of their abandoned terrier.

I decided to attend the scene with the badger expert, Mal Ingham, and we met up with one of the witnesses, who showed us exactly where he had recovered the Jack Russell and the spot where he had seen the men digging. Though he had previously been unaware of this sett, Mal was able to identify it as currently being used by badgers. It was a small outlying sett approximately half a mile from a well established and much larger one. The dog had been down inside the sett and we found that the Daves had actually dug directly into an underground chamber.

While we were carrying out our examination of the scene, I was phoned by the dog wardens who told me that a heavily pregnant woman turned up at the dog pound and tried to claim the Jack Russell. She had claimed that she was walking the dog across farmland and the dog had run off. I later established she had been eight and a half months pregnant and the likelihood of her walking her dog across that terrain was remote. They sensibly had refused to release the dog.

Based on the fact that this was an active badger sett, and that they had dug into it and apparently put a dog underground, I decided to arrest the three men and interview them. All three claimed that they had been hunting foxes, at that time legal, (now illegal under the Hunting Act 2004) although they may have been guilty of trespassing. The three Daves claimed that the dog had been sent into a fox earth and not a badger sett. In law the onus was on them to show that this was not an active badger sett. I was totally confident with Mal Ingham's assessment and this was later borne out by the opinion of another expert.

The men had all shown they had something to hide by denying the presence of a dog underground. One of the Daves had also given the police a false name, although he denied this and claimed the officer had simply misheard him. We were able to prove he had used the same false details when police in Warwickshire stopped him a few months earlier. Perhaps the Warwickshire police officer had also misheard.

All three Daves were charged with offences against the Protection of Badgers Act 1992 for damaging a sett and causing a dog to enter a sett. After a 4-day trial before a district judge they were all found guilty and each sentenced to 4 weeks imprisonment.

I was pleased with the conviction and thought the sentence was a reasonable one, given that the maximum sentence was 6 months and there was no indication that a badger had been harmed or injured.

A year or so after the case I was assisting uniformed officers to search the home address of the cousin of Dave One. I will call him Ken. We knew he was also involved in hunting with dogs and we found all the paraphernalia that you would expect. At his house he had a bitch Staffordshire bull terrier called Bella. She was a lovely looking animal and very distinctive – tan, with a white collar and facial markings. Bella was very submissive and had several old scars around the face and chest. She had obviously fought a round or two.

During the search we found several still photographs hidden behind a television, showing Bella and another dog pulling at a badger. Ken claimed the badger was dead and that the dogs were playing with the carcass. Looking at the features of the badger such as hair and tail, it was quite apparent that the badger had been alive when the photos were taken. We also came across a video tape labelled 'KEN'S TAPE. DO NOT TAPE OVER'. We seized this and arrested Ken.

I later viewed this tape and found it to contain around a dozen clips showing dogs attacking animals. Bella featured heavily in all the clips. Four of the clips featured badgers being attacked by dogs and they remain some of the most savage attacks I have seen. In his interview Ken admitted that he had been present, but that the attacks on the badgers had all been accidents and not intentional. He claimed he had been trying to get the dogs off.

I later viewed and transcribed every second of these tapes and there is no way that these incidents could have been accidental. The men present, which included Ken, could clearly be heard shouting encouragement to the dogs and in some clips can be seen kicking the badgers. At times as many as five dogs are savaging a single badger. The problem was proving when and where the crimes had taken place.

As luck would have it, whoever had filmed the badger incidents had left the date displayed on the video recorder, putting the offences within the six month time limit for prosecutions, which thanks to legislative changes has now been extended to two years.

My second piece of luck was the fact that Ken did not think my police powers extended outside England and was happy to admit that these incidents had taken place in Caerwys in North Wales. So we had an accurate date and a location; without these it may not have been possible to pursue the case. Ken was charged with eight offences against the Protection of Badgers Act 1992. I anticipated that Ken would plead guilty as the evidence was overwhelming.

Unlike a lot of colleagues across the country I was lucky that I could deal with a dedicated Crown Prosecution Service lawyer, who had a great deal of expertise in prosecuting wildlife offences and dealt with all the cases I submitted. I spoke to her about the importance of showing the Magistrates the video footage as a verbal description would not do the events justice. She agreed.

Ken did plead guilty and Magistrates agreed that they would view the footage before sentencing; however Ken's defence solicitor requested that he be excused from the courtroom during the viewing, 'because he finds this type of thing revolting.' Rather bizarrely the Magistrates excused Ken and he waited outside the court while they watched the tape.

Ken was sentenced to 4 months imprisonment for the offences, which were without doubt at the upper end of the scale of animal cruelty.

In another badger-related case an RSPCA inspector was called to an address within sight of Liverpool's football ground. He attended and in the backyard at the address he saw a black Patterdale terrier that had a seriously infected injury to its lower jaw. The injury seemed recent and clearly required urgent veterinary treatment. Unfortunately he could not actually get access to the address.

The inspector recognised the dog, which was called Brick, because he had been to the address previously and knew the owner was someone he would have difficulty dealing with. He phoned me at home for advice and I suggested he photograph the dog and I would try and get him some police assistance.

He managed to photograph the dog, but while I was trying to get assistance to him a group of local youths distracted him, whilst others climbed into the yard and removed the dog. The inspector had been powerless to stop them.

Although the evidence had been lost for now, at least he had some photographs. Luckily for the case – and for the dog as well – it was found abandoned a couple of days later. I visited the dog with the RSPCA inspector at a local vet's, who was of the opinion that the dog had been caused unnecessary suffering and required treatment.

Once again we knew that Brick's owner was also involved in hunting with dogs and I thought the nature of his injury had all the hallmarks of a badger bite: basically his lower lip and the flesh on his lower jaw had been ripped away. It was agreed that Brick should be taken to a specialist vet, who could give expert opinion as to whether this injury had been caused by a badger.

The examination confirmed our suspicions that Brick had been in conflict with a badger. I arrested the owner, who denied Brick was his dog and claimed to have no knowledge of his injury. I must say that the interview was extremely heated and I could understand the RSPCA inspector's concerns about dealing with him. It was obvious we could not prove where or when Brick had been pitted against a badger so we were unable to prefer any charges under the Protection of Badgers Act. He was charged with causing the dog unnecessary suffering under the Protection of Animals Act 1911, which has since been updated by the Animal Welfare Act 2006.

Brick's owner was later sentenced to four months imprisonment, and although he was never charged directly with an offence under the Badgers Act, I am sure the court took into the account the nature of the dog's injuries when passing sentence.

Water Voles v Big Business

Although dealing with individuals involved in wildlife crime can be difficult and protracted, dealing with large corporations can be even harder. One such case involved a large construction company and the humble water vole.

Colliers Moss Nature Reserve lies in the St Helens area of Merseyside. The reserve was managed at the time by the Groundwork Trust. It is divided into two distinct areas, the first with a small lake, which is managed for recreational pursuits such as fishing and walking and the second, the area involved in this case, has been allowed to develop naturally for bio-diversity. The area is regularly visited and surveyed for wildlife. On one such survey Dr Paul Thomas of the Environment Agency identified a significant population of water voles, mammals which are in national decline.

Although in England (since 6 April 2008, though not yet in the rest of the UK) water voles are now fully protected and included on Schedule 5 of the Wildlife and Countryside Act 1981, at the time of this incident they were only protected from disturbance, as were their shelters and resting places. As a result of Dr Thomas's findings a management plan was drawn up. This was aimed to consolidate the existing water vole population and ultimately to increase it.

Adjacent to the nature reserve is a large housing development of around 300 new homes, being built by Company A. On a routine visit to the nature reserve Dr Thomas found that a ditch on the site had been dredged and the banks had been re-profiled and all the vegetation had been cleared. He immediately contacted me fearing that water vole habitat had been disturbed. I went to the scene and could see that a stretch of around 40 metres of the ditch had been cleared. A drainage pipe was running from the building site under an unmade roadway into the ditch. Initially it appeared that the ditch had been cleared to allow a free flow of water off the building site.

Dr Thomas surveyed the ditch and concluded that water voles had probably been killed and that their burrows, shelters and feeding platforms had been destroyed as a result of the ditch work. He concluded that it was inconceivable that water voles had not been disturbed. He estimated that the habitat would take around two years to recover.

I established from the Groundwork Trust that they had not carried out the work and more importantly had not granted permission for anybody else to carry out any work and certainly wouldn't have given any consent because of the presence of water voles. Offences of disturbance and destruction of shelters etc. may be committed either intentionally or recklessly. It was apparent that I was not going to be able to prove somebody intentionally disturbed any voles, but the fact that somebody had carried out work on someone else's land, in this case on a nature reserve, without asking permission showed a high degree of recklessness. The question was: who was responsible?

Initial enquiries on the building site proved fruitless and nobody seemed to have any knowledge of this ditch work. I made enquiries with local residents and traced an 80 year-old lady who, while a ditch was being dredged with a mechanical digger, had actually complained to workmen about the smell. She recalled speaking to a man in a hard hat and a fluorescent jacket, who had told her they had to dredge the ditch so the rain water would flow away from the building site. This confirmed what I had suspected.

I eventually tracked down the site engineer and met him at the affected area, but he said that he had no knowledge of the work. I managed to establish that all road and drainage work was sub-contracted to Company B, who had originally owned the building site and had sold it to Company A with planning permission before building had commenced.

I contacted directors of both companies and asked them if they could establish who was responsible for the ditch work. At this stage Company A did not seem to take the investigation very seriously. Company B were more receptive and I visited their head office and spoke to a managing director, who told me they were having difficulty laying their hands on relevant minutes of meetings to establish who had given the go-ahead for the work to be carried out. Their technical manager at the time had moved and they were unable to contact him. They pointed out that any work would only have been carried out at the request of Company A, or they wouldn't have been paid, which did seem a reasonable point. They told me that they had sold the land on to Company A two years earlier and once Company A owned it was their responsibility to obtain the required consents or permission. They also put me in contact with a digger driver that they had sub-contracted and who they believed may be able to help with the inquiry.

I interviewed the digger driver sub-contracted by Company B, who admitted it was he who had cleared and dredged the ditch, but only under the instructions of the Company B's technical manager and always on the understanding that any required consent had been acquired from the appropriate authority. He clearly had no knowledge of the presence of water voles and claimed he didn't even know what they looked like.

I was able to track down the former technical manager for Company B, who proved invaluable to the investigation. He had been on site at the time and was responsible for the drainage work. He had identified a problem with the drainage of rain water off the north end of the site. The outlet on the nature reserve was higher than the drain on the building site and would not flow effectively. The technical manager offered Company A two possible solutions. Option 1 was to dredge the ditch on the nature reserve to lower the outlet. Option 2 was to siphon the water elsewhere, which he pointed out was more expensive. Company A plumped for the cheaper Option 1 and gave the go-ahead for the ditch to be re-profiled.

It was still not clear who specifically from Company A had given the go-ahead, but Company B's technical manager agreed that he gave the instructions for the work to be carried out on the understanding that the appropriate consents had been obtained by Company A. Company A were still reluctant to be interviewed, but when I pointed out I was considering exercising my power of arrest their position seemed to alter and they suddenly wanted to co-operate with the investigation. A company director attended for interview with a prepared statement, which effectively put the blame on Company B. Although he had prepared a statement, I still put a number of questions to him, which on legal advice he declined to answer.

I had kept the CPS fully apprised throughout the inquiry and they agreed with my recommendation that no individuals should be charged, but Company A should face corporate charges of reckless disturbance and recklessly damaging places of shelter used by water voles.

The company pleaded not guilty, but were convicted following a trial before District Judge Lady Wickham, who was satisfied that they had given the instructions for the work to be carried out and that they had been reckless by not consulting with the landowners. The company was fined £5,000, which was really peanuts for a multi-million pound corporation, but proportionate for the penalties available to the court.

The case took around six months to investigate and at times I seemed to be up against a brick wall, so I was extremely pleased with the outcome.

LINCOLNSHIRE

The third largest and fourth most rural county in England, Lincolnshire covers an area of 2,284 square miles and is policed by approximately 1200 officers as well as 800 support staff in varying roles. Lincoln has the largest population, with 100,000 residents. Other sizeable towns are Boston, Grantham, Skegness, Spalding and Stamford. The population of 660,000 in the county enjoys an excellent quality of life, no doubt enhanced by the wealth of biodiversity on offer.

The coastline of Lincolnshire extends for 70 miles from the Humber to the Wash with the majority of this designated as a Site of Special Scientific Interest (SSSI). The coast attracts many people during the summer months, with Skegness able to boast the largest concentration of caravans anywhere in Europe, an estimated 250,000 on numerous sites. The majority of holiday-makers come from the Midlands, in particular Nottinghamshire, Derbyshire, Northants, South and West Yorkshire.

The coast also boasts some excellent nature reserves with the RSPB Frampton and Frieston in the south and the Lincolnshire Wildlife Trust flagship reserve, Gibraltar Point, three miles south of Skegness. There is also Saltfleetby/Theddlethorpe Dunes National Nature Reserves and Tetney RSPB reserve towards Grimsby in the north.

Inland around the Boston and Sleaford areas in particular the poaching of hares is still a major problem despite this being outlawed by the Hunting Act 2004. The majority of offenders are known to have criminal records and there is a very real fear of associated crime in these areas despite Lincolnshire being one of the safest counties in which to live.

In a similar vein, deer poaching is still of concern, particularly in the south of the county around Bourne and Stamford and to the north of Lincoln around Market Rasen and Caistor. Concerned landowners, farmers and keepers are now members of a poacherwatch scheme which has been in place since 2004 and has proved to be a significant deterrent. Lincolnshire is one of the few counties where all six species of deer can be found.

There are five hunt packs based in Lincolnshire and another two which enter Lincolnshire from neighbouring counties. There is regular police contact with masters of the hunts.

Some areas of the county have a good population of badgers; indeed in some areas they are more numerous than foxes. Badgers continue to attract the attention of criminals who regard digging them out with dogs as some sort of 'sport'. There is also a good number of breeding Schedule 1 birds at various locations and Lincolnshire is nationally important for marsh harrier and little tern in particular. The recent Barn Owl Monitoring Programme revealed that Lincolnshire has 20% of the country's breeding population of the beautiful barn owl, now a familiar sight throughout the county. Add to all this a good population of water vole, otter, natterjack toad, slow worm, great-crested newt, water shrew, over 100 nature reserves and over 100 SSSIs then you will see why the Lincolnshire wildlife crime officer, Constable Nigel Lound, appreciates he has the best job in Lincolnshire Police.

Tortoises in Tesco

A wide range of goods, from begonias to bedsteads and cookers to cars are regularly advertised on the notice boards within supermarkets. When an animal or bird is advertised for sale on their notice boards this always rings an alarm bell with me. There are many people with genuine reasons for selling pet animals but I'm well aware that this number is equalled by the number of crooks involved. If there is no address or landline telephone number provided on the card – or even in a newspaper advert – I become even more suspicious. This suspicion has often been vindicated, and is yet again borne out by the circumstances of a case in Lincolnshire investigated by Nigel Lound.

The investigation began in October 2003 when a man from Lincoln replied to an advert in a Tesco store offering tortoises for sale. A mobile phone number was listed for anyone who was interested. When the Tesco customer rang the mobile number the man on the other end, who called himself Mr Doncaster (later shown to be a false name), agreed to meet him in a supermarket car park. By this time the alarm bells should be loud and clear, if for no other reason that it is an offence under the Pet Animals Act 1951 for a person to sell a pet in a street or a public place.

The buyer and the vendor met as arranged and as a result two tortoises changed hands for £300. Genuine pet dealers, at least with more exotic pets such as tortoises, usually give advice, sometimes in the form of a leaflet, on how to care for them. No such advice here so the buyer contacted the RSPCA and a local reptile expert for advice. The reptile expert subsequently ident-ified the tortoises as Hermann's tortoises (*Testudo hermanni,*) which come under CITES Appendix II, EU Annex A.

The RSPCA inspector, knowing that no paperwork regarding the sale had changed hands, contacted Nigel Lound so that he could carry out further enquiries. The only information Nigel had at this stage was a description of the tortoise vendor, who we'll call Tommy, and the mobile phone number quoted in the advert. Nigel obtained the relevant authority required to carry out a subscriber check on the mobile telephone number, which gave a name and address in London some three years previously with the person 'no longer known' at the address. No progress in tracing Tommy.

With such scant information to go on Nigel approached an

understanding detective inspector and they agreed that the only way towards a successful outcome was for a police officer to ring the mobile, pretend to be interested in buying a tortoise, and arrange to meet this Tommy. The meeting would need to be followed up by surveillance to find out where Tommy lived which is always easier said than done. The first step is to ensure that the surveillance is done legally so that any evidence gained will be accepted in court. Once the necessary authorities under the Regulatory of Investigatory Powers Act 2000 (RIPA) were applied for and in due course approved, Nigel briefed the surveillance team. The next step was to set the trap.

A member of the surveillance team telephoned the mobile number and spoke with a man who he hoped was Tommy. A meeting was arranged. The meeting was recorded on video and the conversation tape-recorded, again authorised under RIPA. The car that the tortoise seller was using was later found to be registered to Tommy, and the Police National Computer gave a Newark address that turned out to be accurate; nevertheless there was a need to follow him back home to confirm this. While all this was taking place Nigel was busy organising the help of the local RSPCA inspector, a reptile expert and a police search team. A search using the powers of a warrant granted under Section 9 of COTES Regulations 1997 would be the next urgent step once they had, in police parlance, 'housed' Tommy the tortoise trader.

Once Tommy's address had been confirmed Nigel attended at Newark Magistrates Court and obtained the necessary warrant. Meanwhile the surveillance team watched Tommy's address to ensure he was at home when Nigel knocked on the door with the warrant in his hand. This ran like clockwork. A woman answered the door and from the beginning was obstructive and uncooperative (in fact, in 23 years of policing, Nigel had encountered no one quite as abusive as this woman). He kept her talking while the search team and others filed in behind him.

It was confirmed that there was just the husband and wife present – Tommy and Theresa – and that they were the only people who lived there. As soon as Nigel entered the lounge of the house he saw three tortoises, identified as Hermann's tortoises by the reptile expert present. Tommy and Theresa said there were no other tortoises anywhere in the house. Tommy was questioned about the tortoises already found and the evidence so far obtained regarding the illicit car park meetings. Evidentially at this point the police had a man using a false name (Mr Doncaster) with an untraceable phone, advertising endangered tortoises for sale at a number of locations, for a substantial amount of money and who would not tell where he obtained them. Yet here he is with three of them in his front room. He admitted he had used a false name, explaining he didn't want anyone to know who he was or where he lived. This is suspicious enough in itself but he couldn't (or didn't) give a reason why. Likewise he wouldn't say where he got the tortoises or how long he'd had them. He did concede he had no paperwork for them; not a difficult admission to make if no paperwork can be produced.

During the search of the house another tortoise was found in an upstairs bedroom secreted in a sealed cardboard box. This was identified as a Kleinmann's or Egyptian tortoise, probably worth up to £5000, and listed on Appendix I of CITES and EU Annex A as it is a critically endangered species, with a ban on its international commercial trade.

When Tommy was asked about it he said he had forgotten about it and 'it must have fallen into the box'. That is the *sealed* box. The expression 'head buttoning up the back' immediately comes to mind, though when someone is backed into a corner any excuse trotted out seems a good idea at the time. It seemed pretty obvious that Tommy had been hiding this particularly valuable animal whilst Theresa was busy trying to obstruct the police officers' entry.

The search of Tommy's house took almost three hours and amongst the items seized were five mobile phones (quite common in scams of this type), numerous books on tortoises, a box of reptile equipment and food for and photographs of tortoises.

Unfortunately for the police operating in 2003 there was no power of arrest for this type of offence (this has since been rectified in England and Wales under the Serious Organised Crime and Police Act, 2005) which meant that the suspects could not be interviewed until – in this case – three weeks later. Hardly ideal, to say the least. With some criminals three minutes is long enough to concoct a story. In three weeks the story is likely to be polished so much that even the inventor of the plausible tale will believe it. Tommy was cautioned and was briefly questioned. Part of the caution contains the phrase 'you do not have to say anything' so he chose this option. He did say that he didn't want to incriminate himself and would require a solicitor to be present. Even when being interviewed in his house if a suspect is not cautioned *and* asked if would like a solicitor present then the questioning can be subject to debate in court as to whether it is admissible or not.

Policing in Scotland is made easier because there is no requirement to ask a suspect if he or she would like a solicitor present when being interviewed. Indeed if a suspect is detained and taken to a police station, where the police can hold and interview him for up to 6 hours, and he requests a solicitor or a solicitor attends at the police station demanding to see his client, the solicitor can be told – politely of course – to clear off. There are some exceptions and in certain circumstances it may be prejudicial to an investigation not to allow a solicitor access to a client. In particular these relate to young people or vulnerable adults charged with a serious crime. I have only once interviewed a suspect in the presence of his solicitor and there was no doubt that the solicitor was the most uncomfortable person in the interview room. The situation changes once a person has been charged, when he becomes entitled to have the services of a solicitor.

Any suspect requires to be cautioned before being interviewed otherwise any incriminatory comments that he makes will not be admissible in evidence. Exceptions are comments made before the police have had an opportunity to caution him. In Scotland the suspect has a right to remain silent and does not have to make any reply to police questioning. This cannot later be the subject of adverse criticism during a trial. On the other hand, in England and Wales an inference can be drawn by the failure of a suspect to say something at the time of police interview and later makes a statement or comment that he relies on as part of his defence. In my view there is value for the prosecution (and the public interest) in this and I'd be pleased to see this arrangement creeping over Hadrian's Wall.

Tommy and Theresa claimed the four tortoises seized were the only ones they had possessed apart from the two sold to the original Tesco witness, and said they had got them about nine months earlier from a man called Chris at a local antiques fair for a total of £600. They paid cash, no paperwork changed hands and they could shed no light on the identity or whereabouts of Chris. Tommy admitted to placing 'four or five' adverts in local stores, and it was also established that in the past two years they had taken holidays to Egypt, Tunisia and the Gambia.

Ever up for a challenge, Nigel obtained a further RIPA authority and examined Tommy's original mobile phone. He was not surprised that the phone log showed that it had received calls from fifty seven different numbers, which he researched and made contact where possible with the subscribers. As a result of visiting some of the subscribers and obtaining witness

Caring for Live Exhibits – and the Cost

When live creatures are taken as exhibits in an investigation they can't just be shoved into a drawer or a cupboard until the case comes to court. It is worth mentioning that the tortoises were looked after by the reptile expert present when the warrant was executed. The Heathrow CITES team (the small team of officers from HM Revenue and Customs who work from Heathrow Airport and are specialists in dealing with the international smuggling of wildlife) were made aware of the case, as was the RSPCA. Nigel made the assumption, wrongly, that the animals would be kept by these agencies during the case and re-homed on its conclusion. He admits that he didn't give it a lot of thought, being busy working on the other issues involved with the case to ensure the correct result at court, as well as the day-to-day investigation of other wildlife crime cases. He was not particularly concerned about the expense involved since, even with limited knowledge of tortoises, he was aware they don't take a lot of exercising or cleaning out and munch away on a few leaves of lettuce every day. Wrong!

The case went to court about a year after the warrant was executed. About six months after the conclusion of the case Nigel found an invoice on his desk from the local reptile expert for the housing of three tortoises for eighteen months. How much would you guess? A lettuce a day, 45p, times 30 for a monthly bill, then again times 18. £243. Doubled to take account of labour, and add on a bit to make the figure even. £500?

Believe it or not the bill was just over £24,000. This caused Nigel great concern, not to say panic, knowing how cash-strapped police forces are. The invoice was eventually resolved with the police, RSPCA, CITES team and the reptile expert coming to an amicable agreement! Nigel wasn't involved with the negotiations, but understands that there was a settlement for about half of the money initially billed, with the Police, RSPCA and Customs paying around £4000 each.

statements he found out that 'tortoise for sale' adverts had been placed in eighteen cities and towns, all in the East Midlands, and that a further four tortoises were sold at prices between £250 and £300. At no time was anyone allowed to visit Tommy's house; he always travelled to meet potential buyers.

In the light of this further evidence Tommy and Theresa were again interviewed and, after a lengthy consultation with a solicitor, they both now admitted they had originally bought thirty tortoises (still from Chris, the phantom wholesale tortoise trader) for the sum of £600. They also admitted to selling twenty four tortoises for a total of £3500. A healthy profit.

When the case went to court, Tommy and Theresa pleaded guilty to a number of charges under the Control of Trade in Endangered Species Regulations 1997 and each were fined £2000.

A Simple Bat Case

I suppose that most people, when asked about what they see as wildlife crime, immediately think of egg collecting, poaching or the destruction of birds of prey. Few might consider that the humble bat is the subject of considerable crime, but the fact is that there is such concern about bats being killed during developments or renovations of old properties that they have been made a species of conservation priority by the Joint Nature Conservation Committee (JNCC – see Note 2).

Constable Nigel Lound was contacted in August 2003 by Lapwings Consultants, an ecological consultancy, regularly used by Lincolnshire Wildlife Trust. They expressed concern that having previously carried out a survey of a bat roost in an old barn, the barn – and naturally the bat roost within – had now been destroyed. Nigel visited Lapwings Consultants and noted statements, including one from the ecologist employed by them, Garry Steele. Noting statements is the boring but essential part of police work never seen on TV programmes. In detective fiction a police officer – usually, for reasons unknown to real police officers, a detective inspector – speaks briefly to a witness without ever taking out his or her notebook, and is immediately on the trail of the suspect. Real policing is about the painstaking noting of crucial detail into statements, collating all the evidence available then typing it for the attention of Crown Prosecution Service lawyers or in Scotland, the procurators fiscal. After thirty years most police officers can type almost as fast with three or four fingers as a trained typist can with eight.

Nigel learned during his statement-taking that Mr Steele had been approached by Lapwings to carry out a 'protected species' survey of a barn in the village of Mareham Le Fen, Lincolnshire. This type of survey is extremely common, though unfortunately does not happen in every case, since some developers want to save the cost of a survey, or in worst-case scenarios they are well aware of protected species being present and equally well aware that if this knowledge were to become official it could hold up their work and cost many thousands of pounds.

The survey was carried out on 23 December 2003 and showed that bats were present, strongly believed to be whiskered bats, a species common in Lincolnshire. You may wonder why a consultant ecologist only *believed* them to be whiskered bats. In fact the characteristics of whiskered bats are notoriously similar to Brandt's bats, the only differences being the shape of the tragus, which is a lobe of tissue inside the ear of certain bat species believed to be connected with echo-location, and in the case of males, the penis. You can see why police officers depend on the evidence of experts in different fields to prove a case in court!

Mr Steele met with the developer on 6 February 2004 to discuss mitigation and further development. He was also able to confirm that the bats were still present on this date. He learned it was the intention of the developer to build four houses on the site, which would sell for £140,000 each.

Mitigation was agreed, and this involved leaving *in situ* the aspect of the building which was being used as winter hibernacula by the bats. It was also agreed that the remainder of the building could be repaired if necessary. These agreements demonstrate that, even when there are protected species present in a building or an area that is to be developed this doesn't necessarily sound the death knell for any improvements. It does, however, mean that recommendations made must be followed otherwise there is no compliance with the law.

Mr Steele again visited the site on 21 April 2004 to ensure that the mitigation agreed upon had worked and that there were no bats present. This would enable development of the site, with mitigation in place, without the need to obtain a licence. (If work needs to be done that goes beyond the terms of agreed mitigation and in effect breaches the law, a licence must be granted for this purpose. In 2004, in England and Wales, Defra was the issuing authority for such a licence, though it is now Natural England.) Mr Steele's recommendations and observations were outlined in a letter to Lapwings and had been faxed to the developer. So far there were no problems.

Mr Steele passed the site on a regular basis and noticed that the barn was still in place up to the end of May 2004. He passed by some time during the following month and noticed the barn had been completely demolished. As has already been explained the roosts of all bats in the UK are protected at all times whether or not there are bats present. All bat workers are (or should be) aware of this. The situation was reported to Lapwings Consultants who in turn made the initial contact with the police.

Having noted the statements from Lapwings and Garry Steele, Nigel visited the site and also spoke to local residents. Unfortunately no one had actually seen the roost site being demolished but all were of the opinion that it was a strong structure and could not have fallen down on its own. The only part of the barn that was left standing was a small toilet now being used by site workers!

It was then just a matter of Nigel tracking down the suspect. This was simple as all his details had been given earlier with his application to Lapwings. I have an innate fear of investigations that are 'simple' and I am sure that Nigel can relate to this. No crime investigation is simple; it is just that some are less difficult than others.

By now Nigel had located the developer, who we'll refer to as Mr Daubenton (the real Mr Daubenton being the person who discovered the species of bats now named after him). He was easily traced, being the resident of a caravan on the site juxtaposed to the ex-barn. He was formally cautioned and the reason for the police enquiry was explained to him. He agreed to be interviewed at nearby Horncastle Police Station on 9 September 2004 therefore there was no need that he be arrested. Simple.

From the onset Daubenton accepted he was responsible for the site as he was the owner of the business and admitted that 'the buck stops with him'. At that time Section 69 of the Wildlife and Countryside Act 1981 covered offences by corporate bodies and appeared to be the most appropriate charge.[1] Still simple.

Daubenton went on to confirm that he had tried to stay on the right side of the law and had instigated the survey with Lapwings and had met with Garry Steele on three occasions. He admitted to being aware there were long-eared bats, whiskered bats and one or two pipistrelle bats present and he had regularly seen bats flying in the area. He was fully aware that the law protects bats and their roosts. Easy. And simple.

Daubenton told Nigel that the actual demolishing of the barn took place sometime in June 2004 but was carried out by a builder employed by him who he very kindly referred to as a 'bloody idiot' and 'an arse'. He said he had been away from the site and on his return he found the barn flattened. When he quizzed Bloody Idiot he told him he did it because he couldn't get a lorry along the driveway so used a bulldozer to flatten the barn despite having been told that it was a bat roost and as such fully protected. Still reasonably simple.

---

[1] Bats were removed from the Wildlife and Countryside Act 1981 in 2007 and are now, as European Protected Species (EPS), given extremely good protection under the Conservation (Natural Habitats etc) Regulations 1994.

When asked to provide Bloody Idiot's name and address Daubenton refused point blank. His response was, 'He's a local guy and he told me if I give him any grief he's going to give me plenty. I'd rather go down the road of taking the brunt of it. Whatever's happened it's down to me.' He went on to say that Bloody Idiot 'hit his woman and was being hounded by police' and believed him to be in either London or Wales. When Nigel asked Daubenton if there was anybody who could confirm this version of events he maintained that he got rid of all builders at the same time after the roost was demolished, 'as they were a nightmare'. His concerns were that since each property being built was valued at £140,000 Bloody Idiot could return and damage windows or set fire to them. There are similar concerns expressed to the police during many investigations. Some may be carried out, some not, but they are usually perceived as genuine threats by the witness or victim reiterating them.

And make an investigation not quite so straightforward.

Daubenton produced two photographs of a new shed he was in the process of building which he claimed was purely for the benefit of bats. Nigel was concerned that when he visited the site to arrange an interview with Daubenton he never saw this new building despite Daubenton's claims that the foundations were put in about two months earlier for this very reason. Despite being asked several times, Mr Daubenton still would not identify Bloody Idiot.

To make sure the enquiry was thorough and fair Nigel researched the police computer and managed to trace a man in a nearby village who had indeed been arrested for an assault on his girlfriend. This is a very small Lincolnshire village and though Nigel couldn't verify this person was Bloody Idiot he thought the likelihood of it being someone else was slim. Nigel spoke to the man, who denied ever having worked for Daubenton and was unaware of any local builder who had worked for him.

The case was first heard at Louth Magistrates Court and was returned to Nigel as the court wished to know whether the new building allegedly being provided by Daubenton was suitable for bat use! It seemed that the court could be intending to minimise the culpability of Mr Daubenton because he had built a shed that *might* suit bats at some time in the future.

What seemed to have been misunderstood by the court was the fact that the offence was complete. The Wildlife and Countryside Act 1981 provided many exemptions but did *not* allow for the destruction of a site used by protected species *on condition* that another site is built in its place. For the usefulness of the replacement roost site to be fully assessed it would require to be surveyed by a bat expert. Nigel, not being an expert, was of the view it was the responsibility of the defendant rather than the prosecution to prove the suitability of the building as a roost site. Daubenton alleged that he had consulted with Gary Steele, the ecologist, in relation to the 'new' building. Nigel spoke with Mr Steele on this point, who denied that was the case.

Nigel established that there were 144 crimes against bats reported to police nationwide over a two-year period. Of these, only two went to court. He reported to the court that this low prosecution rate was one of the reasons bat crime had been deemed a conservation priority, commenting that if we as a nation are to conserve bats and prevent the destruction of their roosts in future then this case surely had to go ahead. He said that it was certainly of public interest that the case was progressed to a successful conclusion and it would serve as a reminder to other developers and builders that such offences would not be tolerated and would be dealt with firmly.

As happens with many wildlife crime court cases they are watched with interest by many members of the Partnership for Action against Wildlife Crime, and many conservation bodies. There would be no doubt that the progress and outcome of this case would be followed avidly by the Bat Conservation Trust and the Lincolnshire Bat Group among others.

Mr Daubenton had already tendered a plea of guilty to the court on a charge of destruction of a bat roost. If the court did not deal with this incident effectively and appropriately, might conservation organisations – and indeed police wildlife crime officers – come to the conclusion that prosecuting offences against protected species were not in the public interest; and that we should wait until species are on the brink of extinction before a view is formed that wildlife is important to the nation?

On his next appearance at Louth Magistrates Court Mr Daubenton was fined £100 with £50 costs. Bearing in mind that each house being built was to be sold for in the region of £140,000, with no doubt a considerable part of that being profit, the question needed to be asked, was anything really achieved by this prosecution? Unfortunately this is a recurring perception of people involved in bringing wildlife cases before the court where the sentence seldom seems to do justice when the full facts of the case are considered! Even in a simple, straightforward case.

NORFOLK

The county of Norfolk, part of East Anglia, is a predominantly rural county with a diversity of habitats. It shares the Fens with Cambridgeshire and Lincolnshire, and the heaths and forests of Breckland with Suffolk. The Wash between Norfolk and Lincolnshire has important wintering grounds for waders and geese, and of course the famous Norfolk Broads are very important wetlands for some species that in the UK are entirely restricted to that area. Add to that the coast on two and a half sides of Norfolk and you have a very unique county. There are centres of population in Norwich, Great Yarmouth, King's Lynn and Thetford but after that Norfolk is populated only by small towns, villages and farms. East Anglia is in fact one of the most important areas in England for wildlife with diversity unparalleled anywhere else in the country. It is a breeding stronghold for such birds as marsh harrier, stone curlew, avocet, woodlark, bittern, nightjar, nightingale, barn owl, little tern and many more.

Policing generally reflects the population centres and so the 1200 officers of Norfolk Constabulary tend to be spread rather thinly across the rural areas. Wildlife crime officers are even thinner on the ground and as in almost all forces their wildlife crime work has to compete with a variety of other policing responsibilities. Leading the team of Norfolk's wildlife crime officers, until he retired in 2007, was Sergeant Alan Roberts. That he is now employed as an investigative support officer with the National Wildlife Crime Unit is testament to his ability.

The plethora of rare nesting birds East Anglia – and of course Norfolk – attracts egg collectors from far and wide, who target traditional nesting sites over and over again. The diversity of nesting birds is welcomed, but there is no welcome extended to the egg thieves who visit to plunder and can in effect home in on what is an egg collector's paradise. At the same time, crime pattern analysis shows the same birds nesting at the same time of year in the same place, and allows some targeted work to be undertaken with a reasonable degree of success. This fits in exactly with the National Intelligence Model process, which now directs most proactive police work towards intelligence-led investigations and operations.

In order to deal with egg thieves in East Anglia, Operation Compass was set up as a ring-around system between the police and the reserves in the east of the area. It achieved some success at preventing egg collecting before being re-launched as a joint police/RSPB exercise using a Ringmaster system normally used for Homewatch. This is a system used by many police forces in crime prevention or detection work where suspicious activity is passed by mobile telephone or text from member to member or by one group call, circulating information quickly and alerting a large number of stakeholders or interested people. It can be used in a number of crime prevention situations including protection of farms, shops and areas of private housing.

This significantly improved efficiency with the ability to send out a warning about suspicious visitors, mainly via Operation Easter to over 70 reserve wardens and other interested individuals all at once. It was extended to cover all of Norfolk with limited coverage in the surrounding counties. It also had the function of letting all the wardens managing reserves with rare breeding birds know how to make effective contact with the police officers who were involved with the protection of wildlife. This led to several arrests and convictions of egg collectors.

A Law for the Rich:
The Case of Banks and Moffat, Egg Thieves

Norfolk has many shooting estates owned by wealthy landowners and managed by gamekeepers. Sadly, there are still those among this community who have little time for birds of prey and will take the easy – or as Alan Roberts might say, the lazy – approach to deal with them. Despite some excellent examples of how predation on game birds can be reduced by increasing cover in pens and eliminating perches for birds of prey, or suspending CDs on string so that they flash intermittently, Norfolk has a high rate of bird of prey persecution. They are shot, poisoned and trapped so effectively that numbers of species such as goshawk and buzzard are few and far between. There have been a number of high profile prosecutions of the persecutors and their employers, including on some of the county's wealthiest estates.

One wealthy landowner encountered by Alan, Michael Banks, lives in a country mansion in Norfolk during the time he spends in the UK. Although he does run a shoot where there have been reports of the odd sparrowhawk having been shot during drives, it is not for this he came to police attention. He is a keen egg collector who also likes to surround himself with taxidermy. Over a period of years the RSPB received several pieces of intelligence that a Michael Banks was involved in egg collecting, but there was never sufficient detail that would link the name to an address. However, an appeal on an unrelated egg collecting incident (the RSPB had caught an egg thief on camera taking chough eggs from North Wales) which featured on BBC Crimewatch UK provided the crucial information. The intelligence was that Banks was an egg collector with several houses in England and abroad and who travelled all over the world. The unexpected outcome of this appeal provided the crucial pointer that allowed Alan to put the wheels of an operation in motion.

The planning of operations is extremely important if the end result is to be worthwhile. Alan decided that he needed a police search team plus exhibits officer, Customs CITES Team officers to assist with any importation offences, and RSPB investigations officers to provide expertise on the egg collecting and other bird offences. In May 2004 Alan turned up on Banks' doorstep with a team of about twelve people.

From the Notebook of *Alan Roberts*:

It was with a certain amount of trepidation that we knocked on the door of Banks' mansion. Most of the warrants I had ever executed had been on houses that would have fitted into the outbuildings of this one; two-up two-down council houses, not places bigger than the council offices themselves. Banks was fishing in Scotland when we turned up so we were let in by one of his staff. His son arrived soon afterwards and showed us around.

It was a daunting task beginning the search of such a big house but we quickly found enough to justify it: lots of photos of his exploits and notes indicating the existence of a collection consisting of many thousands of eggs. There was also a lot of taxidermy. Most was clearly old and there were some impressive displays portraying groups of birds in their respective habitats. There were a number of birds of prey and owls, most of which were CITES-listed and not particularly old. This meant that the items would probably have needed documentation in order to legally import or buy them. There were animal skin rugs and narwhal tusks as well as cabinets of butterflies. Banks was clearly an enthusiastic collector.

The one thing that wasn't obvious was the egg collection itself and we contemplated the prospect of searching the whole building. Bearing in mind that our search team was still on the first room after about three hours, the other two floors, two wings, 11 bedrooms, not to mention the other attached house and outbuildings didn't bear thinking about.

Fortunately, an irate Banks, having been advised of our search, rang up from a Scottish riverbank demanding to know what it was all about. After much protestation about our intrusion without letting him know first he conceded that we would find a collection of eggs in a locked room on the top floor. He talked me through how to find the key and we entered what was clearly his hobby room. There were egg cabinets right around the room and a large display/storage cabinet in the centre of the room. On a desk sat twenty-something stuffed seabirds. These were obviously awaiting further work and we later learned that they were to form a large display like the ones in the shooting room downstairs. Banks insisted on us moving the various animal skin rugs that were scattered around the floor before we started the search, which we agreed, and so we began. One or two of the rugs a little further away were of interest and we moved those as well – into our property store on suspicion of them being smuggled!

It was clear from quite early on that the eggs were not his own collection as recorded in his notes; these eggs were a lot older and obviously an important historical collection. Even so, we began to wonder whether this was the collection that related to our intelligence. We had been in every room we could find and his own collection would have to be about the same scale and not easy to hide, even in a house as big as Banks' mansion.

As we headed into the late afternoon we had to make some decisions on what we would take away. We would need a very large van to take away all the items seized and then, having got them, we would struggle to store them. We had seized numerous display cases of taxidermy; bags and bags of photographs and documentation; some 10ft long narwhal tusks; large bear skin rugs and some eggs in cabinet trays that we *did* manage to find. We decided that we should take a limited amount away and leave most of the larger items *in situ* with an instruction not to dispose of them. We secured the room with a seal and arranged to go back the following day to meet Banks.

The next day we went and explained the events of the previous day to Banks. Though he was not at all happy about the intrusion, he was clearly very proud of his collection and told us quite a lot about the taxidermy and other items in his hobby room. He made a few throw-away comments including the fact that the old collection upstairs had belonged to a man called Peter Adolph. He had been an influential egg collector who was active prior to egging becoming illegal and had gathered several old collections from the turn of the century. Banks told us that he had paid £14,000 for that collection to keep it intact, a statement that was later to work against him.

We left the house again and started the long sifting process. Guy Shorrock, senior investigations officer of the RSPB, was invaluable here as he did most of this painstaking work. There were literally thousands of documents and annotated photographs to be collated. The huge spreadsheets which resulted revealed that Banks had been actively involved in taking birds' eggs for nearly fifty years. This collecting had been undertaken in a number of countries, particularly Spain, but also England, Scotland, Scandinavia, Russia, Iceland and Canada. In Scotland he appeared to have visited some remote Scottish islands including North Rona, Great Cumbrae, Canna and Sula Sgeir (an island with a huge gannet colony where young gannets, called gugas, are still collected for food by islanders today, though now under a specific licence issued by the Scottish Government). The evidence pointed to him having been involved in the taking of over 6000 eggs.

Most of the eggs of rarer species appeared to have been collected outside Great Britain. The only Schedule 1 species he appeared to have taken were several clutches of Leach's petrels from North Rona in 1993 and 1999. The documentation also indicated that two clutches of eggs of CITES-listed species had been taken outside the EU. These were clutches of three (c3 in egg thieves' terminology) rough-legged buzzard eggs from Norway on 28 May 1999 and c4 merlin from Russia on June 20th 2002.

Banks was very interested in taxidermy with numerous antique specimens in his shooting room. However, he was also acquiring modern specimens and documentation clearly suggested at least four specimens, two arctic skuas, a little auk and a frozen sparrowhawk from his freezer had been shot, the latter during a partridge shoot on his estate in 2001. Other documentation indicated numerous live seabirds had been illegally taken from the wild for taxidermy.

The items quickly implicated the involvement of a John Moffat. Documents and photographs clearly indicated that Mr Moffat appeared to have accompanied Banks on at least ten trips to Scotland, Iceland and Scandinavia. Moffat had also been earning money from doing taxidermy work for Banks.

Banks was an excellent record keeper and it was these detailed accounts of his egg collecting exploits, more often than not accompanied by photographs telling the same tale that helped to bring about his downfall.

Banks regularly went fishing in Russia and spent some of each visit searching for prized Arctic species such as Temminck's and Little Stints, Waxwing, King and Steller's Eiders. Dramatic tales of Spanish egging adventures included climbing down cliffs for vultures' and golden eagles' eggs. Iceland and Scandinavia brought waders, ducks and more Arctic species. From our point of view it was the bird of prey eggs that were of most interest as they were covered by CITES and therefore needed permits to be imported. In our view there was no way he would have been granted import permits for wild-taken eggs so these had definitely been smuggled.

The problem here was that we didn't have the eggs. We would have to prove the smuggling by the circumstantial evidence of his photos and records. We felt that photos of him standing at a merlin nest, photographs of the eggs removed from the tree nest, then photos of the same nest in a plastic container was good evidence that he didn't intend to do anything but keep the nest and contents. Add to that records of set marks, (the details egg thieves keep of the eggs they collect and the link to their written record via a mark on the clutch of eggs) clutch size and the state of incubation; all indicators that they had been blown. It was then clear to us – and hopefully would be to a jury – that Banks wouldn't go to that effort and not bring them home. We also found a couple of photos showing the eggs from foreign trips laid out on a table at Banks' mansion. Our case was coming together.

I found during the investigation that whilst Banks had acted on his own for most of his collecting, this interesting association had later developed with Moffat. Moffat had a reputation as a naturalist and taxidermist, and worked for various establishments including Leicester Museum, the Wildfowl Trust and Pensthorpe Waterfowl Park. He had also been a Magistrate in Leicester though had recently retired from that trusted position.

Banks had used Moffat to clean up and create some of the taxidermy displays at his mansion and Moffat had apparently supplied some of the items on display. The two men had begun to travel together on some of the expeditions and there was evidence of their trips to Scandinavia, Iceland and North Rona.

From the trips to North Rona there were dozens of photographs showing nest burrows opened up to expose birds and eggs. Both men were photographed holding live seabirds such as Leach's petrel and Manx shearwater. Part of the evidence from North Rona showed that some damage had been done to St Ronan's Chapel, this apparently being caused during the search for nesting petrels. Since St Ronan's Chapel is a protected ancient monument, damage committed against it is an offence under the Ancient Monuments and Archaeological Areas Act 1979.

Again, Banks' meticulous record keeping told a tale. Annotations on the photographs showed that adult birds had been killed and taken for taxidermy and the eggs taken for his collection. Record cards for two arctic skuas showed that they been shot and the eggs taken. Most of the other taxidermy seabirds were burrow-nesters such as petrels and puffins and as such would have been easy pickings: simply reach into the nest burrow and pull out the incubating female. There were lists of birds in correspondence between the two men that matched the taxidermy seabirds found during the search. Birds taken in circumstances like this are sometimes killed by suffocation: simply grasping the bird tightly and squeezing so that it cannot inflate its lungs. This horrific end for the bird results in a carcass that is completely undamaged and of the best quality for taxidermy.

Then, in the middle of the investigation, we began to think that a room somewhere had been missed in the first search. I needed to check a few things left at the house so that gave me a reason to go back for a further visit. I now suspected that there was a room off the wardrobe in the hobby room and as we still had the hobby room secured I was hopeful that we might find a further egg collection this time. I contacted Banks to let him know we were coming to the house to sort out the taxidermy with a member of the Guild of Taxidermists and arranged a date to do so.

After initial displeasure of a second visit Banks seemed to accept that the police were not just going to confine themselves to the shooting room that contained the taxidermy specimens. When we got into the hobby room, Banks was rather indignant that we were contemplating taking away some of the Adolph collection and so splitting it up. However he remained ebullient and confident. Things changed when we began to poke around the wardrobe, making Banks just a little bit edgy. Banks told us that there was nothing in there but a wardrobe and that there were pipes behind it for the central heating. During the course of the search we realised the floor plan of the hobby room and an adjacent bedroom did not appear to match the outside of the building. It appeared there should be more space behind a wardrobe in the hobby room. This was highly suspicious.

We pushed and pulled, unscrewed a hook rail, but still couldn't work the thing out. What gave us hope was that there was definitely light to be seen underneath the back wall of the wardrobe. Suddenly, as I was applying pressure to the central panel, it gave and sprung open to reveal quite a substantial room containing seventeen display cabinets. Unfortunately, our initial sense of success was tempered when we opened the cabinets. Apart from a few eggs, they had been cleared. The horse had bolted. We then noticed that a panel on the wall behind a heater had been disturbed. It was not fixed to the wall and gave the impression of having been pulled back from the other side. We could only guess that the collection had been removed prior to our arrival. Apart from that disappointment, most of what we set out to achieve had been done. We had logged the Adolph collection, sorted out what taxidermy needed to be taken and what could be returned to Banks and at least, belatedly, sorted out the secret room issue.

Our attention turned for a while to Moffat and a warrant was executed at his house. The evidence here was a very different affair. There was evidence of his connection with Banks but whereas Banks' notes referred to taking eggs and killing birds, when Moffat wrote of the same incident he referred to observations and study with no mention of taking the birds or eggs. In due course Banks and Moffat were interviewed.

Banks wanted to persuade us of his innocence and, at least in part, was honest and cooperative. However, when it came to his eggs and the photos of foreign excursions the explanations became a little less plausible. He tried to convince us that set marks and clutch size records were not an indication that he had taken the eggs. The photos of foreign eggs at Banks' Mansion were more difficult to explain away and he had to concede that he had brought in eggs from some of his trips. He maintained that his own collection had been destroyed on his wife's request.

Frustratingly, most of the incidents where birds had been killed and eggs taken on the Scottish islands were out of time for prosecution for 'taking' offences and so we looked toward charging for 'possession' of the taxidermy seabirds we had found. (See pages 138/9 for detail of Statutory Time Limits).

Banks had some interesting accounts for his possession of the seabirds and tried to convince the police that he had found many of them dead. Anyone who has ever been to an active seabird colony will tell you that whole dead birds are few and far between. There is a constant presence of gulls patrolling the cliffs trying to catch the unwary. A great black-backed gull will swallow a puffin whole, so small morsels like petrels don't stand a chance. That is why they and shearwaters arrive after dark, scuttling into their burrows like little frightened rodents.

When it came to the stuffed birds of prey and owls that we had seized Banks had no hesitation. Most were bought 'as is' from Moffat was his response and when asked for documents, 'The only paperwork was a cheque.' This provided pretty clear evidence of purchase and sale. We only had to prove that the species involved needed documents to cover their sale. One thing Banks now denied was the purchase of the Adolph collection. He suggested that I must have been mistaken: the £14,000 that he spoke of earlier had been for the purchase of books.

Moffat was a little more cautious. He said he had 'given' the taxidermy specimens to Banks. He denied any knowledge of any unlawful activity and was most surprised at any allegation that he might have been involved. He was a little shaken when we produced photos of him digging out Manx shearwater burrows and holding live seabirds with the annotation showing that the birds were taken for taxidermy. He did admit to taking Leach's petrels from their nest burrows to 'study' them. That constituted an offence in itself.

Eventually we were ready to charge Banks and Moffat and we put a series of offences to each of them. In October 2006, the two men appeared at Norwich Crown Court.

As these things go in any justice system, we had lost one or two charges along the way and all the Wildlife and Countryside Act matters had been put on hold until the end of the trial as the higher court had no jurisdiction to hear them until a conviction had been obtained for other matters. Also Banks had entered guilty pleas to a couple of smuggling offences relating to bringing in merlin and rough-legged buzzard eggs from Norway and Russia as well as the offences relating to buying the controlled items in the Adolph collection without documents. A further charge that had fallen was the extremely unusual charge under the Ancient Monuments and Archaeological Areas Act 1979 relating to the damage to the remote St Ronan's Chapel. It had been on the original indictment but Counsel came to the view that the English court system had no jurisdiction on this offence. It may have been able to be tried in Scotland but on its own – even if it had not been time-barred – it was extremely unlikely that a procurator fiscal would have proceeded to court with it in view of the comprehensive case we already had underway.

What this left us with was a series of offences under the COTES Regulations 1997. We had a series of taxidermy Annex A birds of prey and owls that we alleged Moffat sold and Banks had bought without documents.

Banks sat without a word or without calling a witness and relied on Moffat's trial. If Moffat was found not guilty of selling them, how could Banks be guilty of buying them? It was sad to see such a distinguished and respected taxidermist, ex-magistrate and naturalist as Moffat clearly was – according to the testimony of the string of character witnesses willing to stand up on his behalf – squirming like a cornered fox in the witness box.

He tried to convince the jury that he had not sold the items but had given them to Banks. He made the mistake of bringing documents to prove it but unfortunately we were easily able to prove that they had been recently made up to help his story. He

North Rona and Leach's Petrels

North Rona is the most northerly island of the Outer Hebrides to ever have been regularly inhabited. It is 44 miles north of the Butt of Lewis, further offshore than St Kilda. The small community was devastated and probably starved to death after an invasion of rats (probably the black rat after a shipwreck) in 1680 and a raid by the crew of a passing ship, who pillaged their remaining foodstuffs. A resettlement a few years later failed to establish a new community after some sort of boating accident in 1695 and the island was only inhabited by a succession of shepherds until 1844, when it was deserted. It is a National Nature Reserve (NNR) and the site of an Ancient Monument in the form of the Early Christian St Ronan's Chapel. North Rona and the nearby island of Sula Sgeir form the most remote and the least-visited NNR in Britain.

North Rona has a large grey seal colony, while the two islands have important colonies of sea birds; some 130,000 during the breeding season, including gannet, guillemot, Manx shearwater, storm petrel and Leach's petrel. The Leach's petrel is about the size of a starling, predominantly black in colour apart from a white rump, and has a forked tail. It is quite a remarkable bird, spending most of its time at sea and only coming ashore during darkness to breed. St Kilda, the most westerly of the Scottish islands, has the largest colony of Leach's petrel in Europe, with about 40,000 pairs. Since 2007 it has become apparent that the St Kilda Leach's petrels are being taken at night by Great Skuas, a trait that may well cause a serious reduction in their numbers.

told of inheriting old specimens and of giving them away but this fell down on the dates, and also because he mixed up two peregrines and had to admit he had identified one from the other by guesswork. Not the meticulous record keeping associated with the museum curator he claimed to be.

As the trial progressed he did himself no favours and proved himself a liar. Prosecuting counsel was able to wrap him up completely. One classic question sticks out, (when referring to Moffat's claim that notes in the back of a book post-dated picture sales in the front, thus proving his inheritance of several specimens), 'So, Mr Moffat, when you inherited these birds in 1985, just how did you know Peter Scott was going to die in 1989?' Needless to say, the jury was convinced that he was lying and found him guilty. They also found Banks guilty.

I wonder what the jury made of the whole thing. They sat through two weeks of trial about the sale and purchase of a few dead birds without ever knowing about the rest of the case. It was only when they had left that the Wildlife and Countryside Act offences, the Adolph collection purchase and the smuggling offences were aired in court. It was really these that we deemed the more serious matters. The judge agreed and made it quite clear that it was the smuggling that merited the immediate custodial sentence. Banks was sentenced to four months imprisonment and had £30,000 costs awarded against him. Moffat was sentenced to two months imprisonment suspended for a year and had £8300 costs awarded against him.

There was a flurry of press and media interest as one might expect, with television and a full front page story on the *Eastern Daily Press*. Most of the nationals took the story up in some form, making great play of the wealthy landowner having to spend time in prison for wildlife matters.

After all that, however, it was probably Moffat who lost most. He got drawn into a web of lies and deceit through a shared passion that ironically would have led to great respect and achievement had it been a hundred and fifty years earlier. Unfortunately for both men, times have moved on and scientists and lawyers have long since recognised that there is a need to protect wildlife if it is to remain around for future generations. The naturalist Henry Seebohm (who went on horse drawn cart to the areas Banks now flies into to go fishing) may have made hugely important discoveries from the wild birds he collected but this knowledge has now been gained and in the twenty first century we have cameras and computers instead of guns to record data. Moffat lost his peer respect and the credibility that was his life, through bad judgment and a betrayal of his own principles.

WILDLIFE CRIME:
A PROSECUTOR'S PERSPECTIVE

A UNIQUE INSIGHT INTO THE PROSECUTION OF WILDLIFE CRIME
BY NICK CRAMPTON, A SENIOR CPS LAWYER

Beginnings

It was a quiet early autumn evening in October 1993 when I left the main road and found myself on a narrow lane winding through low shrub and down into a shallow valley, across a little bridge and up the other side, towards the unmistakable outline of a Jacobean country house. I parked in the front and enveloped in the silence looked back across the little valley towards the sun, now hidden below the vegetation and bathing all with a bright golden hue. I had arrived at Bramshill Police College in Hampshire for the annual Police Wildlife Liaison Officers' Conference, organised by the RSPB as a training weekend for police officers in wildlife crime enforcement. It was to be a turning point in my prosecuting career and to give it a focus and opportunities that I never dreamt would come my way.

My attendance was due to the interest my then boss David Tomlinson, the Branch Crown Prosecutor for Norfolk, had in wildlife and his decision, unusual in the Crown Prosecution Service then as now, to appoint 'specialist' prosecutors for wildlife matters. Five years before I had joined the then quite new Crown Prosecution Service at its King's Lynn office, new to prosecuting though familiar with Magistrates' Courts having had some 13 years as a court clerk. As the junior of three lawyers I inevitably collected 'responsibility' for anything slightly out of the ordinary, and tachographs, liquor licensing and wildlife made up my unlikely portfolio.

In those intervening five years in West Norfolk we had had a mussel digging case, a CITES offence involving a tortoise (neither of which I had actually prosecuted) and a trial of a man accused of disturbing a nesting barn owl, a bird listed in Schedule 1 of the Wildlife and Countryside Act 1981. The barn owl case had been a trial and I had lost it. Then, the prosecution had to prove that the disturbance was intentional. Proving that the defendant's actions had disturbed the nesting owl was bad enough, proving he intended to do it virtually impossible. Today the situation is much improved in that the offence has been amended to allow the prosecution to prove that the actions were either intentional or reckless. But the case had brought me into contact with the investigations section of the RSPB, and through them I heard of the Conference. I was able without too much difficulty to persuade my boss that I should be allowed to go to the conference to see if it had potential as a training venue for CPS staff in wildlife matters.

Inside the house I found myself in beautiful oak-panelled rooms and corridors. 'Which force are you with?' a cheery voice asked me as I entered the bar. 'I'm not police, I'm a CPS lawyer.' He looked at me in total surprise. Apparently I was the first CPS lawyer he had heard of attending the conference. 'Have you done any wildlife cases?' he asked, clearly anticipating a negative answer. 'Well, yes, a Schedule 1 disturbance case,' I replied. His pleased surprise vanished when I added that I had lost it! My lack of experience in wildlife crime enforcement issues was soon exposed, if only to me, when I discovered that most of the hundred or so delegates were extremely knowledgeable, not only on the law but about the wildlife to which it applied. To them the various statutes were old friends and the contents of their schedules and the offences in relation to each they seemed to know by heart, while the commitment to bringing wildlife criminals to book led most to carry out the job of wildlife liaison officer in their spare time. In later years I was to develop a huge respect for the knowledge and dedication of some of these officers. Without their tireless efforts most cases would never have made it to court.

This annual conference brings together not just police and Customs officers but various conservation organisations and civil servants from the government department (now Defra) responsible for overseeing the legislative programme for wildlife matters. Given the expertise of those attending, it seemed to me that the conference had substantial potential as a training tool for us. The totally unexpected result, however, was that my name went into the conference report, along with other delegates, and I found myself occasionally contacted by officers outside Norfolk. This was to lead over the years to me having to refer matters to CPS HQ in London, and they in turn referred matters to me. Later still I was to be invited to be involved in proposals for law reform of national legislation, speaking at various UK conferences and ultimately to assist in training police and prosecutors in the EU, none of which is normally the fare of an ordinary crown prosecutor.

Following the conference, two matters concerned me. Wildlife crime would only ever be a tiny proportion of the hundreds of thousands of criminal cases prosecuted each year, so it seemed likely that I would see only a handful of cases in my career. Would other colleagues be in a similar position, having to 're-invent the wheel' with every case, since each one could easily be a 'first' for the prosecutor opening the file? In the early and mid 1990s whilst there was internally produced guidance on many criminal offences prosecuted by CPS, there was none for wildlife crime. A few poaching cases were about as familiar as most of us got with anything involving animals, since the RSPCA in England and Wales investigate and prosecute most of the animal cruelty cases. (This is not the case in Scotland where any animal welfare cases investigated by the SSPCA are prosecuted by the procurator fiscal. The situation in Northern Ireland differs still further in that the USPCA have no powers, but have a service level agreement with the Police Service of Northern Ireland, who take over an animal welfare case after a preliminary investigation by the USPCA and report the case for prosecution by the Public Prosecution Service.)

The other difficulty was that until 2002 all but one of the offences under the main statute, the Wildlife and Countryside Act 1981 (WCA) were punishable with only a fine. They could only be viewed as minor summary offences, and thus went to the bottom of the pile always when time was at a premium. The fact that the fine was expressed as attaching to each 'thing' (egg, bird etc.) included in a charge meant that the maximum fine could be multiplied to hundreds of thousands of pounds, but that only made the offences slightly farcical: no court would ever fine at those levels.

Next Steps

Whilst compelling Parliament to amend the sentences available under Wildlife and Countryside Act was not open to me, preparing some guidance notes was. So over one winter in the odd quiet moment, including one Christmas Eve when every one else had gone home and the heating had been turned off and I worked in scarf and gloves, I prepared notes to identify and explain the offences under the main statutes, typing them two-finger style.

The great advantage I now had was that I had a set of notes that I could use to help myself understand and remember! CPS HQ have senior members of staff who take responsibility for keeping a watching brief on the whole range of offences and statutes that cover the crimes and procedures we have to know about. To one such lucky individual 'Animals' was allocated.

Doubtless it was not a topic expected to generate a large quantity of work. Having found out who the person was, I proudly posted off my magnum opus. I received an acknowledgement. It would provide the basis for universal guidance for CPS lawyers.

What happened next was rather unusual at that time. I found myself doing some five weeks secondment to CPS HQ, in the Policy Directorate, and preparing legal resources. Having found the person 'considering' my notes I asked if it might be suitable for my role temporarily to take over such consideration and see what progress could be made. This was agreed. The first thing was to circulate all CPS Areas across the country with a draft. Some helpful suggestions came back, but the result also was that overnight every Area had some Wildlife Crime Guidance notes and this assisted in increasing understanding of wildlife crime issues.

Having done this, my time in London came to an end and I was back in Norfolk as a simple crown prosecutor again, but not long after a lawyer in CPS HQ did produce a form of guidance notes in the accepted format, using mine as a basis. Finally, wildlife crime appeared officially as crime about which CPS would take responsibility, and so it has remained.

First Cases
However, tackling the problem of how to assess the 'seriousness' of these offences was more intractable. My first attempt at trying to do something about this came with a couple of wild bulb 'theft' cases. Digging up snowdrops and bluebells on land not your own has been an activity feeding unscrupulous plant and bulb wholesalers for years, and a large proportion of the trade is located in the East Anglian Fens. Digging trips into Norfolk have thus been common. The sites are identified when the bulbs are in flower, and the diggers return either when the plants are still 'in the green' or in the autumn just as they are beginning to shoot. These activities are potentially offences under the Wildlife and Countryside Act, attracting theoretically massive fines, but they can also be offences under the Theft Act 1968, and here they carry imprisonment. The problem with the Theft Act offences was proving either who they belonged to, or that they had not been abandoned, dug and discarded. Without identifying an owner, could we prove that they had, or ever had, one? If we could not prove this we could not prove a theft. And since the usual story was that they had been bought off someone (sadly

unknown to the unfortunate driver of the van stopped by police with its cargo of bulbs in the back, who said he was 'just the driver'!), we had difficulty in proving 'handling stolen goods'. In considering the options, I received the firmly expressed views of one of the nature conservation bodies that the Wildlife and Countryside Act offences should be employed. 'It will raise the profile of WCA and conservation offences', I was told. I disagreed. The activity deserved a greater penalty than the small fine the court would impose on an impecunious individual who could legitimately claim to be 'just doing what he was told'.

Two cases came fairly close together in time and in both I successfully used the Theft Act. In the second, at Thetford Magistrates Court, we made history: the court imposed Community Service Orders for offences of theft of wild bulbs. Wildlife crime had become 'worth' more than just a fine. Breaching the terms of a Community Service Order was, and still is under the current version of the sentence, a very serious matter: it could, and sometimes does, land the culprit with a jail term. Norfolk magistrates had served notice that they could be persuaded to take conservation offences seriously. This was reinforced when one of the defendants later ended up in the Crown Court where on conviction he received a custodial sentence. About the same time, I became aware of a couple of cases towards the west of England in which offences of theft involving a greater quantity of bulbs than mine had gone to the Crown Court and jail terms had been imposed.

But these cases also revealed a wholly new 'line of attack': publicity, and publicity in two directions.

I noticed that the local media gave some prominence to wildlife crime cases, which clearly had the potential to inform others tempted to commit similar crimes of the penalty to be expected if they got caught. When the court imposed an unexpectedly severe sentence, such publicity was very much to be welcomed. In an effort to be sure the 'correct' message is received, I have done a number of TV and radio interviews. If you think addressing a court must be somewhat intimidating, to me it is a piece of cake compared with the sheer terror experienced in addressing a microphone, knowing that many thousands will hear any mistake that I may make! Over the years, we have had some very good local reporting done by both TV and newspapers of wildlife cases we have prosecuted. I am confident it has had a beneficial effect.

The other area of publicity involved practitioners, both police and CPS. Here the 'vehicle' was initially a thin publication of a couple of sheets of folded A3 paper produced two or three times a year by the RSPB and somewhat grandly entitled 'Legal Eagle'. Successful cases could be written up briefly and included, and then circulated to Wildlife Liaison Officers (now known as Wildlife Crime Officers), and now increasingly to some if not all CPS Areas and individual lawyers. Today, it is a reasonably substantial, multi-page edition that effectively operates as an unofficial 'Wildlife Crime Law Reports,' and it is particularly useful because it covers Scottish cases too. Any case that had some new development could thus be given national publicity within a few months among those who could use it effectively. The possibility now existed of using a case specifically to achieve something new, with a view to such publicity as a means of education. The idea of 'focused' wildlife crime prosecutions was born.

From now on cases I was asked to consider were to be inspected not just for their evidential sufficiency but for any ground-breaking aspect of the law that could be used by others. The result, and more importantly the method, could be given national publicity. Four areas of wildlife crime were to 'benefit' from this more targeted approach: bulb digging, hare coursing, internet CITES sales and pesticide offences. This approach was massively assisted when in 2002 offences under Wildlife and Countryside Act became imprisonable with a maximum of six months in jail. In addition, my colleagues Kevin Eastwick and Tabi Paternoster were to construct and prosecute two major CITES cases, one of which (a joint case with HM Customs) was to become Europe's leading wildlife crime sentencing case when the defendant was sentenced, after appeal, to five and a half years in prison.

Before describing some cases a few words perhaps need to be said about the sentencing procedure in a criminal court and the assessment of 'seriousness' in respect of the offence that a court has to undertake. In the days when most wildlife crime offences attracted only a fine, the court was effectively limited by one factor – the ability of the offender to pay. The concept of grading wildlife crime, of identifying features which made one offence more serious than another in a rational way, was unknown. Once the Countryside and Rights of Way Act 2000 had made Wildlife and Countryside Act offences imprisonable, carrying out this assessment became essential. For the first time courts had to ask the question 'when is a wildlife crime so serious that a custodial sentence is necessary?' For consistency, that required 'seriousness factors' for this type of crime to be identified. In the cases that came my way after 2002 I attempted to provide answers to this question, sometimes drawing on specific decisions reported in 'Legal Eagle', sometimes 'making it up as I went along'! The gratifying result was, however, that the courts generally agreed, and the cases became useful pointers for the future.

Distilling some of the factors now, it is clear that two features provide guidance to the answer in every case. The first is the 'conservation status' of the animal or plant or habitat involved, how rare, what level of statutory protection is provided, what efforts are being made to conserve it, does it fall within the UK's international obligation to protect and enhance biodiversity? The second is whether the crime is committed with a financial motive. Money is the great driver for habitat degradation and taking specimens from the wild. But it includes companies and businesses 'taking short cuts' where acting lawfully would cost money. Linked to this would be situations where the defendant committed the crime in the course of doing his job, where he had a duty to act lawfully and failed to do so. Other factors, taken from other areas of the criminal law, would include a planned offence, a group involved and repeat offending. The cases that follow illustrate these concepts in practice.

Fakenham Bulbs

Bulb digging was the first of the types of crime we dealt with under the new Wildlife and Countryside Act sentencing regime.

In late 2002, a group of men were disturbed in a wood near Fakenham, in central Norfolk, digging bluebells with forks, near to several large sacks and a lunch box. Four men were arrested. The investigation established that they had been driven from the Cambridgeshire Fens and were paid £50 a day to dig the bulbs, and that there had been previous such expeditions, though these men did not admit that they had been involved. It was not disputed that they were intended for unscrupulous traders. Bluebells are protected under section 13 Wildlife and Countryside Act where they have been 'uprooted' and, being listed under Schedule 8, where they are 'possessed for sale'. (Picking the flowers for your girlfriend is not a crime).

Each defendant was charged with both offences. My job was to create a case out of the bare facts which would demonstrate the seriousness of the offence. The most important evidence that I was able to get was a 'conservation status' statement from a botanist which explained the rarity in global terms (confined to north-west Europe) of the English bluebell, which with its flower head delicately falling to one side was to be distinguished from the Spanish bluebell which has a firm upright stance. It is found in ancient woodland, and if destroyed this takes hundreds of years to regenerate. It is also difficult and time consuming to propagate bulbs artificially. This was the ace of trumps, because it allowed me to present the case as commercially-driven exploitation of a rare plant, Norfolk having particularly suitable soil for its growth. When the case came to court, fate took a turn and just for once dealt the prosecution with the perfect hand. One of the four appeared in custody as he was serving a sentence for other crimes. He pleaded guilty to both offences and had a long list of previous convictions. This allowed me to say that here was a serious criminal now turning his hand to exploiting wildlife for his own ends, as he had so many times before with other forms of dishonesty. I invited the court to conclude that the case met the threshold for a custodial sentence. With her client in prison already, his solicitor conceded this, and sought to persuade the court to make any new sentence concurrent with and not consecutive to his present term.

When the court announced the sentence, it was indeed a custodial one, eight weeks on each offence to run consecutively, and consecutively to his present term! With that one safely 'in the bag' so to speak, the next defendant arrived – for some reason he was a little late – and was represented by the same solicitor. Whilst he too had previous convictions, he was not serving a prison term. I rehearsed the same arguments, and my learned friend for the defence could hardly do other than agree with me, having done so barely an hour before! The mitigation was essentially 'Please don't, it'll hurt his family, but if you have to, make it as short as possible'! The court duly did, in exactly the same terms!

These two subsequently appealed to the Crown Court, separately, against their sentences, and I needed to ensure that the judges understood clearly why the magistrates had done as they had. I wanted judicial endorsement of the approach I had used. So I prepared a document setting out the position and served it on the defence and the court. The defence could hardly complain at me seeking to assist the judge's understanding, and sensibly did not do so, though this course is a highly unusual one for the prosecution to adopt on an appeal against sentence. The result was entirely successful from the prosecution's point of view. In the first appeal, the Judge declared that a custodial sentence was 'jolly well deserved' and ordered that the sentence for each of the two offences we had prosecuted be increased to twelve weeks, but then made each concurrent with each other, and then consecutive to any term then being served for other crimes. The second case effectively followed suit. Whilst this had the effect of marginally reducing the overall length of the sentences, it mattered not. The principle of a custodial sentence for this type of crime was resoundingly endorsed. 'Legal Eagle' duly publicised matters.

Hare Coursing: raising the stakes

Coursing hares has been a country pursuit for centuries, but in recent times it has been undertaken by groups of men who bet on the result, sometimes with thousands of pounds allegedly involved. They also indulge in their 'sport' on land not their own and not infrequently with threats, violence and damage being inflicted on farmers who dare to interfere. The police believed that this activity was also used by a criminal element to identify suitable rural targets for later thefts. In East Anglia it had been a serious problem for some time, and despite many complaints, the police were unwilling to commit serious resources to tackling the problem. Illegal hare coursing is not a police priority, and the sentence was rarely more than £100 – even if you did get caught. The offence committed was 'being a trespasser in search of game' contrary to section 30 of the Game Act 1831. However, there was perceived to be a problem about the nature of the proof required: the word was that you had to show the dogs had been chasing hares to prove the offence. This was to change dramatically in September 2003.

A file was sent to me, by an officer clearly quite pleased with the fact that he had a nice case with five men 'bang to rights'. I decided to try and find out how exactly the coursing was done, and about brown hares. With its wide open landscape and no hedges, the East Anglian Fens are ideal hare coursing country. It was obvious that the vehicles used to transport dogs and men were also used as they travelled the country roads to spot hares to course. Sometimes the vehicle would stop on the highway and the dogs released from there if a hare was spotted. This was called 'road running'. Sometimes the vehicle left the highway onto a track on private land and would be driven hundreds of yards before the opportunity presented itself. It was obvious that the vehicle was being used as a vantage point from which to 'search' for hares and was central to the activity. The argument was obvious: the men were trespassers as soon as they left the public highway in the vehicle and were 'searching for game' at the same time! No need to prove any dog set foot outside the vehicle! Take the vehicle away, and the problem would disappear, for many of these gangs came from far afield. The law existed to order forfeiture of motor vehicles under section 4A of the Game Laws (Amendment) Act 1960, which had been inserted by the Criminal Justice and Public Order Act 1994, but it had never been used as far as I could tell. The power was limited to offences in which 'five or more' persons were engaged. How was a court dealing with a minor property crime to be persuaded to take such drastic action? Clearly some other argument was needed than the complaints of dozens of farmers about ill treatment at the hands of violent poachers.

The next step was to approach a brown hare expert. One of the scientists on the staff of English Nature (now Natural England) provided me with a short statement that was to be worth its weight in gold. Brown hares, I learnt, are a 'Biodiversity Action Plan' (BAP) species, with the aim to double numbers by 2010 as part of the Government's commitments to increase biodiversity following the 'Earth Summit' in Rio de Janiero in 1993. Two other game species also have BAPs, grey partridges and black grouse. The statement went on to say that East Anglia with 5% of the land area had 20% of the country's brown hares, and that illegal coursing was believed to be jeopardizing the BAP.

My perfectly ordinary hare poaching case had been trans-formed from a minor property crime into a serious conservation offence, justifying the use of the most serious penalty available, namely forfeiture of the motor vehicle involved. For it now was clear that the only game species requiring conservation measures which criminal activity was jeopardizing was the brown hare, and the BAP was part of an international agreement to enhance biodiversity! When the case came to court I served the defendants with a copy of the English Nature statement, and then expounded the arguments. To say they were 'gob-smacked' would be an understatement: I had simply taken leave of my senses and was inhabiting some other planet! To my eternal gratitude the court was persuaded. The car was forfeit, and very substantial fines, up to £1,000, were imposed as well. From now on the men were going to run the risk of having to explain to their wives or partners how they'd lost the family vehicle, as well as having to pay fines of £500 to £1,000 for their weekend trip into the country.

Local publicity spread the result across East Anglia. East Suffolk was the first area where the new approach was tried, with success. A couple of weeks later I happened to be at a local police-organised conference on rural matters in Cambridgeshire when someone waved a newspaper cutting at the delegates. It was 'that case': 'if they can do it in King's Lynn, why can't you do it in Cambridgeshire?' was the not-unreasonable comment. As no-one else seemed to be able to explain, I got up and did so. All eyes turned. When I finished the explanation the entire room seemed to be applauding. They really believed something good could now be done. Rarely is a prosecutor a popular figure, and this must be one of the most humbling moments of my over thirty years as a criminal lawyer.

Over the next couple of years, until February 2005 when the Hunting Act 2004 reinforced matters, police task forces were to be set up in Suffolk, Cambridgeshire and Lincolnshire to target hare poaching, as it was now worthwhile in policing terms if the courts were going to impose serious sentences. The 'conservation' statement of English Nature was emailed across the country to a dozen Forces. Vehicles were regularly forfeit, or disqualification for driving for a few weeks was imposed instead. Several appeals against sentence were lodged, usually being decided in the prosecution's favour, except where the court had been a little too enthusiastic in imposing the new range of penalties without proper regard to their actual effect on a particular defendant. The effect of the new approach was substantial. The number of reported incidents fell dramatically. The problem may not have been eliminated, but the odds were now with the law-abiding majority and the forces of law and enforcement.

Endangered Species on EBay
CITES seeks to regulate the trade in animals and plants by prohibiting the trade in some seriously endangered species. The resulting EU Directive is 'given teeth' by each Member State passing legislation to provide for enforcement, i.e. penalties for non-compliance. In the UK, this is the Control of Trade in Endangered Species Regulations 1997 (COTES), and offences carry up to 5 years in jail.

Because CITES deals with international trade, enforcement is most obvious at ports and airports. But there are offences under COTES relating to the sale and transport of protected species which can be committed anywhere in the country and are potentially a matter for the local police. This notwithstanding, I was surprised to receive a file on a teenager living in a small hamlet in the Norfolk countryside, some five miles from my house, and who had never left his bedroom, except to go to the Post Office!

When the police visited this ingenious youngster in 2005 and took away his computer they were astonished to find dozens of emails reflecting transactions for taxidermy specimens for over a year. He had been buying and selling on EBay and via private email contact, but unfortunately many of the sales were for CITES-listed species and he could not provide proof of the necessary paperwork to show the specimens could be lawfully sold. Worse, some of the emails clearly suggested that he and the other party knew of the restrictions and had sought to evade them, particularly in the shipping of items from abroad. The defence was later to concede that he had had a minimum profit of £5,000. Not bad for a teenage entrepreneur when so many others were collecting thousands of pounds in student debts!

It was clear that there was potentially a huge enquiry stretching across the country and abroad to trace all the potentially illegal sales and those involved. What Norfolk police wanted to know was how much in respect of this young man did they need to do. My reply was, 'Enough to get this into the custody bracket for sentencing.' My reasoning was this. At the time there was a lot of media attention on illegal internet sales, the International Fund for Animal Welfare (IFAW) had just produced a report suggesting the problem was substantial and the Met Police had been involved in investigations of EBay transactions and discussions with them about controls. It was the 'flavour of the month'. I wanted an internet sales case that was 'good' enough to compel the court to agree that this kind of illegal selling was capable of attracting a custodial sentence and to get the publicity that such a decision was bound to attract.

As it turned out, we judged it about right. The defendant pleaded guilty to several offences, accepting the broad outlines of the prosecution's contention as to the scale of his dealings. Having listened to the mitigation, about his youth and good intentions for the future, the court was inclined to be merciful. Yes, the offences fully justified a custodial sentence, but this one, 8 months custody, would be suspended for two years, and some 200 hours of unpaid work would be imposed as the price for keeping his liberty. It was precisely the result that I had hoped we would achieve.

Pesticides, Gamekeepers and Shooting Estates

The feelings with which prosecutors bring their fellow citizens to a criminal court to answer for their alleged wrong-doings will vary. Most of the time, cases are relatively mundane, sometimes they inspire feelings of real achievement when a serious case is won in the teeth of a substantial defence attack on it. Occasionally cases are brought more in sorrow than in anger, with a feeling that the incident should never have happened, that those involved really ought to know and do better. The cases under this heading belong to the latter category.

The legislation controlling pesticide authorisation, storage and use is the Control of Pesticide Regulations 1986, (COPR) which is enforceable under the Food and Environment Act 1985 (FEPA). Simply put, a pesticide must have a 'ministry approval' before it can lawfully be used, and that approval states the legitimate target species and uses to which it can be put, and the conditions which must be observed by those storing and using it. Those conditions ('label conditions') are printed on the container. What has not always been appreciated is that those printed conditions are the law of the land, just as much as the law against theft or exceeding the speed limit. Step outside them and you commit an offence.

The offences created by COPR are in relation to both storage and use, essentially enforcing the label conditions, but they also have offences that employers may commit if they fail to ensure that their employees are properly trained and equipped for using the pesticide in question. The punitive element of the crime is provided by FEPA, by which, unfortunately, the penalty is limited to a fine (albeit the offence may be tried at the Crown Court where the fine is unlimited.) As with the old regime under WCA, this means the maximum penalty is dictated by the offender's means to pay. However, COPR are not the only Regulations enforced under FEPA, and the enforcement section includes an interesting provision that those 'causing or permitting' offences under the Regulations also commit an offence. Accordingly, they 'bite' on the end user, the employer and anyone else who can in law be described as 'causing or permitting' an offence.

Given the nature of the job, gamekeepers traditionally have worked without a great deal of direct supervision. Like any employee, they quickly absorb the overall 'wishes' of the boss, and if an employer is none too fussed about how his employee goes about fulfilling them, the employee is unlikely to be either. With WCA – at that time – having few offences which could be committed by anyone other than the actual perpetrator, it was impossible to hold an employer criminally accountable where, for example, an employee shot birds of prey. The assumption was that where an employee was illegally using poisoned baits or otherwise failing to comply with the 'label conditions' under COPR his employer was in the same untouchable position. This meant that there was no incentive for any instructions to be issued, or any supervision to see that they, and the law, were complied with. The new millennium was to see that comfortable state of affairs destroyed forever.

A set of circumstances arose on an estate in which an employee 'keeper failed to comply with COPR. The police investigation, however, went much deeper than any previously conducted on an estate, and uncovered the layers of management and the degree and method of supervision. When the file was submitted, there appeared to be defects in that supervision. Since the employer named in the gamekeeper's contract of employment was not one of the figures identified as having some apparent management responsibility, the question arose whether the 'management figures' were potentially liable for 'causing or permitting' the COPR offences committed by the gamekeeper. Had they put in place a mechanism of supervision that was sufficiently complete? Had they monitored that mechanism properly or was it effectively a dead letter residing, forgotten, in the bottom draw of the estate office? Could their actions or lack of action be said to have created a situation which was covered by the word 'permit', since that word has, potentially, in law a meaning of some latitude?

So far as I could gather, such a prosecution had never even been attempted. Not only would bringing such a case cause serious disquiet to the entire estate, it would guarantee a comprehensive legal counter-attack designed to bury the notion of liability in these circumstances six feet under, and permanently. It was not a decision lightly taken, and in no case that I have prepared (or ever will) were the stakes so high. Whilst there were lots of cases giving guidance on the meaning of the word 'permit' under other Acts of Parliament, there was none under FEPA. I decided that there was an argument to be made, and launched a case against three alleged management figures.

In those days, CPS's ability to use technology to track down relevant legal authorities was not what it is now, and my initial researches had failed to locate what turned out to be the most relevant, recent authority! It was the defence solicitors, with far better IT, who found it, thus causing a rewriting of my initial skeleton argument. Round one to them! It allowed them to say that I really had no idea what I was doing!

The case came to trial before the County Stipendiary Magistrate. The presentation of the prosecution took most of the first day, much of it in legal argument, and I concluded it sometime after 3.00pm. It was at that point that the defence team released their full arguments, in writing, seeking to show that there was no case at all against any of the accused. It was indeed a comprehensive demolition job, but far more so than I had even dreamed it could be! The magistrate invited me to reply when he had read it. I glanced at the clock, saw it was 3.55pm, and suggested that he might like to wait till the next day (by which time I might have thought up some sort of reply!) My wish was granted.

A detailed rebuttal of every point was beyond me. I spent many hours that evening poring over it. However, basic criminal law principles state that it is for the prosecution to prove their case. It was my case that was on trial, not their rebuttal of it. That provided the way forward. I picked several issues they raised, and tried to weave them into a re-presentation of why I was arguing for liability to exist. The next morning I did not take too long to reply. The magistrate retired, and then returned with his decision on whether there was 'a case to answer'. The importance for both sides of this decision is hard to overstate. Total victory for the defence would have allowed them to consider challenging the original decision to bring the case at all, on the ground that 'no reasonable prosecutor' could have made the decision that I had. The magistrate found that against the person I had argued as being the most senior management figure there was indeed no case to answer. He made the same decision in respect of most of the charges against the other two. But in respect of three charges against each, he found that there was a case to answer.

The defence decided to call no evidence, but restated the legal arguments, this time relying on the requirement that the court had to be satisfied beyond reasonable doubt before it could convict, not merely that there was some evidence of a case to answer. After a further retirement, the result was announced: guilty verdicts against both the remaining 'management figures' in respect of the charges of 'permitting' the gamekeeper to commit some of the offences he had earlier admitted in relation to the storage of three compounds where they had been obtained by the estate.

There was an immediate appeal lodged, and matters next took

their turn in the Crown Court. Essentially this was a shorter re-run of the Magistrates' Court hearing. The defence team tried very hard to win the 'no case to answer' arguments, but failed. At that point, I had won. We now had a Crown Court decision that liability could be established, and that was the minimum that I had wanted. The way was now clear for other investigations to be conducted in similar circumstances should they arise on any estate from John o' Groats to Lands End. In fact, having heard both the appellants this time give evidence, the Crown Court decided that the evidence fell short of a conviction, and allowed the appeals, but in doing so he expressed the view that in terms of its civil liability the estate might do well to consider its position. And a civil claim following, for example, some injury to another employee or visitor arising from an incorrectly stored or used pesticide, could be very costly, not to mention embarrassing.

The estate's reaction was commendable. It is one with a good conservation record, and undoubtedly supervision by the management improved. A few months later an article appeared in a national periodical circulating among landowners drawing attention to their unhappy experience, and advising land managers to ensure their supervision and procedures were in good order lest they too should be visited by an over-enthusiastic police officer or prosecutor! It is the only time I am aware that an ex-defendant has written about the experience of being prosecuted by me! I have confidence in this estate's current management, which, unfortunately, following a recent, unresolved report of an alleged killing of rare birds of prey, one is not able to say about every estate.

Following the case, a report was prepared by Sgt Alan Roberts, the wildlife crime officer who investigated it, and me, which set out the facts, explained the legal arguments and analysed the result. It provided a blueprint for investigating incidents of this type, and has been sent to numerous forces and other enforce-ment personnel since. It has also been included in the training CD for Scottish wildlife crime officers. Shortly afterwards, the management of an estate in Durham was successfully prosecuted and fines of £10,000 imposed.

Inevitably it raised the profile of this legislation in Norfolk, and another gamekeeper and a farmer were prosecuted for COPR offences. In the case of the latter, he had failed to comply with the label conditions for the fumigant Phostoxin and had used it along a public path adjacent to his own land. The court sentencing him by way of £1,000 fine expressed dissatisfaction that sentencing was restricted to only a fine. The courts were clearly indicating that COPR offences committed by owners and managers were going to be treated very seriously.

In the winter of 2004/05 two dead buzzards found by a 13 year old boy were to lead to another 'management' case. They were found to have one of the largest concentrations of the rodenticide difenacoum found in birds of prey in England. A possible source for the pesticide was identified when the neighbouring landowner's gamekeeper was found to have been using both the liquid and dry bait versions to control rats near where pheasants were fed. The label conditions required users to 'search for rodent bodies and dispose of safely (e.g. burn or bury.)' The elderly gamekeeper accepted he had not been doing this and was duly cautioned. It transpired that his employer had not provided sufficient training for him nor taken reasonable steps to ensure that this task was done. Detailed scientific evidence from a buzzard expert and a university professor who was an expert on rat behaviour demonstrated that it was 'extremely likely' that the lethal doses had been consumed by the buzzards by feeding on affected rats. When the case came to court in 2006, the employer faced charges of failing to provide 'instruction, training and guidance', and 'permitting' offences in respect of the 'keeper's failure to search for dead rats. But, more interestingly, it was possible for the case to be presented as having a likely link to the two dead buzzards, and thus illustrating the 'secondary poisoning' danger of pesticide use, this being the very reason for the label condition being imposed. In the event, a plea of guilty was tendered and a fine of £2,000 imposed. It is believed to be the first case where secondary poisoning has been so closely linked to specific human action. The other unusual outcome was that I became the CPS authority on brown rat behaviour! I am now collecting quite an array of experts on various UK species.

However, the case had another aspect. Defra investigators had inspected a barn used by the gamekeeper and decided that other COPR offences may have been committed. In the normal course of events, that would be something we would readily take on, but on this occasion I declined. I wanted the case focused on the secondary poisoning issue, not diluted with other matters, which if prosecuted could have allowed the defence to 'plea bargain' out of liability for what I regarded as the most serious and most useful aspect of the investigation, namely management responsibility towards their employees and the potential on wildlife that a failure can cause. Defra have their own powers to deal with more run-of-the-mill offences, and I understand they did so.

About the same time, another gamekeeper was being investigated following the finding of an owl in a spring trap, in an open area where there were pheasant feeding stations, within which was a small area of apparently looser ash/soil. The trap was found attached by a chain to near the top of a long post which was shaped to a point at the other end, which showed signs of having been inserted into ash or soil of some kind. Traps of this sort are regulated by the Spring Traps Approval Order, which is reviewed by Defra from time to time. This specifies which traps can be used, against what species and how they should be set, usually in tunnels. It creates an offence carrying a modest fine. However, there is also an offence under WCA where it is 'of such a nature and so placed as to be calculated to cause bodily injury' to 'wild birds'. Game birds for this particular section are included in this definition, as well as owls, one of which it had caught. This offence carries a liability to imprisonment.

The defence in this case were willing to accept the gamekeeper was guilty of the minor offence under the Spring Traps Approval Order, on the basis that he had set the trap on a rat run and failed to ensure it was suitably covered. They proposed that he be cautioned, stating that as he had no previous convictions such a conclusion might be seen as appropriate. I declined the offer. There were clearly questions to be asked about this trap, and it had caught an avian predator of a kind known to take pheasant chicks. I decided to prosecute for the WCA offences, and not leave the Spring Traps Approval Order one as a possible 'plea bargain' escape route. Not guilty pleas were entered, and the race was on to get as much evidence on the habits of tawny owls, rat control practices and to renew my acquaintance with my rat behaviour expert! As witnesses for the prosecution I found a tawny owl expert in Scotland, and a well-known wildlife crime officer from Tayside with considerable experience both of gamekeepers and rat control on his own property!

The suggestion had been made that the pole had been used as a pole trap, and had somehow fallen over. The police conducted an experiment to see if this was feasible, and the result was encouraging. The result was a file of some substance and complexity. Once this was served on the defence solicitors, it did not take very long before I was contacted with the information that the defendant would offer a plea to the offence under WCA of setting the trap in a manner likely to cause injury to a wild bird, but maintaining that it had been set on the ground. Whilst I was pleased with the case that had been built, I was content with the movement towards my position that this represented, and I accepted the offer. Sometimes a point can be made by accepting a lesser outcome than the one that has been prepared for, and prosecutors hope that that point will be noted, and acted on. Sometimes we can be disappointed. He duly pleaded guilty and was fined £500 with costs.

Whilst prosecuting three gamekeepers and three cases involving 'management' figures from the landed community in seven years may seem to suggest some kind of vendetta, or considerable criminality, neither is the case. There are approximately 5,000 gamekeepers in the UK, responsible for about 5 million acres of some of the most beautiful and ecologically valuable countryside. On their beats they hold the power of life and death over every creature that lives on or crosses over them. Their knowledge of that wildlife, in all weathers, all seasons and all times of day, will be matched by only a handful of nature reserve wardens. When it is realised that Europe's largest conservation body, the RSPB, with a million members, manages perhaps 330,000 acres, the potential that gamekeeping has to impact on wildlife conservation becomes clear. Shooting estates and their keepers hold the key to the preservation of the intricate web that is the wild ecology of the UK. They are, potentially, the country's most important 'Wildlife Guardians'. If shooting interests and the conservation bodies are at daggers drawn, it is conservation and Britain's wildlife that will be the losers. They can and must work together, and for this compromises will be needed. But if they do, we can 'build Jerusalem in England's green and pleasant land' (and elsewhere is these islands too!). That is my belief, and this is the lodestone that has directed every case involving estates in which I have had some dealings.

Postscript
As indicated earlier, I am not the only prosecutor in Norfolk to deal with wildlife crime cases, and my colleague Kevin Eastwick and I work together in discussing cases, which has been very helpful. Space prohibits the story of two substantial Crown Court cases under COTES for which he was the responsible lawyer and which were landmark cases in different ways. And there have been some interesting cases involving birds' eggs and disturbance of WCA Schedule 1 species on the North Norfolk coast, one of which led to the first known case of vehicle forfeiture for WCA offences in England (such orders had previously been made in Scotland.) However, a common thread to many Norfolk wildlife crime cases till early 2007 has been the investig-

ating officer Sgt Alan Roberts, to whom has fallen the task of getting evidence to satisfy demanding and perhaps over-cautious crown prosecutors! Possessing diligence and a considerable knowledge of wildlife, virtually all the Norfolk cases to this date owe their success to his efforts. In the words of a CPS colleague who died some years ago at a young age, 'the advocate is only as good as the evidence'. Equally important was his willingness to contact either my colleague or me at the very beginning of the enquiry and discuss possible directions and outcomes. That allowed us to focus cases from an early stage, with considerable success. 'Prosecuting for a purpose' was and is the aim – to find something of potential value to others beyond merely the facts and outcome of the specific case.

Prosecuting wildlife crime cases has been an enormous privilege and has provided some immensely satisfying experiences. But has it all been worth anything more than mere personal enjoyment? I believe that in some measure it has, and I have taken comfort in a comment by a journalist, Conor James, who, in the RSPB's 'Birds' magazine, in 2004, in an article about the problems of wildlife crime enforcement in Cyprus, wrote, 'The tasks of protecting birds in the long term are in the main done by people behind desks, in the corridors of decision-making power and in the courts.' A prosecution can never be a remedy; it is an admission of a failure; of actual or potential damage to biodiversity. But a firm and effective prosecution and enforcement system will encourage voluntary compliance, and that is the ultimate aim of every person who cares for the wildlife of the British countryside and beyond, and its ultimate guarantee.

LEICESTERSHIRE

The two counties policed by Leicestershire Constabulary, Leicestershire and Rutland, have an area of 2,500 square kilometres (965 sq miles) with a population of approx 1 million and approximately 2000 police officers.

The counties are relatively small and are little known, mainly being visited only by people passing through on the various motorway systems to other parts of the country. At their centre is the city of Leicester, the county town of Leicestershire. Radiating out from the city are various market towns such as Melton Mowbray, Market Harborough, Hinckley, Coalville, Loughborough and Market Bosworth.

The east of the county and Rutland are very rural, with Rutland Water being the main wildlife attraction. This sizable man-made reservoir attracts large numbers of birds throughout the year and has an osprey re-introduction programme that has been operating for a number of years. Rutland Water in the past has attracted egg collectors because of its rare species. Rutland also suffers from the attentions of northern deer poachers who are travelling criminals attacking Lincolnshire and Cambridgeshire as well as Leicestershire. The north west of the county around Coalville and Ashby de la Zouch is an old mining area with their traditional love of keeping finches and working terriers. The southwest around Hinckley and Market Bosworth is also rural and adjacent to the West Midlands, and is regularly visited by criminals from this area.

The counties have a total of seven fox hunts that still work in the area. They also have a good mix of indigenous wildlife, with badgers being very prevalent and, though there are no particularly rare species, otters and peregrines are present and in fact increasing. The wildlife crime problems in the counties cover a very varied number of species though there is no particular issue with a single species.

Neil Hughes held the post of Wildlife Crime Officer in Leicestershire Constabulary from 1990 until his retirement in 2000. Most unusually, and to his great credit, he has since carried out this role for Leicestershire Constabulary as a special constable; unpaid apart from expenses but with the same police powers as a regular constable. Such is the enthusiasm and dedication of many of our wildlife crime officers in the UK.

BUTTERFLY CRIME: FIRST PROSECUTION IN THE UK

The chequered skipper, *Carterocephalus palaemon*, a rare and beautiful butterfly, brown with orange-yellow chequered markings on the upper sides of its wings, was once found in England, particularly in the East Midlands area but is now restricted to one or two sites in Scotland. These sites are predominantly in the Fort William area in the North West Highlands, where there is suitable habitat of woodland edge and scrub. It is this species that was the subject of a case dealt with by Neil Hughes, which as it happens was the first prosecution in the UK for the sale of butterflies.

The case involved two people that we'll give the aliases of Smith and Jones. It began in the summer of 1993 when butterflies were taken by Smith – a regular visitor to Scotland to capture butterflies – from the Allt Mhuic Nature Reserve on the shores of the lovely Loch Arkaig in Inverness-shire. As a keen trout angler in my younger day I have lasting memories of fishing on Loch Arkaig. Unusually for a Highland loch its waters are crystal clear with not a hint of peat. It's the only loch I have ever fished where I could see the trout coming up from the depths to examine – and very occasionally to take – my fly. Just watching the trout in this sparkling loch was enough of a thrill; to catch one was a bonus. The butterfly trail moved on from Loch Arkaig to Lincolnshire, as we shall see shortly, then the Leicester Entomological Fair, and finally concluded at Leicester City Magistrates' Court on 2nd November 1994.

The law on some native species is unusual in that it can allow them to be taken from the wild, but not to be sold (Wildlife and Countryside Act, 1981), and the chequered skipper is one such species. Dick Fox, at that time the wildlife officer for Lincolnshire Police, had Smith in his sights for some time in relation to alleged illegal dealings in dead butterflies, and as a result of Dick passing Neil Hughes certain intelligence Neil visited the Entomological Fair held in Leicester. Neil engaged the services of butterfly expert David Shepherd of English Nature to accompany him on his entomological excursion, without whom he admits he would have been totally lost.

As a butterfly collector, Smith regularly visited these fairs and happened to visit the one in Leicester at which Neil was having his butterfly baptism. He found that Smith was exposing for sale fourteen chequered skippers, these being dead and mounted in the way that most would imagine had gone out of fashion in Victorian times. It was learned that he had previously sold some to Jones, who at the same Fair was exposing for sale seven chequered skippers. The butterflies were seized and Smith and Jones were interviewed.

During Smith's interview he admitted taking and selling the butterflies, but then, as many suspects do, pleaded not guilty. In court he came up with a far-fetched story that he had taken a large number of the butterflies from Scotland, but had in fact kept them alive and had bred from them. This is allowed in law but contradicted his initial admission to Neil of taking and selling them. Neil had not been surprised that during interview Smith admitted taking the butterflies, but to admit to selling them was in effect admitting the offence. It may have been that he was over-confident during the interview since there had never before been a prosecution for the sale of butterflies. His confidence would have received a blow when the summons to appear in court was delivered.

He went on to explain in court in great detail the procedures on how to breed them in captivity, expounding that his butterflies would hatch while he was at work and on return he would remove the newly hatched ones. Part of his downfall was that in his defence he called a butterfly expert to give evidence. Unfortunately the expert's procedures differed so much from Smith's explanation that it was clear to the court Smith was not telling the truth. The expert told the court that he regularly bred butterflies in captivity. They always hatched early in the morning and had to be removed from the presence of the others as soon as they hatched or they would damage their wings and bodies as they all flapped about in the confined space – a tactical error from Smith, and fatal to his defence case. Jones admitted offering chequered skipper butterflies for sale but said he did not know that those he bought from Smith were taken from the wild.

At the conclusion of the trial Smith was found guilty and fined a total of £490, which equates to £35 for each of the fourteen butterflies, plus £80 costs. Jones, realising the butterflies he was selling were the ones Smith had taken in Scotland, pleaded guilty. He was given a conditional discharge with £80 costs. The case was competently prosecuted by one of the more senior prosecutors from the Crown Prosecution Service and would no doubt be a learning experience for him. With the butterflies at issue being a rare species in the UK, the Leicester City Magistrates assessed the case with the conservation needs it required and spent considerable time trying to understand the details of which must have been for them a very unusual but interesting trial, and one which, even in the intervening fifteen years, has only been repeated on a handful of occasions in UK courts.

THE COALVILLE BADGER DIGGERS

In 2009 the heinous crime of badger digging (or badger baiting, which has the same terrifying and excruciatingly painful end for the badger) is unfortunately still commonplace in many parts of the British Isles. In a case that Neil Hughes dealt with on 19th May 1998, three men from Swadlincote, Derbyshire, all with previous convictions for dishonesty and violence, were arrested some distance away at Ibstock Coalville. There were two charges involved: one of digging for a badger and one of killing a badger cub. The killing of the cub appears to have taken place as the three were digging into the sett, and the cub had bolted to the surface. Post mortem results showed that the badger cub was probably kicked, resulting in a broken front leg, then struck on the back of the neck, possibly by a spade, which is likely to have been the cause of its death. Such cases are never straightforward, and the lengths to which the prosecution had to go to produce evidence to convict – and the simple but unexpected pitfalls of using 'expert' witnesses – become very apparent in this case.

At the time of the crime Neil's usual badger expert, Bill Cunnington, was away on holiday, but another badger expert, Val Williams from the local badger group, had just as much knowledge but was at the disadvantage of never having given evidence in court as an expert.

The first step in such a case is always to show that a badger sett was 'in use' since this forms a necessary element of the charge. This was done easily by Val, who described various features at the sett; recent claw marks, fresh latrines, the presence nearby of a scratching post, recent digging and the associated heaps of fresh earth or 'spoil.' However the specialist solicitor for the defence managed to get her to admit that as she did not get paid for her 'badger work', that she was in fact only a 'well meaning amateur' and not an expert. In effect the only difference was her lack of court experience. Nevertheless, probably unfairly, this seemed to greatly diminish the value of her evidence. To compensate, on the actual day of the trial Neil had to get Bill Cunnington to visit the sett to establish that it was still in fact 'in use,' then rush him back to court to give evidence to that effect.

The expert used to carry out a post-mortem examination of the dead badger, although a well-known veterinary pathologist and with a number of other badger cases under his belt, was encouraged by the defence to agree that his expertise was in fact in avian pathology. He was unfortunately unable to positively give a cause of death for the badger, which resulted in all three defendants being found not guilty of the charge of killing a badger cub.

If a person is charged with the offence of killing a creature, then the prosecution must demonstrate the means of its death. The best example is possibly the all-too-frequent 'sport' of using hedgehogs as footballs. To do this with a dead hedgehog is not an offence, though most certainly would be offensive. To do this with a live hedgehog almost inevitably results in the wee beastie's death but this must be *proved* to be the case. The hedgehog must be retained by the police and sent for post-mortem examination, which must show beyond reasonable doubt that the animal was alive while being kicked and that the act of kicking it resulted in it being killed or seriously injured. Death by accidental or natural causes must be excluded.

After their arrest by the police each of the three defendants had made no comment to each question put to them during their interviews. The account subsequently given by the defence solicitor at court resulted in the acquittal of one defendant who had escaped from the scene but was arrested some distance away by a police dog handler. When this person had initially been arrested, a dog handler called to the scene, using great initiative, encouraged his dog to track back from the point of arrest, a trail that led right to the badger sett. Unfortunately the magistrate considered this insufficient evidence to demonstrate that this third man had been at the sett. This was surprising, since all three defendants lived about seventeen miles from the sett but in close proximity to each other. It seemed much more than a coincidence they were all in the same area of Ibstock at the same time. So, one off the hook, two to go.

Of the three dogs seized from the defendants, two were Jack Russell terriers. They are typically the size and nature of dogs for putting down badger setts and the electrical impulse devices that had been found on their collars so that they could be tracked underground tended to confirm their use for this purpose. The third dog was a mongrel, but of the size and build of a whippet, and may well have been for chasing quarry on the surface. On its own it would be of little use against an adult badger but if the slower terriers were hot on its heels it could hold the badger till they caught up.

In any part of the UK, and even with the most accommodating prosecutor, cases take many months to come to court. It is a real logistical problem for police officers as to how best to deal with dogs – or for that matter any other types of animal – that are seized. Returning them to defendants charged with an animal welfare issue is not an option. I understand that in England the RSPCA will charge the police for their keep, as will their colleagues in the USPCA in Northern Ireland. I could sympathise with Neil in his quest to find a suitable caretaker for the three dogs until the case came to court. In Scotland we are maybe slightly luckier in that there are no criminal prosecutions other than those at the instance of the Crown Office and Procurator Fiscal Service; none by any other Government agency, non-government organisation or charitable body. This means that invariably an investigation where animals or birds are likely to be seized is carried out as a joint operation, with the police being assisted by the Scottish SPCA. With the Scottish SPCA being an integral partner in the operation they are more than willing to take care of the dogs in a badger digging case as part and parcel of their animal welfare responsibility.

It is typical in the way that police officers work – either with no budgets or limited budgets – that Neil managed to obtain the services of a local boarding kennel that volunteered to keep the dogs, and of a large international pet food company, Pedigree Masterfoods with their headquarters in Melton Mowbray, that provided dog food for almost a year. These were substantial savings in the overall costs of keeping the dogs in the run-up to the trial.

In addition, there was the issue of a request from the defence to see the dogs. There was no guarantee that if the defence solicitor knew where the dogs were kennelled that this would not be passed on to the clients. If they obtained this information there was a real risk that they would visit the kennels and steal the dogs. Neil did not take a chance on this and told the defence he would not be allowed to see the dogs at their kennels but would arrange to take them to a local wildlife hospital for the defence examination.

At the end of the trial the two remaining men from Swadlincote were convicted of digging for a badger and each received a two months prison sentence. In addition their dogs were confiscated by the court. In England and Wales the maximum penalty under the Protection of Badgers Act 1992 is six months imprisonment. In Scotland the legislation has been updated by the Nature Conservation (Scotland) Act 2004 with the maximum penalty now three years imprisonment.

As sometimes happens, the seizure and confiscation of the three dogs from the badger diggers resulted in more of a penalty than the prison sentence. They had obviously spent consider-able time training the dogs to attack and kill badgers (and one shudders to think what this training might have entailed and how many pets may have been used for 'practice') but they would no doubt begin the same schedule of training all over again with new dogs. The original dogs' conditioning was demonstrated when Neil took them from their temporary kennels for examination by the defence. The dogs were so well used to attacking badgers that as they were taken out of the van they all attacked an ornamental stone badger at the wildlife hospital's front door.

Bat Prosecution for Leicestershire County Council

Crime against bats is surprisingly common, very often resulting from the re-roofing of buildings or other development work in the converting of old buildings – particularly farm steadings – to dwellings. In 2009 all police forces in the UK work very closely with the Bat Conservation Trust and with local bat groups.

One of the main problems Neil Hughes found with potential wildlife offences (which happens to be in common with most if not all police forces) was the delay in receiving early notification of the incident. A particularly badly-delayed report in 1997 highlighted the problem. English Nature (now Natural England) had received information regarding a local church where work was being carried out that appeared to be disturbing bats. They spent a considerable time communicating with the people they thought responsible with no success. By the time they passed details to Neil there was insufficient time left for him to obtain sufficient evidence before the statutory time bar was up.

Because of the late reporting of this offence to the police Neil came to an understanding with the local English Nature office that they would contact him directly at home to pass the information, an agreement that is still in place. Such an arrangement mirrors similar agreements made by many wildlife crime officers the length and breadth of the UK and demonstrates the dedication that this singularly thin green line of police officers has in ensuring that wildlife crime is properly investigated and reported for prosecution.

This agreement paid dividends in Neil's next bat prosecution as in August 1999 English Nature contacted him to report the damage or destruction to a suspected bat roost at a school near to Coalville. This information was passed on the day after they had received it.

The English Nature bat expert, Bob Stebbings, was attending the site of the damage the following day to carry out a survey from a licensing perspective, English Nature being the authority that could license work that otherwise would be an offence. He asked Neil if he would like to accompany him. During the examination of the bats' share of the school building Neil could see first hand what Bob was looking for and was thereby able to gather ideas for future investigations by following suggestions of the most relevant evidence to gather. Four dead bats were collected, which Neil would have collected in any case. Bob was able to advise Neil that bat species can sometimes be identified from their droppings, so there had to be an examination of those. (Not really a task that is too unpleasant as they are mostly powdery versions of insect bodies and wings.) He also pointed out oily marks and smooth woodwork on the central beam, indicative of long-eared bats. As well as evidence-gathering, the whole experience was, as far as Neil was concerned, a practical lesson in the ecology of long-eared bats that he could make good use of in his next bat case.

The school at the centre of the investigation was owned by Leicestershire County Council and was having roof repairs carried out by a local insulation company. Bob recommended that the company stop work until a proper survey was carried out. Meantime he and Neil crawled all through the roof, Bob leading the way since he best knew what to look for. It was apparent there was a large brown long-eared bat roost in the roof space and it was clear that many of the bats had been disturbed or killed by the work. The workmen removing the insulation from most of the roof space had caused so much disturbance to the roost that it was impossible for Bob to estimate the number of bats affected. From the evidence available he was able to conclude that it was not only a substantial brown long-eared bat roost, probably with one or more hundred, but there was also evidence – from examination of the ubiquitous droppings – of whiskered bats.

Bob Stebbings produced a report on his findings and, armed with this and some assistance from Jenny Harris, a local bat expert, Neil interviewed the company carrying out the work. The company representative claimed ignorance of the bats. This is not uncommon in a bat-related investigation and indeed sometimes can be true. However it is not an escape hatch through which a suspect can disappear and avoid prosecution. As it was Neil's intention to use the provisions of the Habitats Regulations in this case, he didn't have to prove that the bat roost had been damaged or disturbed either recklessly or intentionally or even that the company had knowledge of the presence of a bat roost. Indeed it would have mattered not a jot if no bats were present at the particular time, since a bat roost is protected at *all* times. Some may consider this severe – even unjust – but it is the role of the police to enforce the law as it is and for the court to assess the extent of the culpability of the person charged.

When Neil contacted the Department at the County Council, also suspects in this case, he suggested they might wish to have their legal representative present during the interview. The legal department of the County Council initially showed no interest but quickly changed their minds when they realised that it was the council that was being prosecuted.

In due course when the case came to court (the first ever under the Habitats Regulations in Leicestershire) the company carrying out the work pleaded guilty and was fined £1000 with £225 costs. The County Council was found guilty since the school had been their property and they had a degree of responsibility. They were fined £2,500 with £400 costs and subsequently appealed to the Crown Court. The appeal was not contested by Crown Prosecution Service, most likely since this would involve public money being used against a public council, but the damage to the Council's reputation in the field of conservation had been done.

There are always learning points for others in these cases, in this instance the alerting of other county councils and other local councils of how they must review their procedures to avoid becoming embroiled in a similar incident. Increased professionalism and awareness by local authorities leads to better conservation. Sounds like the beginnings of a slogan!

Statutory time limits

In 1997 there was a six month limitation on prosecutions under the Wildlife and Countryside Act 1981, beginning from date of the offence. This time bar was common throughout the UK. This put a severe time restriction on the investigation of many cases that were reported to the police. As the reader will have seen even by this time the gathering of evidence in some wildlife crime investigations is complex and time consuming. Normally six months would provide sufficient time for most cases to be completed provided the incident is reported as soon as the time bar clock starts ticking. A classic example where public interest did not seem to be served by this short time span was in the recovery of victims of poisoned baits set out to kill wildlife. In some cases it was evident from the state of the victim that it had already been dead for some months before being discovered, leaving little time left for the investigation.

Since the Countryside and Rights of Way Act 2000 this has thankfully been extended in England and Wales to six months from the date

LITTLE OWL CASE

During the months of August and September 2000 Neil received a number of complaints about a man displaying birds of prey at a car boot sale. The concerns of many customers to this particular stall related to a small bird in a box that was repeatedly taken out so that people could be photographed holding it. The person displaying the birds was a bird of prey keeper from Leicester, who we'll call Mr Low. Mr Low clearly required a visit from Neil so that the mystery bird could be identified, and to establish if there were illegal practices taking place. For this job Neil obtained the services of an expert, Graham Taylor, a bird of prey keeper from Derbyshire.

When he was visited, Mr Low claimed he was keeping a number of birds for Birdline, an organisation that rehabilitates injured or ailing birds. Included in the assemblage of nocturnal avian predators was a little owl, which unfortunately was in a very dirty state. Mr Low explained that the little owl was hand-tame but when Graham tried to handle it, the owl came to the hand right enough but that was for the purpose of attacking him. It was a real feisty wee character, no doubt completely fed up with all the handling forced upon it.

The owl had a ring on its leg which caused some confusion: if the details inscribed on it were to be believed then this should have been a barn owl. The owl was most definitely a little owl so to mitigate any blame for the confusing – and illegal – ring Mr Low said that he had obtained the bird from another falconer in Leicestershire, who when interviewed later, told Neil he had

sufficient evidence is passed to the prosecutor but not more than two years from the date of the offence. In Scotland, the time bar was extended under the Criminal Justice (Scotland) Act 2003 to six months from the date sufficient evidence is passed to the prosecutor but not more than two years from the date of the offence then further extended to three years under the Nature Conservation (Scotland) Act 2004. Northern Ireland, in their consultation in 2008 to update their wildlife legislation, is meantime considering the same time extension as in England and Wales.

In 1997 bat cases could also be dealt with under the Conservation (Natural Habitats etc) Regulations 1994 (the Habitats Regulations). The time bar here was also six months but could be extended to a year if a bat had been killed in the incident being investigated. Since legislative changes in 2007 crime committed against bats is now dealt with under the Habitats Regulations, with the time bar extended as in the Wildlife and Countryside Act to two years in England and Wales and three years in Scotland.

been given the bird by a falconer from Derbyshire. In turn the Derbyshire falconer was seen and admitted having the bird knowing it had been taken from the nest. This is probably why it had been fitted with a ring meant for a bird substantially bigger.

Coincidentally, it turned out that the little owl started life in a nest in Derbyshire near to where Neil's expert, Graham Taylor, lived and while the case was being prepared it was looked after by Graham back in Derbyshire. As part of the evidence Graham produced a video of the owl attacking his hand and compared it with a video of his own tame little owl which would come readily to hand. The staff in the Police Prosecutions Department developed a soft spot for both owls and loved to watch that video. Sadly, the little owl died before the end of the case, and before it could be released back into the wild.

All three of the falconers pleaded guilty. The two who had the itinerant owl prior to the unfortunate photographic period of its life were each fined £100 but the real punishment was the withdrawal by Defra of their licences to keep Schedule 4 birds. As a consequence they were forced to get rid of many of their own birds. They were devastated at this ban and realised then the seriousness and consequences of what at first seemed a minor offence.

As is the case with captive-bred finches, captive-bred birds of prey are used to people and are quite happy and confident in their company. The little owl in this case, taken from the wild as a fledgling, must have had a pretty miserable life.

MYSTERIOUS MERLIN

In August 2004 Neil contacted a woman living in Nottingham. She had bought two barn owls from a man we'll call Mr McCloud from Coalville and, once she had obtained them, asked Defra what documentation was required. Defra staff had given the appropriate advice on bird registration requirements but also made Neil aware, suggesting that it may be worth speaking with her.

Neil found out that Mr McCloud had given the lady no documentation for the birds and that he had other birds at his house including one that he said was a merlin. Merlins are birds on Schedule 4 of the Wildlife and Countryside Act 1981 requiring registering with Defra and ringing if kept in captivity. Neil wondered about the legality of Mr McCloud having a merlin and contacted a friend and well-known falconer from Coalville called Pete to try to get some background on Mr McCloud. Pete confirmed McCloud had a merlin, and Neil mistakenly assumed that Pete had actually seen the bird.

Neil checked with Defra to see what birds of prey Mr McCloud had that were registered on their database, but there was no word of a merlin. Armed with the answers he then went to see Mr McCloud who, when seen, admitted selling the two barn owls without any documentation. He was also happy for Neil to view his other birds. Neil started the dialogue:

'Can I see your merlin?'

Mr McCloud produced a bird that to Neil looked like a kestrel, (though Neil admits that birds of prey identification had never been his strong point).

'It looks very much like a kestrel.'

'No it's a merlin.' (Obviously Mr McCloud's identification of birds of prey was also in need of re-certification.)

'Then why is it not registered with Defra?'

'What?'

Quizzing of Mr McCloud revealed that the barn owls and 'merlin' had been obtained from a man called Bill, who took birds for rehabilitating.

Neil's next visit was to Bill, who revealed he had a stack of barn owls, two of which he had given to Mr McCloud because he had run out of space to keep them. Neil again began the dialogue.

'Bill, tell me about this non-registered merlin you gave to Mr McCloud.'

'What merlin?'

'The merlin he's got: the one he says you gave to him.'

'What bloody merlin are you talking about?'

'The bloody merlin he says you gave him.'

'Oh you mean the kestrel called 'Merlin'!

FRIENDS OF THE GREAT-CRESTED NEWT

In 2004 a developer purchased land on which he intended to build two executive properties. There was a pond on the land and a local resident advised the developer of the presence of great-crested newts. Great-crested newts are a European Protected Species and though it is not believed they are particularly rare, certainly not in the Leicestershire area, they are under-surveyed and therefore actual numbers are unknown. These newts usually live in small ponds in fields and gardens. They do particularly well in ponds that dry out during the year because these are less likely to contain predatory fish. As well as telling the developer, the resident also informed Neil who, in true tradition of police wildlife crime officers, sought out his resident expert for the species at issue.

In due course, along with his great-crested newt expert, Neil visited the proposed development site and saw the developer. Since no offence had been committed at that point Neil advised the developer to obtain an ecological survey, which he did. As it happens, some local authority planning departments will as a matter of course ask for ecological surveys in planning applications, which is not only good practice but likely to keep them on the right side of the law. The ecological survey advised him of the presence of great-crested newts in the pond and of action that could be taken in requesting a licence from Defra to re-locate the wee amphibians which in due course would allow the work to go ahead. This advice was ignored by the developer, possibly because of the cost and he continued with work in the vicinity of the pond.

Neil was contacted a year later when this work was underway. The ecology company revisited the site and completed a report showing the work carried out by the developer was in contra-vention of their survey. After gathering evidence Neil charged the developer, who was summonsed for three offences under the Wildlife & Countryside Act 1981 and the Conservation (Natural Habitats etc) Regulations 1994. His company was summonsed for the same three offences. The charges were intentionally or recklessly damaging or destroying a structure or place used by great-crested newts for shelter or protection, which of course was their pond, and intentionally or recklessly disturbing a great-crested newt. These offences are under the Wildlife and Countryside Act 1981 but the newts, as European Protected Species (EPS) are also protected under the Habitats Regulations 1994, and a charge under these Regulations was added for the damage or destruction of their habitat.

On first appearance at court in January 2007, the developer asked, on behalf of himself and his company, if he could plead guilty to four of the six offences. This was accepted by the crown prosecutor and he was fined a total of £8,400 plus £70 costs, the highest fine currently for offences involving great-crested newts.

An interesting aspect of this case is the number of conservation organisations that became involved, so much so that the developer probably had no option but to plead guilty. Neil involved the Local Authority Ecology Unit, a local newt expert, an ecology company based in Nottinghamshire and the Wildlife Trust. The basis for this was it was they who had completed the survey for the defendant, then in rejection of their advice on the action that needed to be undertaken, had been told by him that they weren't required. Neil had them revisit the site after the work had been carried out, and they saw that the work had been carried out in disregard of their survey advice.

Letters were also sent to the court from more newt allies: the local Amphibian Network and Froglife, which helped to persuade the magistrates of the seriousness of such conservation matters. The Environment Agency also produced for the court a very detailed survey of water quality showing how the work had effectively killed the pond. This survey was carried out by a senior analyst free of charge since the Environment Agency was keen to become more involved in conservation.

Newts obviously have lots of friends.

LONDON

The Metropolitan Police is by far the largest police force in the UK and the range of crime it deals with is colossal. That the list includes wildlife crime is not surprising but the type of wildlife crime, and the way in which it is tackled, is different to almost any other police force.

For a start, the Metropolitan Police is the only police force in the UK that has a full-time wildlife crime unit. Headed by Andy Fisher, it comprises Sergeant Ian Knox and Constable David Flint. If a full-time wildlife crime officer can make a difference in a provincial force, a full-time unit can, and has, made a huge impact in the Met in enforcing their share of an illegal international wildlife crime trade estimated by the US State Department, in global terms, at being worth more than £5billion a year.

While other police forces are dealing with such wildlife crimes against bird of prey, songbirds, badgers, seals or great-crested newts, international wildlife crime trade forms the bulk of the Met's work. It follows therefore that officers in the Metropolitan Police have to be much more aware of international wildlife than the those in the rest of the country. The illegal trade in some traditional medicines, for example, is a threat to tigers, rhinos, musk deer and bears. The trade in furs made from the endangered big cats and shawls made from the soft belly fur of the chiru are bringing some of these species to the edge of extinction. And London is part of the problem.

CHIRU AND SHAHTOOSH

The trade in shahtoosh is completely illegal and has resulted in the murder of State Forestry Administration guards and the destruction of local people's livelihoods. Many Tibetans are actively involved in protecting chiru and some have paid for this with their lives. As a result of lobbying by the Tibetan people the chiru was adopted as one of the mascots for the 2008 Beijing Olympics.

It was against this background that the Metropolitan Police wildlife crime unit, in February 1997, seized 138 shahtoosh shawls worth £353,000 from a London trading company. In April 2000 the company pled guilty and was fined £1,500, which would hardly put them into liquidation. The fact that the chiru is listed on Appendix 1 of the Convention on International Trade in Endangered Species of Wild Fauna and Flora (CITES) and that shahtoosh is banned from international commercialisation initially did little to prevent attempts at slaughtering the remaining 75,000. In the year 2000 the Chinese authorities confiscated hundreds of chiru pelts and thousands of rounds of poachers' ammunition. Unfortunately armed poaching gangs greatly outnumbered the anti-poaching patrol staff and for a time an estimated 20,000 chiru were being killed annually in China.

This first class result by the Metropolitan Police was one of the earlier successes of their innovative 'Operation Charm', a pioneering scheme that has inspired similar operations in a number of other countries. It was launched in 1995 and is a combination of law enforcement, partnerships and education to deal with the illegal trade of endangered species. Since its launch Operation Charm has led to the seizure of more than 30,000 items (including in 1996 the world's largest seizure of rhino horn) as well as the prosecution and conviction of a number of traders. It has also markedly reduced the number of illegal products openly on sale. In addition to enforcement, an important aspect of Operation Charm is the development of initiatives to increase public awareness and reduce the demand. The Met, in conjunction with the International Fund for Animal Welfare (IFAW), has gone on to develop a kit to identify shahtoosh or similar products. This kit was successfully used in 2004 to identify ninety shahtoosh shawls and ten shahtoosh scarves from Kashmiri-owned shops in Dubai.

ENDANGERED SPECIES: Chiru

Most people will never have heard of chiru; if that is the case they are unlikely to have heard of shahtoosh. The chiru is another name for the Tibetan antelope, the producer of wool so fine that it is worth more than gold. It is unfortunate that the chiru can't be rounded up and sheared of the fine underbelly part of its fleece once a year like sheep. It is a totally wild animal so has to be killed in order that this extremely fine wool can be cut off to be woven into shawls so fine that they can be passed through a wedding ring. The finished ultra-fine material is termed shahtoosh.

Shahtoosh is coveted by the super-rich and means 'king of wool' in Persian. It makes cashmere feel like horsehair. It has become a common currency among crime gangs and terrorist groups, such as the Kashmiri separatists. It is also a key part of a complicated transaction involving tiger bones being smuggled into China, where the smugglers are paid in shahtoosh. Reputedly, as a result of this two-way trade, a tiger is killed in India every day.

So how many £5,000 to £15,000 shawls can be made from the killing of one chiru? None. In fact it takes 100 grams of hair from the soft fleecy stomachs of three chiru to make a single shawl. To bring this despicable trade into a more local context, shahtoosh parties are known to have been held in the UK, with the well-heeled meeting to show off their shawls and to buy the latest designs. There is a romantic claim that the wool for the shawls is gathered by locals from bushes that the Tibetan antelope have used as scratching posts, all part of an industrious 'cottage industry'. In truth bushes are exceptionally scarce in the Tibetan uplands and their presence must be in inverse proportion to the naivety of anyone who believes this fairy tale.

The real villains of the piece are the rich consumers in the developed world. The perceived need for some wealthy people to have an exclusive fashion accessory has meant that the Tibetan antelope numbers have fallen, through full-scale slaughter for its wool, from several million a hundred years ago to less than 75,000 in the early part of the 21st century.

In 2009 poaching continues but at a reduced level and shahtoosh is harder to find in the West. Chiru numbers in Tibet and Qinghai appear to be increasing slightly. In a way the chiru is turning into a success story, which shows what can be achieved by range states and consumer nations working together to attack the problem from both ends – poaching in China and consumer demand in the West.

TRADITIONAL MEDICINES

Operation Charm has continued to yield successes. In May 2002, the Met wildlife crime officers took possession of traditional medicines (TMs) from a London business. The 25 seized packets of medicated bandages claimed to contain leopard bone. This seizure came about by chance. Ian Knox and Andy Fisher had decided to visit a street market in East London which supplies African food and had been found to sell bushmeat. Having had no success in their search for bushmeat they popped into a small Vietnamese shop nearby to buy some cigarettes. On the way out they stopped to look in the window where they saw a range of medicines including a number of packets of medicated plasters made from leopard bone. A short time later they returned armed with a search warrant under the COTES Regulations and made the seizure. When questioned, the shop owners said that whenever they were in Vietnam they always bought these plasters because they knew that people in London were keen to buy them – this supports the team's viewpoint that it is important to curb consumer demand. There were no other illegal products in the shop so the plasters were seized and the shop owner was cautioned. This offence was at the lower end of the scale but all species of leopard are protected under Appendix 1 of CITES and any commercial trade in their body parts is illegal, with a maximum penalty on indictment of five years imprisonment and/or an unlimited fine.

Chinese traditional medicine has become extremely popular in the UK today as many people turn to alternative medicines and therapies. Whilst most are from sustainable sources, some continue to be made from derivatives of animals or plants which are endangered. Particular favourites are tiger bone, rhinoceros horn and bear bile. This illegal trade is one of the biggest threats facing many endangered species and, like any trade, works on the basis of supply and demand. Because endangered species are rare there is a limited supply, thus pushing up the prices and providing considerable profits for criminals.

In October 2005 a further search was carried out for traditional medicines on a Chinese medicine supplier in central London. On this occasion several hundred medicinal products, mainly bottled pills, believed to contain endangered species derivatives, were seized by the wildlife crime officers. The species included tiger, bear, rhinoceros and musk deer. Some raw plant material was also recovered. This case was lost at court when the judge upheld the defence argument that, in the case of species that are included in more than one of the CITES Appendices (e.g. bears

ENDANGERED SPECIES: Saiga Antelope

The saiga antelope is found in the Great Lakes basin area of Mongolia, with another sub-species in Russia and Central Asia. It has always been hunted for meat, horns and skin, with tens of thousands being killed each year without dramatically lowering the population. After the collapse of the Soviet Union a lucrative market for Saiga horn opened up, with hunters using motor cycles and high-powered rifles to chase and kill their quarry. Subsequently the use of saiga horn, exported to China to be used in fever cures as a substitute for rhino horn, received a degree of official support but no-one seemed to foresee the extent of the slaughter. It is now critically endangered, with the Mongolian sub-species now occupying less than a fifth of its historical range. It is on the verge of extinction, with biologists stating they have seen the most sudden and dramatic crash of a large mammal ever witnessed. From over a million in 1993, fewer than 30,000 remain, mostly females as the males have been decimated for their horns. Now that there is such a scarcity of males it can only be hoped that the animal's famed fecundity may be sufficient to allow a recovery, in time, to a stable population.

and musk deer), it was necessary for the prosecution to prove which species or geographical population the actual seized product was derived from. It is virtually impossible to be specific about which geographical population of an animal is involved when all that the product lists as ingredients are bear bile or musk. The Metropolitan Police Wildlife Crime Unit is working with Defra at present to amend the COTES Regulations to ensure that they can properly be enforced in cases like this. Frustration stalks a high proportion of wildlife crime cases.

Operation Charm's continued success is linked to their joint work with Trading Standards Officers. In June 2006, the Met wildlife crime unit executed a search warrant at a traditional medicine shop in Deptford, south-east London, where a number of items were seized. They then went on to search an outlet in Eltham, where more products were seized and the shop owner was arrested. The products claimed to contain ingredients derived from protected species including tiger, bear, saiga antelope, musk deer, monkey, seahorse, and rare species of orchid and tree fern. If these species are protected under CITES it is not necessary to prove that the ingredients actually contain the species; simply that they state that they do and that they are being offered for sale. The proprietor later pleaded guilty to eighteen charges under the COTES Regulations 1997 and was fined £300 on each charge, a grand total of £5,400.

The Trade in Ivory

The sale of traditional medicines is only one of many wildlife crimes taking place in London. Ivory is also in demand. In November 2004, officers from the Unit executed search warrants at three London premises. Two other premises in Somerset and Gloucestershire were searched simultaneously by the wildlife crime officers from these forces. In London, twenty-four ivory items were discovered that were being kept for sale. Most were shaving brushes stamped 'real ivory' and with a retail price of around £1,100 each. Other ivory items found included an elephant tusk, glove stretchers and hairbrushes. Almost two years later the gentleman's grooming accessory company implicated pleaded guilty and was fined a total of £10,000, with the ivory items being forfeit. Despite an ivory trade ban, it was estimated by the International Fund for Animal Welfare that 10,000 elephants are still being killed each year for their tusks. In this case we in Britain are helping to fuel this bloody and illegal trade by being willing end users.

The Fur Trade

In less enlightened times the fur trade was a booming business and fur coats were popular and fashionable. Now that the fur coat enthusiasts realise that animals have to be killed for their furs, most have given up the idea and prefer to see the animals wearing the coats. Nevertheless there is a hard core who cast conservation concerns aside in the lust for fur. The problem hasn't disappeared. Because of this greed the trade in rare animal skins is still simmering.

In November 2006, after receiving intelligence, the Met Wildlife Crime Unit carried out a search under warrant at a fur dealer's premises in London. Seven coats made from highly endangered cat species were seized; they were identified by the Natural History Museum as tiger, leopard, snow leopard and ocelot. The shop owner later pleaded guilty to being involved in their trade and was fined a total of £900, with the coats being forfeit.

After this case, Andy Fisher said, 'This case has shown once again that the illegal trade in endangered species is not just something that happens in Asia or Africa. Endangered species are on sale here on the streets of London and they will be for as long as we continue to buy them.'

It beggars belief, almost a decade into the environmental enlightenment of the twenty-first century, that anyone is prepared to walk about swaddled in a tiger skin (or any other rare animal for that matter) thinking that they are indulging in the height of fashion.

In a search of a taxidermist's premises a year earlier the wildlife crime officers recovered two stuffed tiger cubs, tiny and pathetic victims of the black market trade that exists in London and elsewhere. There would be little doubt that their mother had also been killed.

Trade in Live Animals, Bushmeat and Animal Skins

Millions of animals, birds, fish and reptiles are bought and sold in the world every year. Hundreds of thousands of live animals enter the UK every year as part of a legal wildlife trade. Alongside the legal trade, there is a high volume of trade in endangered species filtered in by wildlife criminals (reckoned by some authorities to account for a quarter of the trade) making this one of the world's most lucrative types of crime. Much of this trade is dealt with by HM Revenue and Customs officers as it enters the country, using the powerful Customs and Excise Management Act. Once inside the UK, the illegal trade in protected species is the responsibility of the police to enforce under the COTES Regulations 1997.

In October 2007 the Met Wildlife Crime Unit received intelligence that a number of the endangered fish, Asian Arowana, had been imported by air from Singapore. Acting on this information they visited the east London home of a dealer in exotic fish species and seized eleven live Arowana fish that were clearly being offered for sale. They had been working closely on this case with the local officers, HM Revenue and Customs and the National Wildlife Crime Unit. These endangered fish, which grow up to at least 18 inches long depending on the species, are worth up to £2,000 each and are sought after by keepers of exotic fish. There is a belief in the far-east that owning an Arowana will bring about good fortune.

In this case there was a degree of good fortune. The importer did have permits to import the fish but was not allowed to sell them. At Crown Court he admitted two offences, was fined £2,000 and ordered to pay £800 costs.

In January 2008 the Met wildlife crime unit officers visited a well-known auction house in central London after an allegation that items derived from endangered species were being offered within the auction. Three sea turtle shells, a tiger skull and three narwhal tusks were removed from the sale. The items were unworked, which means that licences should have been obtained to trade in them. Some investigations can be dealt with by warning rather than by prosecution and since there was full co-operation with the police from the auction house the matter was dealt with on the basis of crime prevention and awareness-raising, objectives of Operation Charm.

A more recent example of the Met Unit's successes was in June 2008, when an antiques dealer was convicted of trading in endangered species. He was part of a network that took ivory and whales' teeth from Africa for processing in China then via Eastern Europe for sale in the Western world. To obtain this conviction the Met Unit had worked for three years with the American authorities investigating the operation, which they thought had been ongoing for ten years. The dealer had pled guilty to seven charges under the COTES Regulations and was sentenced to two years imprisonment, suspended for two years. He also signed a disclaimer for a further eighteen ivory items. The dealer now faces prosecution in America.

The illegal trade in bushmeat – meat of animals mainly from the tropical regions of Africa that are killed for human consumption – is also of concern. Many are relatively common animals such as forest antelope and cane rats but others killed for this trade are highly endangered such as gorillas and chimpanzees. In recent years this trade had expanded and some bushmeat is now sold in London.

There is also a huge worldwide trade in products made from reptile skins, particularly snakes and crocodiles, which are made into handbags and shoes. In addition, one of the priorities of the National Wildlife Crime Unit (formerly based in London and now based in North Berwick near Edinburgh) is the illegal trade in caviar, the unfertilised eggs of the sturgeon. Tropical fish, parrots and snakes are among the many exotic species that are popular as pets, though several of these species are endangered and can only be sold if they have been legally bred in captivity in the EU or if they have been imported under a Government licence.

THE ILLEGAL INTERNATIONAL TRADE IN PLANTS

Invariably when people think of wildlife crime it's rare that they think of plants being 'at risk'. Plant trade is big business, and of course much of it is legitimate; forestry alone, a major global sector, accounted for $160 billion gross production worldwide in 1998. However, illegal plant trade, both in a UK and an international context, is one of the factors that contributes to species' decline. In one trade sector alone, logging, the World Bank has estimated that some governments are losing over $16 billion per year from illegal logging. Plant crime and smuggling have been on the enforcement radar for many years and over 30,000 species of plant are listed on the CITES Appendices – nearly five times as many plants as animals.

The cases throughout this book clearly illustrate that the police cannot tackle wildlife crime alone; in almost every case another agency is consulted for specialist advice. More and more these agencies and organisations are cherished members of the Partnership for Action against Wildlife Crime (PAW). One PAW member invaluable not just to the Metropolitan Police wildlife crime unit but to all UK police forces is the Royal Botanic Gardens, Kew. Kew leads the world in assisting enforcement officers in the UK and internationally on plant trade and plant crime. It has world-leading expertise in plant and fungal science and holds globally important resources that span a vast range of the Earth's plant diversity.

The principal contact at Kew is Madeleine Groves, a member of the Conventions and Policy Section (CAPS). CAPS play an important role in assisting enforcement agencies in regulating the illegal trade of wildlife by providing expert advice and identification skills. As the UK CITES Scientific Authority for plants, Kew is in a position to provide expert scientific advice and capacity building to other PAW partners in combating wildlife crime. CAPS co-ordinate Kew's role and won the PAW Partner of the Year Award in 2009, an award presented annually to the organisation or individual contributing most to the work of the partnership.

As part of its training commitment Kew hosts a week-long training course for Police and Customs twice a year, introducing law enforcers to the plants in trade and to the pertinent issues. On an EU scale, between 2003 and 2009 Kew has trained over five hundred law-enforcement officers in the UK, Poland, Ireland and Sweden. The training is often put into practice.

Orchids are considered by many to be the most beautiful and

exotic flowers on earth – and they are also amongst the world's most endangered plants. In June 2004 smuggling orchids led to the downfall of a senior scientist working for a British drugs company. He was attempting to bring 130 orchid specimens taken from his native Malaysia into Britain concealed in his luggage when he was apprehended by Customs officers. The haul included plants of *Paphiopedilum rothschildianum*, named after the eminent Victorian orchid grower, Baron Ferdinand de Rothschild. Of all the species in the *Paphiopedilum* or slipper genus, this is one of the rarest. Despite extensive searching for more than a century, it has been located only in a small number of sites on Mount Kinabalu in Borneo. A site recently discovered outside this area has been reported to have been stripped by illegal plant-hunters. He also had *Paphiopedilum sanderianum* and *Paphiopedilum gigantifolium*. *Paphiopedilum gigantifolium*, discovered in 1997, is confined to Sulawesi, Indonesia, and is now thought to be extinct at its original location because of over-collecting. All Asian slipper orchids are strictly regulated by CITES, where they are placed on Appendix 1 of the Convention, banning their trade from the wild. Slipper orchids are distinguished by a voluptuous lower petal, or lip, and are closely related to Britain's rarest wild flower, the lady's slipper. Some specimens can change hands for thousands of pounds. This species survived in a secret location, guarded round the clock, until British collectors nearly wiped it out. It has now been planted elsewhere. Some Asian slipper orchids, including those in the scientist's haul, are only known from a single location. Others – only recently discovered – may now be extinct in the wild, such have been the plant-thieves' activities.

The scientist was charged on thirteen counts under Article 4 of Council Regulation (EC) 338/97 as amended by Commission Regulation (EC) 1908/01 and Commission Regulation (EC) 1497/03, contrary to Section 170(2)(b) of the Customs and Excise Management Act 1979. This sounds serious, a view clearly held by the judge.

After pleading guilty at Isleworth Crown Court the scientist was sentenced to four months imprisonment. Judge Richard McGregor Johnson told him, 'I am satisfied that you did bring in these orchids with a view to commercial gain. It is essential the courts make it plain that such behaviour will not be tolerated in order to discourage others who might be tempted to follow in your footsteps.' Dr David Roberts, an orchid expert at the Royal Botanic Gardens, Kew, who helped to identify the haul and acted as an expert witness in court, said that illegal collecting and trade was pushing the rarest orchid species to extinction.

In July 2007 at a further hearing the scientist was ordered to pay £110,331 (the proceeds of his trade) and £15,000 in costs (including research that had been carried out by Kew).

Various sections of Kew are used by enforcement officers and agencies when plant material and their parts and derivatives require identification as part of an inspection or to add to an enforcement case. This includes the Wood Anatomy Lab in the Jodrell Laboratory where staff identify timbers in trade, and the Biointeractions Team, who have developed tests to identify medicines in trade, for example ginseng. Kew also houses the Chinese Medicinal Plant Authentication Centre which authenticates traditional medicines and assists with the identification of relevant plants, their parts and derivatives. Royal Botanical Gardens Kew has also been actively working to identify some of the major CITES timbers as traded and have worked with Wildlife DNA Services to develop a validated forensic test to identify ramin (*Gonystylus* spp.) in trade and are currently working on widening this test for other CITES timbers.

Ramin is the common trade name given to a number of light-coloured tropical hardwood tree species native to peat swamp forests, including those in Indonesia, Malaysia and the Philippines. It is prized for its fine grain and is commonly made into picture frames, blinds and pool cues. There is concern at the over-exploitation of ramin from prime orang-utan habitats in south-east Asia. Links have already been demonstrated between policing wildlife crime in the British Isles and the risk of extermination of species many thousands of miles from our shores: this is yet another such link.

In February 2002 Felixstowe Customs' officers seized a consignment of ramin that had been illegally imported from Indonesia. The consignment consisted of 38m^3 of picture mouldings with a retail value of £171,713. The company responsible, Arqadia, is one of Europe's largest manufacturers of picture frames. The case was investigated by Custom's National Intelligence Section, and Kew was called to give witness statements and assist with the identification of the picture mouldings. All of the identification of the material was carried out by the wood anatomy team in the Jodrell Laboratory, Customs requiring identification of a comprehensive range of samples from the consignment. The case was resolved with Arqadia being fined £80,000 and their consent to a press release being issued by Customs outlining the case and naming the company.

Public Opinion Wins the Day

Operation Charm has gone from strength to strength and in 2006 it became a partnership involving the Metropolitan Police Wildlife Crime Unit, the Greater London Authority, the Active Conservation Awareness Programme, IFAW, WWF-UK and the David Shepherd Wildlife Foundation.

Despite the incredible successes of the Metropolitan Police Wildlife Crime Unit, in 2007 in a cost cutting exercise, it was announced by the Met that they intended to cut core funding for two of the posts (there are now four posts, two police support staff and two police officers) within the Unit. This was not well received by the public and after an incredible 6,000 letters and emails the Met reversed the decision. Wildlife crime detection has always been near the bottom end of policing priorities but that is not necessarily reflected in public opinion. In this case, rightly, public opinion won the day.

It is a decision that was quickly vindicated. In February 2008 the unit, along with local police officers and officers from HMRC executed a search warrant at a traditional Chinese medicine shop in South London. On this occasion 300 medicinal products that appeared to be made from endangered species of animals and plants were seized. The species included musk deer, tiger, sea turtle, seahorse, Tibetan wild ass (Kiang), yak and a number of endangered plants. This is the first time that Tibetan wild ass, which is found in the remote mountains of Western China, has been found on sale in London.

Whilst most police forces in the UK are working hard at reducing crime committed against our own wildlife, nowhere better than in London is it demonstrated that we also have a responsibility beyond our shores. Andy Fisher's comment is well made: 'Ultimately, as long as we continue to buy these products, endangered species in other countries will be at risk.'

Red kites demonstrating their aerobatic skills
(Photo: Neil Macdonald)

REPUBLIC OF IRELAND

The Republic of Ireland has its own distinctive flora and fauna. The native red deer is Ireland's largest land mammal, with the earliest record of red deer in Ireland about 26,000 years ago. The rest of the red deer in Ireland were introduced in the 1800-1900s from Scotland, England and France. In 1860 Lord Powerscourt introduced Japanese sika deer to his estate in County Wicklow, one male and three female. Many of subsequent generations of these deer escaped or were released into the Wicklow hills where they flourished and have now hybridised with red deer. As a result, red-like hybrids are mostly found in the upland areas and most sika-like hybrids (new evidence now suggests that these may be pure sika) are found in woodland habitats. The Normans introduced fallow deer to Ireland in 1244 from England to County Wicklow. Quite surprisingly there are no roe deer in the country.

Though there are brown hares in Northern Ireland (they were introduced to a number of estates in the Republic in the late 1800s but do not seem to have established populations) the island has its own unique mountain hare. *Lepus timidus* is the species found in Britain, but the Irish version is *Lepus timidus hibernicus*, the main difference being that the *hibernicus* sub-species do not normally change their coat to white or mottled white in winter.

The other mammal noted for its change of coat to white in winter is the stoat, which though present in Ireland is considered a sub-species of that found in Britain. The stoat is protected under the Wildlife Acts but there are some problems on shooting estates where many gamekeepers are UK-trained and continue to trap stoats despite their being protected in Ireland. Its smaller cousin, the weasel, is absent from Ireland.

Like its neighbours, Ireland has not been immune to the spread of non-native pest species: mink and grey squirrel. More recent attempts have been made to introduce muntjac deer and wild boar by unscrupulous and misguided hunters. Whilst there have been unwelcome imports, there have also been regrettable losses of iconic birds.

Return of the Natives: Eagle and Kite

Golden Eagles last bred in Ireland in 1910, in Glenveagh, Co Donegal, and became extinct after the last breeding attempt in County Mayo in 1912. In 2001, as part of a reintroduction programme headed by Lorcan O'Toole, eagle chicks, collected from nests in Scotland and reared in large aviaries for a further five to seven weeks without direct human contact, have been released into Glenveagh National Park. Between 2001 and 2006 the project has released 46 birds in Donegal. The birds bred for the first time in 2007, this being the first Irish-bred golden eagle for 100 years. I first met Lorcan in the late 1990s when he headed the release of red kites into the central belt of Scotland and his knowledge of red kites and his determination that they succeed was inspiring. I'm sure these qualities will be no less evident in his latest project.

In 2007 another eagle that disappeared from Ireland more than 100 years ago took flight again as part of a scheme to reintroduce native birds of prey to the country. This time the reintroduced birds were fifteen young white-tailed eagles, donated by Norway and released into a national park in the southwestern county of Kerry. Ireland's Environment Minister, John Gormley, who released the birds, said, 'These eagles had pride of place in the cultural and natural heritage of Ireland for hundreds of years but due to trapping and shooting in the nineteenth and early twentieth centuries they became extinct.' This of course was little different to Britain. Ireland – and Scotland – has had to rely on the generosity of Norway so that these majestic birds can fly again in our skies.

Mr Gormley had a busy year in 2007 and was present when thirty young red kites from Wales were introduced to the wild in County Wicklow. It had been 200 years since red kites were last seen in Ireland. The Red Kite Project Manager is Damian Clarke, and as I, along with my editor Sean Bradley, began a two-day trip to Ireland in September 2008 courtesy of Damian and Lorcan O'Toole, I wondered if these new releases would fare any better than those in Scotland. Had there been a sea-change of policy in respect of birds of prey by land managers and game managers, or were those who use guns (or worse, pesticides) still just as disrespectful of conservation, biodiversity and public opinion as their predecessors?

I was reasonably optimistic when one of the first mammals I saw was an otter on the Vartry river in the town of Wicklow. It was in the middle of the river and oblivious to the passers-by, most of whom in any case were too interested in jogging or dog-walking to notice the mysterious ripples in the river, the dark shiny head that was their cause or the brief view of an arched back as the otter dived.

I was even more optimistic when Damian told me of the spread and diversity of National Parks throughout Ireland and the fact that shooting is not permitted in Irish National Parks.[2] Any person found in breach of this is prosecuted. Deer hunting licences are granted by the National Parks and Wildlife Service for hunting activities on other lands. Licences to shoot hares and game bird species are issued by An Garda Síochána with an endorsement on the shotgun owner's certificate. When activities are licensed, and a licence can be revoked for a breach of the licensed activity, this tends to ensure those dependant on the licence obey wildlife laws.

One of my visits was to a Wicklow shooting estate and this served to reinforce my view. Pheasant poults were present in numbers I have seldom seen in Britain and buzzards and red kites soared in the sky overhead. I chatted to the two gamekeepers about their rearing programme, about their comparatively modest shooting days with around 250 birds per day despite the thousands I saw round my feet, and their views on buzzards. 'Buzzards', they said, 'take one or two pheasant poults but nothing really to cause great concern except when they panic young birds in a pen and some can get smothered. Red kites are no problem at all.' If this was the dominant view across Ireland then the red kites, golden eagles and white-tailed eagles being re-introduced might build up to decent numbers quite quickly.

---

[2] The National Association of Regional Game Councils, an affiliation of the country's gun clubs with 27,000 members, has taken a High Court challenge on the prohibition of shooting on state lands. As at January 2009 the case has still to be determined.

WILDLIFE LEGISLATION

The main relevant legislation is the Wildlife Act 1976, amended in 2000. Under this, enforcement powers are given to An Garda Síochána and any other person authorised under the Act, which of course includes conservation rangers, a remarkable body of men and women that I'll come back to. Much of the Act is similar to UK legislation: protection is given to badger, bats, otter, deer, hares, pine marten, red squirrel, natterjack toad, seals, cetaceans and, somewhat surprisingly, the stoat and the hedgehog. Hare coursing with greyhounds is permitted under licence, as is the hunting of hares with a pack of beagles. Coursing is carried out at 'regulated coursing matches' during which the dogs are muzzled. The reality is that hares are unlikely to be killed by being crushed or torn apart but may well die of stress, a death with a more benign effect on the conscience of participants and spectators. Licensed Course meets are attended by conservation rangers. All injuries and deaths are recorded and this information is used for deciding whether a licence should be granted the following year. Despite this licensed coursing anyone would be naive to think that illegal coursing does not also take place.

When I read in the 1976 Act that licences could be granted to hunt otters I wondered how this could be, since otters have complete protection as European Protected Species under EU legislation, which of course informs legislation throughout the EU. A check on the more recent Wildlife (Amendment) Act 2000 showed that the hunting of otters had been banned in 2000, though in reality there had been no licence issued to hunt otters since well before that.

Penalties under the 1976 Act were incredibly low. The highest fine I could find in the Act, even in a case taken on indictment, was IR£500. A dramatic change came with the 2000 Act, and now penalties of IR£50,000 and/or two years imprisonment are at the top of the range.

THE INVESTIGATION OF WILDLIFE CRIME
AND THE ROLE OF THE CONSERVATION RANGER

It was surprising to learn that most wildlife crime in Ireland is not investigated by the police but by the conservation rangers of the National Parks and Wildlife Service. Powers are broadly similar to those of the police in Britain. A member the Gardai or an authorised person may at all reasonable times enter any land (other than a dwelling) to which the suspicion relates if there are reasonable grounds for suspecting that a person is committing or has committed an offence under any provision of the Wildlife Acts, 1976 and 2000. This effectively means that anywhere other than a dwelling house or a lockfast building may be entered.

The developing role of the conservation rangers is best explained by Val Swan, one of the longest-serving rangers, who works in the North-East Region.

'When I started working as a ranger with the Forest and Wildlife Service away back in 1979 we were then called wildlife rangers. Our duties were mainly concerned with the implementation and enforcement of the Wildlife Act, 1976 though we also dealt with all wider countryside wildlife issues. In the early 90s the Wildlife Service parted from the Department of Forestry and became part of the Office of Public Works (OPW). At the time, OPW had responsibility for managing our National Parks and employed park rangers to look after the parks and the public visiting them. The OPW then merged the grades of wildlife rangers and park rangers into one grade called conservation ranger. We were told at the time that management decided to call the grade 'conservation ranger' so that neither grade would feel that they were been taken over by the other. However, we later found out that the real reason was to facilitate a serious attempt to get the new grade to look after national monuments as well as wildlife.

'In our North-East region we cover the counties of Louth, Meath, Dublin, Kildare, Laois and Offaly. The region is divided into two districts, each managed by a district conservation officer (DCO). We have ten rangers in the region with five reporting to each DCO. Each ranger is assigned to an area that usually corresponds with an area controlled by a Local Authority.

'About 40% of our rangers' time is taken up dealing with planning referrals and licence applications, much the same role as carried out by the statutory nature conservation organisations in the UK. Rangers also comment on forestry applications within or near designated sites or other ecologically sensitive areas.

'Application for licences under the Wildlife Acts are referred to the rangers, who start the process by interviewing the applicant, checking the situation on the ground and making their recommendation to their DCO. Licences applied for include those for hunting deer species; hunting the foreshore and state lakes; engaging in falconry and keeping birds of prey. In addition they are issued for ringing, tagging or marking protected species, or capturing or killing them for scientific or educational purposes; for capturing, killing or scaring protected species where they are causing serious damage to crops or fauna; or lastly for cutting, picking, collecting or interfering with the habitat of protected flora.

'Only about 10% of our rangers' time is dedicated to the enforcement of our wildlife laws. During this they carry out anti-poaching patrols, particularly for late-night and weekend deer poaching. Other activities they patrol for and investigate include crimes against birds of prey, bats, badgers, hares and so forth.

'The remainder of our time is taken up with the surveillance and monitoring of areas designated as protected sites, the monitoring of which form the basis of Ireland's submission to the EC on the conservation status of these sites. Where damage is found rangers are required to investigate and this may lead to a prosecution. We also make recommendations on applications by landowners on protected sites (including raised bogs) to do works which are notifiable actions requiring the written consent of the Minister.'

The designation of these sites did not receive the universal approval of landowners, especially where it impacted on farming activities and other developments. It is part of a ranger's duty to monitor these sites to ensure that they are being maintained at a favourable status. Where damage is discovered or works found to have been carried out without the consent of the Minister the ranger may initiate a prosecution.

Val Swan continued to describe his varied and demanding role: checking records of wildlife dealers, pet shop owners, attending regulated hare monitoring coursing events and even a licensed carted stag hunt.

'There is one carted stag hunt in Ireland, the Ward Union Hunt in County Meath, which keeps and hunts farmed deer. On hunt days deer are loaded into a trailer and transported (carted) to a release point where one is duly released and hunted by people on horseback with hounds. Once the deer tires and stands at bay it is recaptured and carted back to the deer farm. Not without justification there is considerable opposition from animal welfare groups. Thirty-four separate conditions of compliance are now attached to the licence. Without the licence the hunt would be subject to the provisions of animal welfare legislation and could not take place.

'Rangers are also involved in species and habitat surveys undertaken by NPWS, carrying out the legwork and collecting data from the field. It is an area of their work that rangers love and the bonus to the public is that it saves on fees to independent contractors. There were 32 research projects scheduled for 2009 that involved ranger participation. In the North-east region we manage approximately 6000 acres of NPWS owned lands. It mostly comprises Natures Reserves and other areas such as bogs and wetlands that we have acquired for conservation purposes. Rangers are very much involved with the management of these sites and the supervision of contract staff doing works such as woodland management, visitor facilities, pathwork etc.

'Rangers are offered a number of training courses each year. Some are mandatory and their participation in others is usually decided in consultation with their line manager. Somehow we seem to manage to keep busy!'

There is a strong view from conservation rangers that NPWS staff members do not get adequate training in relation to the enforcement of wildlife crime. They occasionally have refresher courses in wildlife legislation but very little that deals with the practical situation in the field when they actually confront a wildlife criminal. One ranger commented that he had a lot more training on managing a safe office environment than in dealing with people involved with wildlife crime! Enforcing wildlife law is a specialised area and if conservation rangers are to remain efficient enforcers of wildlife laws their training needs to be much broader than classroom-based legislation.

One ranger observed, 'I feel that even though we have rangers who are very qualified in the natural sciences they may not be able to recognise a badger baiter or know what he is doing, even if they fell over his terrier and spade, or I sometimes wonder how many would recognise a finch trapper if he met one with his clap net under his arm. Rangers have no ready access to advice on legislation and it generally falls to the more experienced rangers to impart the knowledge they've gained. It might help if we had a unit in HQ specialising in wildlife crime.'

So here we have a statutory body that in the UK might compare with English Nature or Scottish Natural Heritage but with powers nearly equivalent to the police in relation to the enforcement of wildlife crime. On the positive side rangers will be much more experienced on the identification and ecology of wildlife than most Gardaí. The rangers I met are enthusiastic about their job and there is no doubt that they get some very good results. On the negative side rangers can only spend 10% of their time in enforcing wildlife law, they are few in number and some have limited experience. Because they do a good job with the wildlife crimes reported to or discovered by them it seems that the Gardaí pretty much leave them to it and abrogate their own statutory responsibilities under the Wildlife Acts. Joint working would be so much more effective not only in securing convictions but in deterring those who participate not only in wildlife crime but in other types of criminality.

CRIMES AGAINST BATS

I was interested in comparing the types of wildlife crime encountered in Ireland with the UK experience and where possible looking for direct links that would confirm cross-border criminality. My first port of call was to the offices of the Department of the Environment in Dublin, in particular to Peter Carvill and Gerry Leckey of the National Parks and Wildlife Service (NPWS). Peter and Gerry are administrators in the legislation and species protection sections but only have certain cases referred to them. Most cases under the Wildlife Act would be taken in the District Courts by field staff without passing through their offices. The range of wildlife crime that they deal with is not quite as broad as that dealt with in Britain but it was clear that crime committed against bats was a real issue. This is an extremely difficult area in which to gain a conviction unless every agency involved is knowledgeable about the evidential requirements to prove, for instance, that a particular place is a bat roost or of the powers that can be used to secure evidence. A range of experts can bring various knowledge and skills to a case, in particular that of bat ecology. A strategy is required well in

Raised Bogs

The protection of designated raised bog sites has generally proved to be contentious and difficult for rangers. The Republic of Ireland has some of the best examples of raised bog remaining in the European community. Raised bog formation began in the post glacial period and covered much of Ireland's central plain; the original area was approximately 310,000 hectares or 5% of national territory. Today only 139 bogs containing approximately 18,000 ha of uncut raised bog, which is of conservation interest, remain. Their preservation requires that all turf cutting activity be brought to an end. Commercial turf cutting and moss peat extraction has been stopped and compensation paid but the problem of turf cutting for domestic supply remains. Cutting turf from the bog as a household fuel is a tradition that has continued for centuries in Ireland. Until the 1980s it was cut by hand with an implement called the slane. It was then a labour-intensive operation requiring three or four people to dig it out and spread it to dry. Since then it has become a mechanised process, usually carried out by a contractor who can cut and spread many people's turf in one day. Unfortunately the advent of this mechanised method seriously hastened the decline of the bogs and brought an urgency to protect the remaining bogs of conservation interest. This has been met with considerable resistance by many rural folk who still depend on turf for heating and cooking and who have no wish to change to other sources of fuel. Unfortunately the ranger is the face of the Department on the ground and has to bear the brunt of people's anger. On occasions this has resulted in rangers being threatened and even physically assaulted. (This is just one of the reasons that in Wales, and more recently England and Scotland, these investigations are generally carried out jointly with a police wildlife crime officer.)

In some ways one can sympathise with turfcutters, as until recent times in Ireland bogs were associated with hardship and seen only as a source of household fuel and a place to dump old cars and domestic rubbish. The good news is that people are beginning to appreciate bogs for their conservation value and see them as magical places to visit and to see wildlife. The concept of the need to protect these places is becoming more widespread. There is no doubt that in the not too distant future examples of raised bog ecosystems will be fully preserved for posterity in Ireland. Conservation rangers are playing an important role in bringing this about through their educational work and through their enforcement work under European and National legislation.

advance and it is only through everyone knowing what part they should play and preparing the groundwork that a conviction can follow. It has taken us years in Britain to get anywhere near this stage, but we are making progress. As yet I don't see Ireland, north or south, with the necessary training or awareness-raising in place that would lead to more successful investigation, or better still, that may deter people from committing crime against bats.

Developers and builders must be made to consider the threat that their work may pose to wildlife. Unless there is a threat to profit or livelihood, bats – as well as badgers and other protected species – are unlikely to be considered during demolition or construction. Through their involvement in the vetting of planning applications, conservation rangers can determine which properties are likely to have bats, for example, and request further information by ordering ecological surveys to be carried out. After assessing these survey results, conditions can be attached to any planning permission granted. The same happens in relation to habitat protection. NPWS can insist that an Appropriate Assessment under Article 6 of the Habitats Directive be carried out.

I suspect that in Ireland crime against bats will seldom cross the mind of the vast majority of Gardaí yet they have the statutory power under wildlife legislation to investigate it and are responsible for strategies to prevent *all* crime.

CRIMES AGAINST BADGERS

It came as no surprise that in Ireland crime committed against badgers featured heavily. I was interested in researching criminal activity over the previous decade or so and the first crime that I encountered was the interference with a badger's sett in 1997 near the town of Trim, on the River Boyne in County Meath. Three men had been caught by wildlife rangers who had seen the men at the sett. They had by that time dug a metre and a half into the sett and had two dogs with them and another in their car.

The first thing that surprised me was that despite that fact that, probably without exception, anyone involved in badger digging in the UK has a background of violent behaviour, the crime was being dealt with by conservation rangers, without baton, handcuffs or any of the protective equipment carried by Gardaí. One criminal had given a false name and I wondered what facility wildlife rangers had to check names and address. Did they carry radios? Did they have access to any database that could assist? I learned that all conservation rangers carry mobile phones and those that work in the National Parks also have radios but that, in practice, they don't have facilities to check names and mostly only informal arrangements exist to enable them to run car registration checks.

Whatever the restrictions under which conservation rangers operate it is to their great credit that they gained a conviction and the three men involved pled guilty to a number of offences. Two were fined IR£100 and IR£150 respectively, and they were ordered to pay IR£100 witness expenses. The third was remanded in custody for a week. I was pleased to learn that one of them was also disqualified from driving for a year for using his car in the commission of this crime – that really was a significant penalty.

Cross-border wildlife crime didn't take long to come to light, and I found out that in the year 2000 men from the north of England had been travelling to Wales and Ireland for 'badger-baiting holidays' with their Irish counterparts often making return trips to the north of England. Sergeant Eddie Bell, wildlife crime officer of Durham Constabulary had been investigating this ring of baiters, and was of the view that there are a substantial number of people involved. Because of the torture they were inflicting they had to be secretive and there was great difficulty in gaining intelligence, but they were found to have their own publications and were using coded messages to communicate on the internet. One group in Ireland was even bragging that they bred badgers, advertising on one site, '*We breed 'em, you bait 'em*' and badgers available for '*death by baiting.*' It is doubtful that they had been breeding badgers: much more likely had been taking them from the wild.

Badgers are also at risk from some farmers, who consider that their presence may spread bovine tuberculosis to their cattle herds. This is also the fear in many parts of the UK, though less so in Scotland where the incidence of bovine TB is much lower. In 2000, a farmer from Newtownmountkennedy had set a live-catch trap for a badger. The trap was discovered by conservation rangers and in it they found a barely-alive badger, with another decomposing badger carcass lying nearby.

The farmer was interviewed and claimed that he had checked the trap two days before the rangers found it and that it had been empty. In the case of the decomposing badger he claimed that he had caught it in the trap and that when he checked the trap on that occasion the badger had been asleep. He admitted to having shot it.

Since there was suspicion that cruelty had taken place the police were involved and the farmer was charged with a number of offences: hunting a protected wild animal without a licence; injuring a protected wild animal and cruelty to a protected wild animal. He pled guilty at Wicklow Court to the charge of hunting without a licence, giving the reason that he was trying to protect his pedigree herd of charolais and limousine cattle and was fined € 35. This is a paltry fine and would hardly deter anyone from breaking the law, but the judge pointed out that the maximum fine available to him was € 50. Defence solicitors are sometimes more aware of maximum penalties than prosecutors. Had a guilty plea been tendered for one of the other two charges the outcome may have been entirely different.

A case at Roscrea District Court, County Tipperary the following year confirmed my suspicion that badger digging was commonplace. Two men had been caught – again by conservation rangers – and charged with interfering with a badger sett and baiting a badger with terriers. The two, plus another couple of young teenagers, had been found walking away from the sett with terriers, one of which was bleeding and had a gash between its eyes and nose. A sett nearby had been partly dug but the two men who were charged had admitted to the rangers that they could get down no further because of rocks. In court the defence solicitor told the usual story (perhaps thinking it was a unique defence) that a dog had entered the sett after a rabbit. The lady judge virtually told him not to be so stupid and convicted his clients, ordering them each to pay £1000 to be divided between Badger Watch Ireland and the Irish Society for the Prevention of Cruelty to Animals (ISPCA).

In another incident in 2003 two stray terriers, each with severe injuries to its jaw and mouth, were taken in by a woman in the Oughterard area of Kildare. The dogs were taken to a vet by the ISPCA dog warden and received treatment that included the lower jaw of each dog being wired in place. The vet had no doubt their terrible injuries had been inflicted during badger digging. Thankfully most badger diggers' propensity to violence and cruelty is in inverse proportion to their Mensa rating. The owner of the dogs phoned ISPCA and reported his loss. This information was passed to the Gardaí, and when the dogs' owner, from Ballyfermot, near Dublin, came to collect the dogs, he was arrested.

In another case with abandoned dogs, this time in 2006, two severely injured terriers were found close to a badger sett in Kilkenny after men were chased from a field. The dogs – one of which had sustained facial wounds – were reportedly being used to pull badgers from below ground. A spade was found beside the sett. This incident was reported in the media with a request for information to be passed to the Gardaí or to the National Parks and Wildlife Service. It is unfortunate that no-one with information came forward.

Having met a number of conservation rangers, I recognise that they are doing a terrific job, but it is an extremely dangerous one. In my view, it is a job that they should be doing *alongside* the Gardaí, not *instead of* the Gardaí, combining the expertise in wildlife with the expertise in law enforcement. Conservation rangers would generally welcome this opportunity and would be grateful for better investigative powers and training to match.

Any wildlife crime officer in Britain would agree that dealing with wildlife crime is a really specialised role, and without training (especially joint training with other law-enforcement agencies and then putting that training into practice to gain expertise) the chances of getting a case to court and gaining a conviction are low. Wildlife crime in the Republic of Ireland could be reduced, and the crimes that occur dealt with very much more effectively, if there existed a network of Gardaí trained as wildlife crime officers and they worked closely with conservation rangers.

In early 2009, how many wildlife officers does An Garda Síochána currently have? The answer is one.

FINCH TRAPPING

A second type of crime against wildlife where there are known to be Irish/UK links is in the lucrative trade in finches taken from the wild and then sold on to breeders. (As recently as February 2009 information was received from the NPWS that resulted in a man from central Scotland who had recently visited Ireland being charged with finch-trapping offences.) Links are also suspected with Malta, islands which are infamous for their capture of finches on their bi-annual migration.

In one case in Ireland in 2005 the Spanish son-in-law of one of Ireland's wealthiest business dynasties was caught in an operation involving wildlife rangers, Gardaí and staff of the Dublin Society for the Prevention of Cruelty to Animals. A dawn raid saw wildlife rangers scaling the walls of the family estate, where they caught their suspect in the act. He was busy gathering up a clap net that had been set to catch the valuable finches attracted to seed set out on the ground. He also had a Larsen-type trap set and baited with a feral pigeon, which the rangers suspected was set to catch a bird of prey. He may have already been successful at this as there were a few sparrow hawk feathers already in the cage.

They then went on to discover dozens of wild birds, including redpolls, goldfinches, bullfinches, chaffinches and greenfinches housed in an aviary. Some were also trapped in small cages and some had string harnesses fitted around their bodies. The harnesses were referred to as 'braces' and consisted of a harness fitted closely to the bird's body. The brace had a swivel ring attached to it and it allowed the bird to be secured to a perch, where it was unwittingly decoying its wild brethren into the trapping area. The conservation rangers had never seen these encumbrances before (not indeed have I) though they had heard of them. Val Swan, one of the rangers involved had caught finch trappers in the past using a goldfinch tethered to a perch by a short string from a jewellery clasp around its leg. A long string attached to this allowed the illegal operators to disturb the captive bird, making it flutter and thereby attract other finches.

After the search, the wildlife rangers secured an order allowing them to release the birds into the countryside. Some were completely disorientated but it was hoped that most would survive. Whatever the case, their chance of survival was considerably better than it would have been as terrified captives.

One of the wildlife rangers, commenting on the activities of the man captured, was of the view that this had been an extensive operation, but that a number of people were involved and this case was only the tip of the iceberg. 'There is a serious amount of trapping in Ireland involving all sorts of illegal or unapproved cages, nets and traps. In recent months we have seized mist nets, clap nets, cages, trap cages and even glue traps. As a result, we now have a number of cases pending in the courts.'

A district court in Dublin fined the man €800 which, considering the extent of the cruelty involved in this particular case, the scale of the problem and the apparent associated wealth of the man accused, seemed remarkably lenient and must have been a disappointing result to those involved in the investigation. There appears to be major inconsistencies in the sentencing of wildlife crime in Ireland, with some judges treating it seriously while others seem to put it on a par with a parking offence.

DEER POACHING

Deer poaching is particularly common in Ireland, and the conservation rangers collectively spend many hours on anti-deer poaching patrols. It is suspected that some of the poached deer find their way into the Scottish venison market, a link that is currently being investigated by Scottish wildlife crime officers in conjunction with the conservation rangers.

In the late evening of January 2001, conservation ranger Damian Clarke and two colleagues were carrying out an anti-poaching patrol in the area of Mucklagh, Aughrim, when they saw the occupants of a vehicle using a handheld spotlamp. They later managed to stop the vehicle and the two occupants claimed that they were lamping foxes using a .22 Hornet. The rangers searched the vehicle and discovered a dead sika deer in the back. The poaching pair alleged that they had shot the deer much earlier on land where they had permission to shoot, but they were unable to account for the deer being warm and clearly newly-shot. They then changed their story to having accidentally run in to the deer and injured it with their vehicle, then shot it with the .22 Hornet 'to put it out of its misery'. Before concocting this story there was no consideration that there should have been damage to their vehicle and also some damage to the deer!

The two were charged with a number of deer poaching offences, including the use of a vehicle and an artificial light source to shoot a deer, and taking a deer with a rifle of unsuitable calibre. The rangers later skinned the deer and found that it had been shot in the neck and that there were no other injuries.

During their trial the men continued their story-telling. They had simply been going for a pint when they decided on the spur of the moment to go lamping for foxes. They had accidentally hit the deer when rounding a bend and decided to capitalise on the deer's bad fortune and use it as free food for their dogs. The lamp had coincidentally been in the vehicle for checking farm stock and on the night when the rangers saw them they had not been lamping into fields but in fact had been innovatively using the powerful beam to search for a cigarette lighter that one had dropped. Quite why the court did not believe this story is beyond me! The men left the court poorer by €300 and €180 respectively. They may well by now have recouped this loss many times over by collating their fairy tales into a children's book. I suspect that had I spent the last 40-odd years policing in Ireland rather than Scotland it would have been much more entertaining!

DISPOSABLE GREYHOUNDS: IRELAND'S SHAME

The Irish are well-known for their interest in racing, and many of the best racehorse bloodlines in the world can be traced directly back to Ireland. They are also keen on greyhound racing, with some €90 million spent in recent years upgrading Ireland's seventeen venues. In 2007 the tracks drew more than one million people, a quarter of Ireland's population. Because of the callous and ruthless nature of some of the people involved, greyhound racing results in unbelievable cruelty to many dogs and, of course, a great deal of work for the Gardaí and the ISPCA. In many cases the dogs are bred for one purpose only and once that purpose is fulfilled they are disposable.

According to the UK-based public interest group Greyhound Action International, globally 'tens of thousands of dogs are disposed of every year by the greyhound racing industry, either because they fail to make the grade as racers or because their racing days are over. These dogs are bred to die. Ireland has created a glut of greyhounds and other countries are being left to mop up the problem.' The spokeswoman concluded: 'Ireland is a drastic place for animals.'

As if to vindicate this final remark, a number of discarded live greyhounds have been found with their ears cut off, so that they cannot be identified by the tattoo inside the ears.

Are the Irish really any worse than some greyhound owners and trainers in the UK? I suspect not. In May 2004 a black and white greyhound was found by a hill walker on a Welsh mountainside. It was still alive despite having been shot in the head, probably with a nail gun, and its ears had been cut off. Not surprisingly the animal was extremely distressed and had to be taken to a vet where it was put down. A post-mortem examination showed that the dog had brain damage and had a shard of metal embedded in its cheek.

In July 2006 every UK newspaper covered the greyhound disposal factory in the back garden of a house in Seaham, County Durham. The main photograph in the newspapers showed two dogs that had been shot being brought in a wheelbarrow to their last resting place.

Each year in the UK trainers retire around 10,000 licensed greyhounds from racing, but homes are only found for about a third of them. Probably around 6000 greyhounds are slaughtered every year because they start to lose races. Provided that the dogs are killed humanely no criminal offence is committed but is it not taking us back hundred of years in terms of civilisation that dogs can simply be discarded at a relatively young age when their commercial purpose has been served? Mutilating them by cutting off their ears is of course barbaric and most definitely a criminal offence.

The point is this: the ill treatment of greyhounds is a scandal, whether it takes place in Ireland or the UK. It sickens the vast majority of the population yet investigation into cruelty to greyhounds is way down the priority list for the police in mainland Britain. To their credit it now appears to be taken more seriously by An Garda Síochána and the Police Service of Northern Ireland (PSNI).

HUNTING THE FOX

Cruelty can also be associated with foxhunting. Banned in Britain in its traditional form where the intent is for the hounds to catch and kill the fox, it is still legal in the Republic of Ireland. This situation attracts hunts over from Britain whose members are not content with driving the foxes forward to people waiting with guns to shoot them, or drag hunting, where the end game is for the hounds to follow an artificial scent laid in advance. Though I used to take part in rough shooting and occasionally driven game shooting – much less so now – I have no issue with field sports where the creature killed as part of the sport is eaten, or the true objective of the day is pest control. I have no issue with foxhunting as it is carried out in Scotland (and some other parts of the UK) where the intention as part of pest control is to have people on foot with hounds chase the fox forward to be shot, or with the use of terriers in fox dens in spring. I have never been an advocate of foxhunting on horseback that purports to be pest control but in reality is sport. If those who took part ate the foxes they killed I might change my views.

What makes this sport worse is when the fox being hunted 'goes to ground' and is dug up. This happened during a hunt in 2008 with two Irish foxhound packs, with a pack of hounds and their followers from Cumbria taking part as guests in what was described as an act of barbarism by a witness. The witness described how a group of men dug foxes out of their underground refuge with spades and iron bars, then killed them in direct violation of what the witness described as 'the good sport' of leaving foxes who have outwitted the hounds alone once they are underground. The allegations included one man tossing a helpless captive fox from a bag to the waiting dogs. The witness said that he 'thought bagged foxes were a relic of darker times and consigned to the history books. The anti-foxhunting brigade can hang up their boots; foxhunting will end as a result of the actions of its own followers.' That may well turn out to be the case.

This incident was not reported to the Gardaí though it appears that they knew about it and were waiting for an official report so that they could investigate the allegation of cruelty. There is no doubt that had that taken place in Britain, full-time wildlife crime officers would have made it their business to elicit a complaint.

And foxhunters wonder why public opinion is against them.

Hare Coursing

Hare coursing is still practised in Ireland, but with the greyhounds muzzled. Again this is a 'sport' that I have little truck with as the end result is not for the pot. Hares are netted under licence and brought to enclosures, where they are released singly for the dogs to chase.

In September 2006 a farmer from Raharney, County Westmeath, was charged with trapping hares without a licence. He held hare coursing meetings on his land and was found guilty of hunting eighteen hares without a Department of Environment licence. A licence granted to the Irish Coursing Club by Environment Minister, Dick Roche, allowed the Raharney-based coursers to take hares from the wild after September 1st. The hares in question were found at the end of August when National Park and Wildlife Service officers inspected the club's premises. The farmer concerned stated that the hares had only been caught the day before but a conservation ranger stated that in her experience the hares at the farm appeared to have been in the pen longer than a day and that it was unlikely that so many hares could have been trapped in a single day.

The coursing club were fined €300 for hunting hares without a licence and the club's chairman, the farmer, was found guilty of the same offence but was not fined since the fine had been directed towards the club.

I am full of admiration for the conservation rangers who investigate these wildlife crimes. They have little or no training in interviewing skills yet have to counter a parcel of lies in many of their investigations. They cannot arrest a suspect and place him or her in a cell to be interviewed at a pace that best suits the investigation[3]. Yet they frequently can put together a watertight case that will satisfy the high standards of evidence in court. But how much more effective would this be with the conservation rangers and Gardaí working in tandem.

Another very experienced conservation ranger, Enda Mullen from Wicklow, has had many encounters with hare coursers. Enda is now a District Conservation Officer with a number of conservation rangers working directly to her. She related the following tale while we relaxed in the bar after attending the National Wildlife Enforcers' Conference at the Scottish Police College in November 2008.

[3] Strangely neither can the Gardaí except for an offence under Section 14A of the EC Natural Habitats Regulations 1997 and 2005. The Gardaí are also empowered to arrest a suspect under Section 72(2A)(b) of the Wildlife Acts 1976 and 2000, a power not given to conservation rangers.

'It is amazing sometimes how paths converge and how seemingly trivial events lead to something more significant. When I was a young ranger, we had a regional manager who didn't like to say no to people, so, one day, when a woman rang up to say that her dog had been stolen, he asked me to contact her. Finding lost dogs is not part of the remit of the NPWS, but I rang her nevertheless. This is the tale she told me.

'This woman, Mary, and her husband lived in a relatively remote area and had 'adopted' a rather large lurcher from the county dog pound. Being responsible owners, they had had it neutered and had shared their house with it for several years. Mary had worked for the Wildlife Service when it had been part of Forest & Wildlife, but was now a teacher in a second level school in Bray, about ten miles from her house. One day she arrived home from school to find the door of the dog pen open, and the dog missing. Having searched high and low for the dog for several days, and having placed posters throughout the locality, there was still no sign of him.

'One of Mary's classes at school was a group of 13 year-olds that she took for personal development lessons. As they were discussing emotions, one child asked her if she was ever sad. She told the class that she was very sad at that moment because someone had stolen her dog. After class, one boy hung back to talk to her. 'Miss,' he said. 'I know where your dog is and I can get it back for you.' He went on to say that it had been stolen by two of his neighbours who wanted a lurcher for hunting competitions. He described the competitions, telling her that the men and dogs would go to different parts of the country, and used their dogs to bring down whatever animals they could find. Different points were allocated to each species; so many points for a deer, a badger, a hare, and so on. The prize for the winner was a holiday for two in Spain. The child named Tinahely in Co. Wicklow as one of the locations where coursing took place.

'A few days later when Mary returned home from work, she met her dog trotting up the road. There was nobody around and none of the neighbours had noticed anything. She went out and bought the thickest chain and the biggest lock she could find and used these on the dog pen from then on.

'All was well for a number of weeks until Mary came home from work once more to find that the chain had been cut with a bolt cutter and that her dog had been stolen again. This time the child in school was not so forthcoming, saying he had been in 'awful trouble' for 'squealing' to her on the first occasion.

'I kept in touch with Mary for a number of months, but to the best of my knowledge, she never saw her dog again. I made enquiries around Tinahely and spoke with colleagues around the country but we never managed to find any useful leads to these groups.

'There is absolutely no doubt that such illegal coursing takes place. We had a case recently where one of my staff investigated some lamping at night and discovered that four men were using dogs but had no guns. He seized a deer and photographed the lurchers. We had an autopsy done on the deer which concluded that it had been killed by dogs and that it had not died quickly. Our powers under the Wildlife Act meant that we could prosecute them on two charges: for hunting at night using dogs, and hunting on land without permission. The Gardaí added charges of animal cruelty under different legislation.

'The case came before the district court in Carlow on several occasions where there were arguments about jurisdiction and the statute of limitations. Eventually it came to a hearing and the defendants said they would plead guilty to the animal cruelty charge if the Wildlife Act charges were dropped. The prosecution agreed to do this without consulting us. Ultimately the men were fined €400 each and ordered to pay a further €250 to the NPWS for expenses. Interestingly, a brother of one of these men was up on more conventional deer poaching charges at the same time.'

'About two or three years after I had spoken to Mary, there was a Mountain Rescue call out in very cold, icy weather, to Djouce Mountain, a few miles from Bray. Some young men and their dogs were missing having failed to return home the previous night. Their families gathered in the car park at the base of the mountain, praying, crying and keeping vigil. The young men were eventually found, dressed only in tee shirts and suffering from the early stages of hypothermia. They were accompanied by, yes, you've guessed it, their lurchers. I believe that the biggest difficulty in stopping illegal coursing is lack of information. The coursers move in different circles entirely and even disaffected coursers are highly unlikely to ever share anything with the authorities.'

THE GALWAY BAT CASE

Enda had knowledge through a colleague of a wildlife crime of a completely different nature in June 2007, when a national newspaper ran an article about a bridge in County Galway that had been closed for some time as it was in danger of collapse. The river beneath it had been diverted during the 1960s and consequently its five arches spanned a dry bed. The newspaper reported that there were bats roosting in the bridge and that the local people, whether out of concern for disturbing the bats or not, really did not mind the six mile detour imposed on them by the closure.

A week later, on a Friday morning, an engineer with the County Council arrived at the bridge to discover that someone had placed a number of tyres under each arch and set them on fire. Some of the fires were still burning and the bridge was covered in soot. Only one arch was relatively undamaged.

The engineer immediately reported the matter to the Gardaí and also rang the bat expert who had been advising the council on the repair works. She made contact with the local conservation ranger, who told her that he was going on a month's holidays that day but would try to get someone out to the bridge the following Monday. The bat worker was aware that three Daubenton's bat pups had been born in the bridge's maternity roost the previous week. These young bats would certainly not have been able to fly and probably would have crawled further into the crevices to try to avoid the toxic fumes and smoke.

The following day a local man phoned members of the Galway Bat Group saying that he had found five bats under the bridge. Three were dead and the remaining two were barely alive. The bat group members visited him and saw the bats, and were distraught to see that their wings were so badly burned that they looked as though they were melted. Nothing could be done for them and they had to be euthanased.

Subsequently the bat worker employed by the County Council found a further four dead bats, and this under the arch which had not been too badly damaged. She was infuriated that the worst fires had been under the two arches containing the maternity roost and the most-used crevices.

On their visit to the site the Galway Bat Group people saw tractor tracks leading to the bridge from a nearby silage pit. Tyres, of course, are regularly used by farmers to hold the cover on top of the silage. By Monday the Gardaí had spoken with a local farmer, but he denied having had anything to do with the incident. He said someone else must have taken the tyres from his silage pit. There were no witnesses who could contradict this.

Bat Conservation Ireland (BCI), the national umbrella group for bat groups and bat workers took up the cause and contacted the NPWS head office in Dublin. There was much dissatisfaction with what they perceived as an unwillingness to prosecute on the part of local NPWS staff in Galway. BCI ran a very successful media campaign about this incident with articles in many newspapers and both local and national radio interviews. One can only hope that the perpetrator of this crime felt ashamed of his actions and suffered embarrassment in the locality.

A number of issues arise from this case. The first one is the interplay between the responsibilities of the Gardaí and NPWS. In most cases the NPWS are the first port of call, gather the evidence, put the case together and then present the file to either the Gardaí Superintendent or the Chief State Solicitor's Office for prosecution. In this case the Gardaí were the investigating body as the crime had been reported to them. It seems logical that the role of NPWS then becomes one of support to An Garda Síochána, giving advice about sections of the legislation, the life cycle of the bats etc. and assisting them in whatever way possible. This distinction was not understood by the public or the NGOs involved in this case.

The second issue which arises is the lack of understanding by the public of the standard of evidence required to bring a case to court. On our TV screens crime scene investigation teams can solve cases from DNA and fibres in fifty minutes and so there are often unreasonable expectations around the successful outcome of real live cases. The evidence against the suspect in this case was all circumstantial and it would be difficult to prove 'beyond reasonable doubt'. All in all these expectations create a huge level of frustration for both the NGOs and the Law Enforcement Officers. Joint training between investigative agencies and public awareness-raising immediately springs to mind.

DEAD KITES, DEAD EAGLES

The year 2007 brought good news – and then some bad – to Ireland. The good news came first with the celebration in late May of the first golden eagle chick to have been hatched in Ireland for 100 years. A nest in Donegal – part of the Glenveagh National Park introduction programme – hatched two chicks. Often with golden eagles, unless there is food being brought to the nest in abundance, one succumbs and helps its sibling out of hard times by being a menu item. I had a particular interest in these golden eagles since some were collected as chicks in my own area in Tayside, Scotland.

And the bad news? In August 2007, ironically during National Heritage Week, one of 30 red kites released in County Wicklow just six weeks earlier was found dead. Following common practice the kites were radio-tagged, which is why it could be located in a field near Arklow, County Wicklow. It was x-rayed and was found to contain shotgun pellets. The incident was

---

Insane Law needs to be changed now!

It's an unfortunate fact that under the provisions of the Protection of Animals (Amendment) Act 1965, section 14 it remains lawful to lay poisoned baits in Ireland providing the person doing so places a notice of the laying of the bait which is clearly visible from the public road and gives a notice in writing to the local Gardaí. When the Wildlife Act was enacted in 1976, section 34 made it unlawful to lay any poisonous or poisoned substance in any place frequented by wild birds and wild mammals which is calculated or likely to injure them or facilitate their capture. This provision was very obviously in conflict with section 14 of the Protection of Animals (Amendment) Act 1965. Legal advice to the Department at the time was that the legislature would have had in mind the provisions of section 14 of the 1965 Act when enacting section 34 of the Wildlife Act, 1976. Therefore, so much of section 14 of the 1965 act is by implication repealed as incompatible with section 34 of the Wildlife Act 1976. To say this is ambiguous is an understatement but when the chance came to clarify the issue of poisoned baits in the Wildlife Act 2000 the opportunity was missed. Instead, a subsection to section 34 of the1976 Act was added which states "the other provisions of this section are without prejudice to sections 7 and 14 of the Protection of Animals (Amendment) Act, 1965." It is hard to believe that in 2001 when the Scottish wildlife authorities were so generous in commencing a programme of relocating some of their precious golden eagles to Ireland the Irish authorities were commencing the Wildlife (Amendment) Act, 2000 which included a subsection to remove any obstacle to the continued setting out of deadly poisoned baits!

Pressure on the Irish Government to reverse this archaic law is required now from the governments of Scotland, Wales and Norway.

reported to the Gardaí in Wicklow, who were investigating. I appreciate how difficult these cases are, even for someone in a full-time capacity and I would not hold out much hope of anyone ever being charged. As in the UK, there is good support for the reintroduction of red kites from farmers, landowners and shooting syndicates. Unfortunately a single unscrupulous – or even reckless – act can ruin years of planning, work, expense and goodwill.

Despite this setback it is hoped that in time a viable breeding population can be re-established in County Wicklow. As Damian Clarke, Project Manager with the Golden Eagle Trust, which runs the project, said, 'It's hard to believe someone could have accidentally shot a kite. They are a difficult bird to confuse with anything that you can legally shoot.'

This is exactly the case, and with their distinctive forked tail they are very different from any game bird or pest species. Even if the criminal who pulled the trigger was aware that the kite was a bird of prey, he was ignorant of the fact – or chose to be – that red kites are no threat to game shooting, living on carrion, very small mammals, insects and worms. The shooting of the bird, which had seven shotgun pellets visible in an x-ray, sparked widespread outrage and condemnation locally (and no doubt in Wales where the fledgling birds came from) but the real point is that in 2007 this type of incident just should not be taking place.

And there was more bad news. In late October a further red kite, called 'Purple N' because of its wing tags, was found almost dead by a farmer near Dromahair, County Leitrim. He had found it in a very weak condition on a road verge at his farm and put it under an infra-red heat lamp that he used for heating chilled lambs. Damian Clarke was contacted and arranged blood and faecal samples to be taken by the Sligo Regional Veterinary Laboratory. The samples were tested at Cork Institute of Technology and evidence of the pesticide alpha-chloralose (formerly marketed in Ireland as 'Kill Crow') was detected. Alpha-chloralose lowers the body temperature of a victim, which eventually dies of hypothermia, in this case averted by the action of the farmer who knew to heat the bird up.

A red kite was undoubtedly not the target of whoever laid the poisoned bait. Nevertheless it underlines the danger posed by the indiscriminate use of poisoned baits, still legal in Ireland for 'vermin' control. The use of alpha-chloralose unfortunately remains legal and is one of the biggest threats to the success of the golden eagle, white-tailed eagle and red kite re-introduction schemes in Ireland, as well as to indigenous birds of prey. Signs for display beside the bait stating, 'This bait should be consumed by pest species only' are not supplied with the pesticide!

Further bad news completes the 2007 saga. The red kite, 'Purple N' saved from death by poisoning was killed on 8 November. It had been feeding on a carcass on a railway line in County Wicklow when it was hit by a train. Kites, unlike cats, obviously have less than nine lives. Regrettably, though perfectly logically, birds of prey and poisoned baits don't mix. Ever since I heard that young golden eagles were being taken from Scotland to a country that still allows the use of poisoned baits this has been my fear. People in Wales who have donated red kites and likewise Norwegians who have given white-tailed eagles must have had the same fear. It was unfortunately no surprise to me that two white-tailed eagles were reported to have been poisoned in February 2008 in sheep farming country in the foothills of MacGillycuddy's Reeks in County Kerry. A third bird that had been found in December of 2007 and initially thought to have died of natural causes, was also confirmed as having been poisoned.

One of the birds had been killed by alpha-chloralose, while the other two had taken a bait laced with Trodax, a liver fluke and worm infestation medicine for sheep and cattle. The scientist in charge of the reintroduction project had received a tip-off that farmers were dosing carcasses with Trodax in order to kill off foxes in advance of the lambing season.

So is there less regard for wildlife law in Ireland compared with the UK? The population of Ireland is certainly more rural-based than in most of the UK apart from the northern half of Scotland and this may influence thinking on hunting and killing wildlife. The difference in Ireland is that there are very strong lobbying groups of whom the politicians and their civil servants are wary, if not afraid.

The farming lobby is very strong in Ireland and any mention of prohibiting the laying of poison would be vehemently opposed by them. The farmers would most likely also be supported by the National Association of Regional Game Councils in this matter. As a conservation ranger told me, 'Their reasoning may not make much sense or be backed up by science but they'll shout and roar and will usually win the day.'

POSTSCRIPT:

As this book goes to the publisher in April, 2009 I have just been notified by Lorcan O'Toole and Damian Clark of the recovery of a four dead birds of prey: a poisoned golden eagle, one confirmed and one suspected poisoned red kite, and a suspected poisoned white-tailed eagle. Difficulties were being experienced in Ireland in completing the tests for certain pesticides and I helped organise that this work be done at the Science and Advice for Scottish Agriculture chemistry laboratory in Edinburgh. Hopefully these birds have not died in vain and their deaths may now trigger legislation that finally bans the use of poisoned baits in the Republic of Ireland.

NORTHERN IRELAND

Northern Ireland has 17% of the land area of the island and 31% of the island of Ireland's population, the border with the Republic stretching for 220 miles. It is often described as bowl-shaped, with mountains – the Antrim Mountains to the north and north-east, the Mourne Mountains to the south-east, the uplands of South Armagh to the south and the Sperrin Mountains to the south-west – surrounding flat land with loughs in the centre. Lough Neagh is the largest freshwater lake in the British Isles and holds a huge stock of a distinctive whitefish called the pollan, also found in Upper and Lower Lough Erne. The Giant's Causeway is found near the northernmost point, an unusual formation of basalt rock columns created by the cooling of an ancient lava flow. Just off the northern coast lies Rathin Island.

In winter, Carlingford Lough – a sea inlet rather than a fresh-water lough – for a time holds virtually all of the world's population of pale-bellied brent geese. They are attracted by the rich feeding of eel grass at the lough's edges after leaving their summer quarters in north-east Canada. They feed until the eel grass supply diminishes under the onslaught of thousands of hungry bills, then disperse south to areas round Dublin, Wexford, Cork and the west of Ireland.

Like the Republic, Northern Ireland has Irish hares and brown hares, plus the three deer species found on the island: red deer mostly along the Donegal border, sika deer mostly in Fermanagh and Tyrone, and fallow deer scattered throughout.

The legislation relating to wildlife crime in England, Wales and Scotland is broadly similar, all relying on the Wildlife and Countryside Act 1981 variously amended. The Police Service of Northern Ireland works to the Wildlife (Northern Ireland) Order 1985, in its time no less efficient than, but since 2004 falling considerably behind, the wildlife legislation of the rest of the UK. On my fact finding visit to Northern Ireland in May 2008 their Wildlife (Northern Ireland) Order 1985 was out to consultation with a view to bringing it into line with the rest of the UK and I'll return to that later.

It is notable that the variety of crimes seems much narrower than in England, Wales or Scotland. Until recent times the police

– and indeed the people – of Northern Ireland have had many issues of concern that were far higher in their priorities than that of wildlife crime. It may be that this has narrowed the range of wildlife crimes committed. Or did the Troubles simply provide a barrier, albeit an unintended one, obscuring a wider range of wildlife crimes yet to be discovered?

Despite the extraordinary demands on the then Royal Ulster Constabulary in dealing with the terrorist atrocities and sectarian violence, it is quite commendable that they gave a firm commitment to the investigation of wildlife crime earlier than did many UK police forces. Sergeant Mark Mason was installed as part-time RUC wildlife liaison officer in the early 1990s. There is no doubt that fewer wildlife crimes would be reported to the police at that time than today but Mark was the forerunner of a policing strategy in Northern Ireland that was considered effective in its time and has continued to improve year on year. He has now been replaced by Emma Meredith, a full time wildlife liaison officer in a support staff role (Northern Ireland retain the term wildlife liaison officer rather than wildlife crime officer).

Of the 80 or so wildlife crimes committed between 1985 and 2007 where prosecutions have been brought, 31 have been related to offences against badgers. There seems little evidence of these offences being connected to the brutal pastime of badger baiting, where the strength and biting power of the badger – often deliberately injured first of all – is pitted against a variety of fighting dogs. It appears that in Northern Ireland many of those involved in badger-related crime simply want to dig badgers up and kill them – an extremely odd and cruel pastime. It is known that a number of badger diggers from England, Wales or Scotland visit Ireland for the purpose of badger digging and it would be surprising if none visit Northern Ireland, though neither the statistics nor police intelligence have confirmed this so far.

Bird crime is next on the list, with 18 offences relating to finch trapping and 18 relating to the possession of or the killing of wild birds. Since it is likely that one or two of the 'possession' offences relate to finches, this probably puts finch trapping in second place. This is hardly surprising since the laundering of wild songbirds into the captive-bred trade can be a lucrative business. The killing of wild birds in Northern Ireland revealed no financial incentive, with some being killed for 'fun' by stoning or shooting with air weapons.

Of the remaining offences, seven related to birds of prey,

including the taking of peregrine, kestrel, sparrowhawk or barn owl (an extremely low number in comparison with other parts of the UK), one deer poaching offence – an offence included under the 1985 Order – and one poisoning offence. Even this was of a substantially different character – using pesticides without a licence as opposed to the utilisation of pesticides to deliberately poison wildlife. There are no known egg thieves in Northern Ireland.

So is Northern Ireland different in the scale and type of wildlife crime committed? Sporting shooting is certainly much less intensive; in the rest of the UK wildlife crimes that occur on land utilised for sporting shooting are unfortunately still far too common. Badger crime and bird trapping is pretty much on a par with the rest of the UK but many other wildlife crimes seem uncommon or even absent. Is this because the presence of a full-time wildlife crime officer in Northern Ireland is a relatively recent development? After all, in the 1970s, there was very little drug-related crime being uncovered until there were drug squads to do so. So is there really very little poisoning of wildlife in Northern Ireland or is it simply not being either recognised or reported?

Certainly in October 2006 a male peregrine was found shot and a buzzard was poisoned with the pesticide alpha-chloralose. The peregrine, still alive, was found in a field near Sprucefield, County Down, with four shotgun pellets lodged in its leg, wing and shoulder blade. It was taken to the vet but died a few days later. It had been part of a scientific study and was identified from the ring on its leg as having been hatched earlier in 2006 in County Antrim. The buzzard, also still alive but suffering from the effects of being poisoned by pesticide, was found in the Drumbanagher area near Newry, County Armagh. It also died. Is this the tip of the iceberg? Only time will tell.

There does however appear to be one wildlife crime, especially in County Armagh, East Londonderry and West Belfast, that seems out of kilter with the rest of the UK: that is the use of tethered pigeons laced with poison used to kill peregrines, most likely connected to the hobby of pigeon racing. In June 2002 two dead peregrine chicks and one on the verge of death were found in a peregrine scrape near to Cloughmills, County Antrim. Suspicion fell on pigeon fanciers having shot or poisoned the parents and, as would happen on mainland Britain, the police, under the supervision of (the by now) Chief Inspector Mark Mason, investigated the deaths. Despite a reward being offered, no conclusive evidence came to light.

Returning for a moment to legislation, Emma Meredith and her police colleagues in Northern Ireland are similar to the rest of us in that they use a mix of legislation to carry out their role to full effect. One of the Acts they utilise regularly is the Welfare of Animals (Northern Ireland) Act 1972. This legislation was well ahead of the rest of the UK which had until very recently in England and Wales the Protection of Animals Act 1911 and in Scotland the Protection of Animals (Scotland) Act 1912. In Scotland this legislation was updated in 2006 to the Animal Health and Welfare (Scotland) Act, and in England and Wales to the Animal Health Act. Learning from each other and leap-frogging is the way to make progress. Any one country is usually either in the lead or lagging behind only for a short time.

Providing regular expert advice to the police, the Northern Ireland Environment Agency (NIEA), whose Countryside and Wildlife department is responsible for nature and countryside conservation in Northern Ireland, is empowered by three main pieces of legislation: the Nature and Amenity Lands (NI) Order 1985; the Access to the Countryside (NI) Order 1983; and, of course, the Wildlife (NI) Order 1985. Since the expertise of the police is law enforcement, not conservation or natural history, they rely on guidance and advice from experts in different fields, none more so in Northern Ireland than the Northern Ireland Environment Agency. In effect the NIEA – at least in the earlier days – probably carried out the main investigation, calling in the police once evidence was obtained and someone needed to be arrested or charged. John Milburne was a wildlife inspector with the NIEA since the legislation was enacted in the early 1980s and has been involved in many of the investigations. This policy was little different to the lead that RSPB Investigations Section took in Great Britain until the police eventually got a grasp of the legislation and their statutory responsibilities in the early 1990s.

Traps in Glen Lark and the Mistaken Swan

One of John Milburne's first investigations in 1986 related to the use of pole traps. He had received information that the traps were in use in Glen Lark, Country Tyrone, and drove to a farmhouse near the reported location. John received permission from the farmer to walk over the land 'to look at birds' and soon found a total of five fence posts driven into the ground with a trap on top of each and secured to the post by a short chain. These traps are circular, fitting snugly on top of a post with their serrated jaws agape waiting on an unwary bird landing on the metal plate inside the jaws. At the point that weight is put on the plate, the catch is released and the jaws spring up and catch the victim round a leg, both legs or, in the case of smaller victims, round part of the body. The trap and victim then fall off the post and hang halfway to the ground until the victim dies of shock, exposure, starvation or at the hand of the person setting the trap. They were barbaric and as cruel as the gin traps that used to be set at burrow entrances to catch an emerging rabbit by the foreleg.

In John's case, he found that three of the traps had been sprung and one held a dead male kestrel, caught by both legs and part of the abdomen. Scattered around within feet of each trap site he found the remains of at least one further dead kestrel, a dead raven and several small birds. These were mostly skylarks or meadow pipits; birds which regularly like to make use of a post on which to perch and survey or protect their territory. John collected the dead birds, along with the traps and two of the posts, and returned to his car.

As he was loading the items into his car he was met by the farmer. John reported, 'I asked him if they were his property and he said that they were. He explained that he had been losing lambs to crows and ravens and was simply protecting his property. I identified myself as a wildlife inspector and explained that the use of the traps was illegal, telling him that ravens and kestrels were protected. At that point he became very agitated and abusive, waving his stick in the air and calling to the house for some assistance.' John rightly decided that this was the time to make a quick exit and did so, making his next stop the police station at Omagh, where he handed over the evidence to the police officer on duty.

Unfortunately, this case was dismissed at court on a legal technicality. A mistake had been made in the wording of the summons, but as the court date was still within six months of the offence the police were prepared to correct this and serve the summons again. However, their divisional commander would not allow this as the serving of the original summons had necessitated the use of an army escort and a helicopter because of the security situation and he could not justify this expense a second time. In the troubled times of the mid-eighties wildlife crime, as well as any other type of crime, had additional problems in Northern Ireland that colleagues elsewhere never really appreciated.

John's expertise was called on a few months later when the police were investigating the shooting of a swan. The bird was identified by John as a mute swan, the most common species and the only one, apart from a handful of whooper swans, that breeds in the British Isles. The swan had been shot in Ballykinler, Co. Down, and at the trial at Newcastle Magistrates' Court the accused gave evidence that he had mistaken it for a crow. His excuse was that he had fired a shotgun only once before and that he was at the bottom of a small valley when two or three crows came over. He said, 'I aimed, closed my eyes and fired. I never saw the swan.'

We all know that in the tale of the Ugly Duckling, what appears to be duck turned into a beautiful white swan. Was this a variation on the theme with a diminutive black crow suddenly altering its colour and size to become a mute swan? Giving evidence, John Milburne didn't think so: 'In the open against a clear sky I would find it very difficult to conceive how anyone could kill a bird as obvious as a swan by mistake.'

At this point the defence solicitor took issue with the magistrate, claiming that his client was not getting a fair trial: 'I take the view that the court and the attitude of Your Worship is less graceful than a court must normally allow and I must ask you to disqualify yourself from this case.' His argument must have been convincing because a new trial, under a different magistrate, was set. However, the new magistrate was no more swayed by the defence argument than the first and found the accused guilty, fining him £70.

In the next case a chough, one of the two protected members of the crow family, was shot. It was alleged that two of the extremely rare birds were shot but only one was recovered, the culprit being a farmer on Rathlin Island off the Antrim coast. Indeed the chough appears on Schedule 1 of both the Northern Ireland and the GB legislation as one of our rarest birds and in need of extra protection. Again the allegation was mistaken identity with the person who carried out the shooting claiming he thought it was a hooded crow or 'hoodie'. The chough is similar in size to the hooded crow but has widely splayed feathers at the wing tips giving a finger-like appearance. The chough is all black, whereas the hooded crow appears to have a light grey 'waistcoat.' In addition the chough is longer and thinner in silhouette but the main characteristic is that its feet and bill are a bright red/orange colour and the beak is slightly curved downwards almost in the fashion of a curlew. Even the calls of the two birds are different, the hooded or carrion crown being much lower pitched than the chough.

The farmer claimed that he had lost 75% of his lambs that season to hooded crow predation, which appears to be a claim in the extreme. He elaborated that he had lost all but 28 of 115 lambs born. There is no doubt that carrion crows, hooded crows and ravens predate weakly lambs, and indeed maybe even in some years might predate a number of strong lambs that would certainly have survived to market size and be part of the annual farming income. These members of the crow family, whenever the chance occurs, pick out the eyes, the tongue, the genitals or the back end of lambs or sheep that are incapacitated due to lambing or being over on their back. It is a terrible sight, and these injuries are often fatal. Nevertheless the law protects one of these birds, the raven, though licences can be applied for to control ravens if extreme damage can be evidenced.

In any case, the dead chough had been found by a keen bird watcher. He had been watching a flock of about a dozen choughs feeding on the shoreline near his house. He then heard two shots from a shotgun, and took his boat out to the bay, where he picked up the dead bird but had seen another flapping about in the sea. He had been extremely annoyed and had delivered the dead bird to the police station. During the trial the defence solicitor had asked the witness whether he could be certain that the birds were shot by the defendant. 'Unless they committed suicide I don't see how they could have got there,' he answered. I was impressed by the dark humour of the trial and there was more to come.

John Milburne had earlier received the bodies of the birds from the police and of course was keen to make the distinction between choughs and hooded (or grey) crows for the court. He produced from his briefcase a dead bird, with glossy black plumage, a bright red curved beak and red feet, which he identified as the carcass received from the police sergeant on duty at the time the complaint was received. The magistrate remarked that it appeared smaller than a grey crow, whereupon John brought out the carcass of a hooded (grey) crow and held up the two bodies to point out the difference. One must wonder if John had a white rabbit in his briefcase for the next trial. I hope that he kept his sandwiches in his pocket!

There had been discussion that crows would hop about amongst healthy lambs then suddenly descend on one and pick out its eye before killing it. John agreed that this old argument existed but contended that there was no evidence justifying it, saying, 'Certainly in all the years this theory has been in circulation no photographic evidence has been produced to support it.' The golden rule of defence and prosecution solicitors is that they should not ask a question unless they know the answer.

The defence may have given this some consideration but in any case asked, 'How would you expect photographic evidence to be obtained.' Wrong question by the defence but brilliant answer by John: 'With a camera.'

At the end of the trial the magistrate accepted the evidence that the defendant shot and killed two choughs, protected birds. There may have been confusion but at the very least the defendant did not take much care in identifying the target. The defendant may have felt justified, in view of some degree of predation to his lambs, but the law was quite clearly against him. This mitigated against the highest penalty of a fine of £2000 for each bird. He imposed a fine of £50 with costs of £39. Since the year was 1988 I would not disagree with the magistrate though in similar circumstances today a fine of £2000 or even £3000 may be nearer the mark.

BADGER CRIME

In 1992 Mark Mason, the part-time wildlife liaison officer, and John Milburne visited a badger sett in the town of Clontanagullion, Co. Down, to find that the two visible entrances were overflowing with what was clearly cattle slurry. Vehicle marks indicated that it had been deposited within the previous few days but nothing suggested that it had accidentally found its way into the sett as there was no slurry-spreading anywhere in the contiguous field or indeed anywhere nearby. They found several badger setts in the next field some fifty yards away and some evidence of badger activity in the surrounding fields. They could therefore come to the conclusion that the slurry-filled sett had been a badger sett that was 'in use' – at least until visited by the liquid sludge. Whether or not some unfortunate badger was trapped forever underground or drowned in the contemptible concoction of cowshit, cow urine and water, a wildlife crime had definitely taken place.

The investigation resulted in the farmer being charged under the Wildlife (Northern Ireland) Order 1985 (different legislation to the Protection of Badgers Act 1992 used by England, Wales and Scotland.) In evidence during trial the farmer told the court that a pedigree bull had recently broken a hind leg at the sett. Having studied the entrances and concluding that no badgers were in residence, he had disgorged the contents of a slurry tanker into the sett. He was 'shocked and surprised' that he had done anything illegal. The court heard from the police that in effect he had now probably made the sett even more dangerous whereas a fence built round it would have prevented access by stock.

The magistrate was satisfied that the act was a 'callous, calculated act to rid himself of badgers' and fined him £300. Whether or not he accepted the 'prize bull' story is not known, though it is strange that in any argument either for compensation or compassion it is always the most valuable animal that is injured.

The next badger crime, again in 1992, must have been one of the forerunners to crime against badgers today that revolves round the development, and redevelopment, of buildings. This case related to a derelict property in Baillies Mills, Co. Antrim, where outline planning consent had been given for a replacement building subject to certain conditions: the applicant had been informed of the protected status of the badger and its sett. It transpired that the eventual owner of the property carried out a total demolition without heed to these conditions.

In January 1992 Sgt Mark Mason and John Milburne had visited the property and both witnessed an active badger sett with a number of entrances in an around the property. At that time planning permission had been refused and the farmer assured Mark and John than nothing other than a general cleaning up was going on.

Shortly after, the farmer entered into a verbal agreement to sell the land to an architect provided outline planning permission was first sought and approved. It was during this phase that John became aware and instigated the conditions necessary to protect the badger and the sett. Further wording on the protection clause advised the developer of the steps he must take to avoid breach of the wildlife legislation. In April that year transfer of the property, now with outline planning permission granted and conditions and advice regarding the sett, was made to the final client, who assumed total responsibility as from that date.

Work began and on 16th June Mark and John again visited the site. Demolition was almost total – this despite the planning conditions issued which stated: 'The developer must inform this Branch before any work commences. Demolition work cannot begin *until after 30th June* and only thereafter when the badger has been barred access to the site.'

Only one of the active entrances could be found, the others having been filled in by rubble and debris. Some damage was found at the one remaining entrance, which had been partly protected by a sheet of wood. In due course the owner of the property was charged with damage to the sett, damage to anything concealing or protecting the sett (in this case the building) and disturbing the badger while it was occupying the sett. In some cases the contractor or the person carrying out the machinery work may also be charged, but in this case there was no evidence that they were aware that they should not proceed.

The property owner met with Mark and John and made a statement. He claimed that he had taken some measures to protect the entrances to the sett by placing boards over them. He also stated that he had used a track machine so as not damage tunnels and did not allow the track machine closer than twenty feet from the main two entrances. He disputed that the sett had been damaged and claimed he liked badgers, having two setts on his farm, one being under his lawn and another within 300 metres of his house.

In the end only one charge was put forward by the police to

Badgers may be killed or injured by being trapped underground during development or demolition work. Some burrows are often fairly near the surface and tractors and diggers can easily crush the burrow. This way it is relatively easy to block a badger in a blind end of a sett, where it will die of asphyxiation. In the case described here the badgers most certainly would have been disturbed by the demolition, plus the access to their place of refuge was obstructed. The logic in relation to the date of 30th June for work to begin is that when badger cubs are young lactating sows will only leave them at night while she goes off to forage for food and the cubs remain down in the sett. Biologists generally agree that by 1st July in any year all badger cubs will be weaned and will leave the sett each night with the sow to forage along with her. If badgers have to be excluded from a sett it is during this time that a fence with one-way gates should be built round the sett so that once they leave they cannot return. Provided they are informed (one of the conditions), this is done under the terms of a licence from Environment and Natural Heritage Service and demolition or other work can only begin when it is known that the sett is empty.

There have been many examples of developers and contractors flouting the law, whether in relation to badgers, red squirrels, nesting birds, bats or great-crested newts. In England and Wales prior to 2000, and in Scotland prior to 2003 only monetary penalties were available to the courts. An unscrupulous developer may risk a fine of a few thousand pounds if the profit that can be made by ignoring the law is many times that amount. Even then the illegal action carried out may not be noticed or there may not be enough evidence to prove a case; after all if the creatures are displaced or buried in a pile of rubble evidence is extremely hard to obtain.

Now that imprisonment is available as a sentencing option for courts in Britain (and almost in place in Northern Ireland) there has been a marked change in attitudes and there is no question that it is a deterrent. More and more companies are obtaining environmental impact assessments or ecological surveys before they go ahead with work, which is a major step forward. Some others who go ahead with demolition or alterations appear to be genuinely ignorant of the damage they may do to protected species but there is most certainly a reduction in people who are well aware of the risks yet still proceed.

the Crown Prosecution Service: that of damage to the building concealing the sett. There are differing views when police are reporting cases for prosecution with some officers more inclined to report only the most serious charge that there is evidence to support. Three charges is not an inordinate number and I may have been inclined to put all three forward since there appeared to be sufficient evidence to justify them. However without having involvement in the case I can't make comment on why two charges were dropped. The main disadvantage of course in not putting all three charges forward is that evidence could not be led in relation to disturbing the badger or damaging its sett.

The property owner admitted the single charge and the defence rightly claimed that there was no evidence before the court of actual disturbance of a badger in the sett or of damage to a sett. He claimed the sett was a subsidiary of the main sett, which was more than 100 metres away, and put forward his client as a friend of the badger. The magistrate took the view that while the offence contravened the letter of the law it was not against the spirit and there was no ill will towards animals. She fined the accused £20.

ANIMAL CRUELTY AND PARAMILITARIES

In Northern Ireland, possibly to a greater extent than in the rest of the UK, the police have the role of investigating all animal welfare-related crime. In 2003 it was suspected that Loyalist paramilitaries were raking in hundreds of thousands of pounds from betting on organised dog fighting. Fights were known to be taking place all over the country in Newcastle, Warrenpoint, Bangor and Ballyhoran and animal welfare groups had been alerted to the development of a new dog fighting ring in County Down.

The barbaric training tactics were no different to the mainland, with the thugs involved stealing family pets for the purpose of 'bloodying' – giving the fighting dogs a taste for the blood of another animal by using the pet as bait.

Mark Mason explained, 'Because organised dog fighting is such a secretive practice, it was extremely difficult to uncover. The extent of paramilitary involvement was hard to gauge – again because of the degree of secrecy – but it would be safe to say there was a cross-over. There are undoubtedly some individuals who breed fighting dogs and organise fights who are also paramilitary members, and there is a great deal of money to be made, but until we'd cracked a ring, we couldn't say whether paramilitaries ran these rings or not.'

The PSNI and the Ulster Society for the Prevention of Cruelty to Animals (USPCA) were convinced that, although most of the organisers were city-based, the dog-fighting took place in barns or fields in remote countryside. The place and time of a fight was a closely guarded secret and at the slightest hint that the location had been leaked, fights would be cancelled at the last minute. Secrecy was paramount, and the dogs were known to be kept away from the owner's house.

Mark said: 'This is vicious, illegal activity and these thugs are more secretive than your average paramilitary group. Information was very difficult to come by. A few times we had solid information and we put a great deal of time and resources into trying to catch these people but when we got there, there was no fight. They'd either shifted the venue or cancelled.'

In one incident a large terrier went missing after escaping from his run at his Bangor home. Three weeks later, it was handed in to a pet shop, where his owner had placed a missing dog poster. The dog was thin and disorientated and didn't even appear to recognise its owner, bolting out the door in an effort to escape. The dog had bites and cuts around his throat, neck, ears and front legs which had become infected. The vet confirmed that the injuries were caused by canine teeth and they had been inflicted at different times. There was little doubt that this was one of the lucky pets that had survived attacks by fighting dogs.

Cruelty in the name of dog-fighting is bad enough, but the following year, 2004, an act of unbelievable barbarism took place: a dog had been tied up as part of a Halloween bonfire in County Tyrone and was burned to death. People attending the bonfire in the Glebe area near Sion Mills tried desperately to rescue the animal but were beaten back by the flames.

There were calls at this time from the Dogs Trust for better training of police officers to deal with cruelty, even for a special department within the police. The Trust made clear that they were aware that police resources were overstretched, but said, 'It's under their jurisdiction and it has to be taken seriously. We can't rely on voluntary organisations or charities.'

In Scotland, England and Wales, animal cruelty is investigated by the police, the RSPCA or the SSPCA, or a combination of those organisations working together. In Northern Ireland the situation is slightly different. The USPCA can take animals into care on the PSNI's behalf, but the PSNI then carries out an investigation aimed at a possible prosecution. This is closer to the situation in the Republic of Ireland and, to a lesser degree, Scotland where a relatively high proportion of animal cruelty cases are investigated by the police, often alongside SSPCA. In England and Wales RSPCA appear to investigate and prosecute most animal cruelty offences.

SONGBIRDS, RACING PIGEONS AND RED KITES

The keeping of songbirds is a popular hobby but the law is slightly different in Northern Ireland. A person keeping a song bird such as a bullfinch or siskin in England, Wales or Scotland must have bred it in captivity and must also have fitted a closed ring while it is still a fledgling, with the ring being supplied by and the details of the birds being kept by either the British Bird Council or the International Ornithological Association. In Northern Ireland each individual songbird must be ringed but must also have a licence that corresponds to that ring.

As a spot check on the system in late 1993, John Milburne and Mark Mason visited a bird show in Coleraine, Co. Londonderry. They introduced themselves to show officials and had a general inspection of the birds on show. They then decided to make a closer inspection of twenty-one birds and found that fourteen of them, including siskins, linnets, bullfinches, goldfinches, a yellowhammer and a redpoll were not correctly ringed under the terms of the licences held by their owners. The birds had rings that were either of the wrong size or had been tampered by stretching or filing. These are traits that immediately conjure up suspicion that the birds had been taken from the wild, therefore further investigation is required.

The fourteen birds belonged to two suspects and a check was made on their aviaries by John and Mark, though there were no other birds there that aroused suspicion. The two men were not charged, but an application was made to (and granted by) Coleraine Magistrates' Court for an order to release the birds into the wild. The two had been incredibly lucky; in fact I can't imagine anyone in Scotland being let off so lightly.

More recently, in July 2008 four buzzards, a crow and a rabbit were found dead in suspicious circumstances. Alpha-chloralose was later confirmed as having been the pesticide involved in the death of the birds. Interestingly they were again found near Drumbanagher, County Armagh, the location of the poisoned buzzard found in 2006. No doubt Emma and her police colleagues will be looking closely at this repeat incident as possibly part of a series crime. I was pleased to see that Bessbrook PSNI sector inspector had told the media: 'Wildlife forms an important part of our natural heritage, and we don't intend to tolerate incidents such as this. Anyone with information should come forward as doing so will help make sure those responsible go before the courts.'

The PSNI certainly have the right approach, but I know how

difficult it is to have a successful outcome to these investigations without proper training and experience. Perhaps this will be on their future agenda.

Hot on the heels of this crime, in August 2008, members of the Northern Ireland Raptor Study Group (NIRSG) discovered a live tethered pigeon at a peregrine nesting site near Glenarm on the north Antrim coast. A single chick had fledged from the site and it had disappeared at the time the pigeon was found, creating the suspicion that the pigeon had been used to lure the peregrines into gunshot range. NIRSG's Chairman, Jim Wells, told the press: 'The group has confirmed over fifty incidents of persecution during our peregrine studies and we suspect over a hundred more. There is no place in society for such illegal activity targeting raptors. We suspect these incidents are all linked to individuals within pigeon racing communities and their perception that peregrine falcon impact on racing pigeons.'

The comment about the scale of the problem is interesting and mirrors many areas of mainland Britain where raptor study groups built up this vast knowledge of wildlife crime but only started to report the incidents to the police once they knew that they would be taken seriously and thoroughly investigated.

A month earlier, in July 2008, as part of a three-year reintroduction programme, twenty-seven red kites were released in Northern Ireland. These birds had been absent for the previous 200 years – apart from an occasional visitor from mainland Britain – having been killed off by shooting and poisoning. In April 1997 one of these visiting kites from mainland Britain, a bird with yellow wing tags that had been released as part of the reintroduction programme in central Scotland and had been present in County Antrim since December, was found poisoned in County Tyrone. This was the first twenty-first century case of a kite being deliberately killed in Northern Ireland. It was not to be the last.

In September 2008 one of the kites newly released in Northern Ireland was found dead in a field near Castlewellan in County Down. Its wing tags and leg ring had been removed, perhaps to thwart the investigation, perhaps as trophies. This red kite would have been no more than four months old and represented a threat to no one. Gamekeepers in the rest of the UK where they are much more accustomed to red kites see them flying over young pheasant poults, which take little notice since they appear to know the birds are not a threat. There seems little doubt that it had been shot deliberately, to the fury of everyone involved in the release programme and the disappointment of primary school children who had been looking forward to tracking the life of the bird as part of the RSPB's 'Adopt a Kite' initiative.

Again the PSNI stance was encouraging, with the investigating officer, Constable Alex Beck, saying, 'Wildlife crime is taken seriously by the PSNI, and its significance can not be under-estimated. Red kites, like all wild birds, are protected by law under the Wildlife (Northern Ireland) Order 1985. As such, any person involved in this type of crime could find themselves subject to a report to the Public Prosecution Service. I would ask anyone with any information to contact their local PSNI station.'

This is typical of police comments to the media throughout the UK to try to obtain evidence to convict. In many crimes witnesses do make contact with the police after they read a press article. Witnesses can give statements that can lead to a conviction. Unfortunately in most wildlife crimes there are no witnesses and the best the police can hope for is some intelligence that may point them in the right direction.

It is enormously frustrating for conservationists, forward-thinking members of the public and police officers that 200 years after the annihilation of a species there are still a minority who are stupid, inconsiderate and selfish enough to deign to repeat a shameful crime that should have been consigned to history. Unfortunately this is a battle we need to keep fighting, utilising every possible weapon including strengthened legislation, effective policing, enlightened judges and changing the attitudes of the next generation.

Returning to penalties, when I visited Northern Ireland in May 2008 the government had yet to decide on including imprisonment as a court option for wildlife crime. I was disappointed to learn that in the consultation to update wildlife legislation they were not calling for imprisonment as a court option, which would have made the maximum penalty for a wildlife offence £5000. This may be appropriate for most of the wildlife offences committed but it is totally inadequate for repeat offenders, for the violent criminals who abuse animals, particularly badgers, in the name of 'sport', and as a deterrent for unscrupulous developers who might see wildlife as a hindrance to a massive profit. However, more recently, though I have yet to see it in print, I was assured by a very reliable source that in the face of considerable opposition the Department were forced to reconsider and imprisonment will now be an option for a court disposal, as it is in the rest of the UK.

It is probably not in dispute that wildlife crime investigation in Northern Ireland is still some years behind the rest of the UK. Mark Mason was a part-time wildlife liaison officer but was allowed to devote a large part of his policing duties to wildlife crime. Since her full-time appointment in May 2007, Emma Meredith has been able to devote all of her attention to the prevention and detection of wildlife crime and has made huge strides forward. She is the central point of contact within the PSNI and, though not involved in investigation, is responsible for offering advice, support and assistance to local police officers in relation to wildlife law and animal welfare. The PSNI have demonstrated that they take incidents of wildlife crime or animal cruelty seriously and encourage the public to report these to them.

Emma is from a rural background and therefore came to the force with a good grounding in wildlife issues. She draws on a wide range of sources (including from wildlife crime officers in England, Scotland and Wales) to improve her knowledge base. Once her role is better known and recognised within the PSNI Emma hopes for executive support to take wildlife crime investigation a further rung up the ladder. It is her desire to have police officers appointed as part-time wildlife liaison officers in each of the eight areas of the force.

Clearly there is considerable will from the PSNI and from the many organisations associated with wildlife to ensure that there is a reduction in related crime. In the forefront of this environmental purge is Jim Wells, Democratic Unionist Party MLA for South Down, chairman of the Northern Ireland Raptor Study Group and a member of the Northern Ireland Partnership for Action against Wildlife Crime. Jim is committed to preserving as much wildlife as is possible for the benefit of the next generation.

STRATHCLYDE

Encompassing twelve local authority areas Strathclyde Police covers an area of 5,371 square miles and a population of some 2.3 million, almost half the population of Scotland. It has an extensive coastline of 1,760 miles and 5,500 square miles of coastal waters.

The force area varies greatly from Glasgow, the largest city in Scotland, to the Hebridean islands of Coll and Tiree; this variety is also reflected in the types of wildlife crime occurring. In Greater Glasgow with a population of around 2 million the types of wildlife crime reported are similar to other major towns and cities. There are many problems associated with development and crimes against badgers, bats and nesting birds. There is a particular issue in these urban areas with deer coursing. Perhaps surprisingly there are large numbers of roe deer even in the centre of Glasgow and they are targeted by criminals with dogs and air guns and, on occasion, even crossbows.

Throughout the old mining areas from Ayrshire through to Lanarkshire and the force boundary with Lothian and Borders Police finch trapping and badger baiting still occur.

Strathclyde has some of Britain's rarest breeding birds such as white-tailed eagle, red kite, corncrake and chough and additionally golden eagle, osprey, peregrine, hen harrier, divers and Slavonian grebe. In the past they have all been targeted by egg thieves but the illegal disturbance of these Schedule 1 birds by photographers now appears to be a bigger problem.

Poaching of salmon and trout takes place in most areas of the force and the full-time wildlife crime co-ordinator and eighteen part-time wildlife crime officers work closely with the Marine Policing Unit to tackle this and other marine issues, such as disturbance of dolphins and porpoises.

Joe Connelly, formerly a welfare officer with Strathclyde Police, the full-time wildlife crime co-ordinator (a support staff post), became the second full-time wildlife crime officer in Scotland.

McSlurry the Badger Criminal

In April 2005 Joe was notified of a fairly unusual variation on badger crime. Two men walking through farmland near Strathaven, a picturesque town in Lanarkshire, saw a tractor in an adjacent field, with a farmer who was known to them standing beside it. Attached to the tractor was a slurry tanker with a grey hose which seemed to have been placed into the ground. The two men then saw the farmer move the tractor and slurry tanker forward a few metres and replace the hose into the ground. It became clear to them that the farmer was pumping slurry into the ground.

The men were aghast, as they were aware that where the farmer was working was an active badger sett. They saw him remove the pipe from an entrance of the sett, having disgorged the disgusting cargo of the tanker and return with his tractor and its trailer towards the farm.

When the he was out of sight, one of the witnesses went to the sett and confirmed his fears: the entrances were full to the top with a green, pungent, revolting sludge. Any badgers in the sett, if they were not drowned in this awful stuff, would be unable to dig out and would eventually be suffocated. The police and badger experts were notified and as an initial response two uniformed officers arrived. They were able to confirm that two large holes were full of sludge but they had little knowledge either of badgers or their setts and left the scene, knowing that wildlife crime officers were to attend later.

Before either badger experts or wildlife crime officers arrived at the farm the farmer returned to the sett, this time with a JCB-type tractor with a large bucket on the front filled with earth. He dumped the earth on top of the sett and levelled it off. Not satisfied with this, next on the scene were two contract tractors and ploughs, and the area was quickly ploughed, leaving no trace of the farmer's murderous deed. It is likely that the contract workers were unwitting assistants in the cover-up of a crime, one that probably would have gone undetected had there not been two people conveniently passing.

Only minutes after the contract workers had left with their tractors and ploughs, two of Strathclyde Police wildlife crime officers arrived with John Derbyshire, a badger expert. Luckily, John had carried out a badger survey on this land eight months earlier in the summer of 2004 and had recorded several active badger setts on the errant farmer's land, including one on the fence line bordering the field in which they now stood. He and the police officers could see no trace whatsoever of a badger sett now. There was not even a trace of slurry. However, because the sett was along the edge of the field, and the fence was the boundary between the farmer and his neighbour, there were entrances visible on the other side of the fence. These showed signs of very recent badger activity and confirmed that the sett was indeed active.

To date there had been no badger investigations in Strathclyde – or indeed any other part of Scotland – where police officers had felt the need to excavate to obtain evidence. If ever there was an investigation that would benefit from an excavation this was it, and that required a search warrant.

The evidence in the case so far was so good that a warrant was not too difficult to obtain, but there was a cost to be considered: JCBs and an operator don't come cheap. The Partnership for Action against Wildlife Crime (PAW) came to the rescue here. One of the members of PAW is North Lanarkshire Council and they were good enough to supply a JCB and a driver for the job free of charge. This is the value of having a variety of interested partners on board. Most are not able to contribute financially to the interests of the partnership but many from time to time can contribute in kind. The help in-kind this time was warmly welcomed.

On 5th May 2005, ten days after the introduction of the slurry to the sett, police wildlife crime officers called on the farmer and showed him the unusual search warrant. He admitted being the owner of the field but said that he was too busy to attend at the excavation of the sett. Under the direction of John Derbyshire, the badger expert, the digger driver began his work, filmed by the police.

Within five minutes the digger had exposed one of the sett tunnels, still filled with farm slurry. Police officers have to take samples of many substances during their service but a sample of slurry must rate as one of the more unusual. The excavation continued and slurry flowed freely from the underground cavities. Evidence became available of badger guard hairs, black and white hairs unique in that if rolled between thumb and forefinger they are very clearly oval rather than round. In addition, fresh badger bedding in the form of dried grass was found, another indicator of the recent presence of badgers.

As the excavation progressed, Ian Hutchison of Scottish Badgers mapped the progress, ascertaining that at least 75% of the chambers exposed so far had been contaminated with slurry.

There was a welcome surprise when the face of a badger was suddenly seen in one of the drier chambers. This needed gentle excavation by the JCB operator to gradually inch his way towards the badger, which suddenly bolted when the bucket of the machine got too close for comfort. This was a badger that would be extremely hungry and almost certainly would have died had it not been for the decision to excavate.

The following day the farmer was interviewed by the police wildlife crime officers in relation to the sorry incident. He denied any involvement in the insertion of slurry into the sett. Maybe a farmer from elsewhere had transgressed on to his field, dumped the slurry, then returned and spread earth on top? The presence of the contract tractormen ploughing the field immediately after this was probably an unfortunate coincidence!

The farmer was charged with wilfully attempting to kill, injure or take a badger, cruelly ill-treating a badger, interfering with a badger sett or alternatively destroying it, and disturbing a badger when it was occupying the sett. He appeared at Hamilton Sheriff Court and pleaded guilty to two of these charges and was fined £800 for what must have been one of the most despicable crimes of the year.

ANGRY SPOUSE SYNDROME
– A SPECIAL REPORT BY CONSTABLE FINLAY CHRISTINE, WILDLIFE CRIME OFFICER, ISLE OF MULL

Although most crimes are solved by using diligent police work, witnesses, local knowledge, crime trends or, increasingly, forensics, there are other ways to catch your criminal. Quite often, the best way of getting a result is from an aggrieved spouse wanting a break from a quarrelsome, drunk or irritating partner.

I remember one well-known criminal who was caught because of his devotion to his children, but not to his ex-wife. When he phoned their home every night to speak only to his kids, she would dial 1471, retrieve the telephone number he had called from and pass it onto the police. The police then contacted the local force, informed them that they had a notorious thief on their patch and the man later spent some time in prison – all due to his angry ex-wife.

I have come across 'angry spouse syndrome' a number of times in my career, but few as obvious or calculating in their use of the police service as the lady in the following story. This was not the first time, nor would it be the last, that this lady would use the police to lock up her partner, though I find it strange that she didn't consider getting rid of her criminally-minded drunk partner with a legal separation.

There were two renowned fish poachers on my patch. I'll call them Lenny Tatterson and Stew Pott. Through the years, I often found their nets discreetly hidden along river banks or near to estuaries where they would be netting salmon. The local farmers and anglers were also a good source to help find their mono-filament nets. I had locked both men up on numerous occasions. On a good night and at the right time of the year, they could net many large salmon, earning them a handsome reward, which would keep them in whisky for a couple of months.

A diminishing retail market in the mid 1990s meant that times were not as good as they had been. This was due to the availability of cheaper salmon from fish farms and the courts imposing large fines on buyers of illegally caught fish. Salmon caught in this way have easily identifiable tell-tale net marks around the head and gills.

My two poachers had been getting into some trouble lately, not only due to their poaching activities, but for some other minor offences, mostly related to drink. The men had been on the drink more often than not of late, and this can get tiresome to partners and the local population who have to put up with their drunken antics.

One October day in the mid 1990s, I was sitting in the office doing some paperwork when I took a phone call. The female caller introduced herself as 'Mrs Anonymous', going on to tell me that Stew and Lenny had been out poaching the previous evening and had salmon in various freezers around the village, including in each of their houses. Stew's partner, let's call her Carol, had a very distinctive voice. No matter how hard she tried to disguise it, it was obvious that Carol was my 'Mrs Anonymous'. So I said, 'Thanks Carol,' and she hung up.

An hour later, after having obtained a warrant, I attended with a colleague at Stew and Carol's house to search for the poached salmon. The door was answered by Carol who asked what I wanted. I said that I had information that there were some poached salmon in the house and that I intended conducting a search to recover them. She remonstrated with me quite fiercely stating that I would not get in without a warrant. When I then produced a warrant she smiled, let us into the house and shouted to Stew, 'The police are here, and they have a warrant!' He was in his bed at the time sleeping off a hangover after celebrating a good night's fishing on the river.

I informed Stew of the reason for my visit. In silence, and smelling of fish, he walked me through to the freezer and opened it. Inside there were a number of recently-caught salmon with the tell-tale netting marks. A search of the house produced fish scales, nets and various other items they had used in their nocturnal wanderings. Stew put out his arms in anticipation of the clink of the handcuffs. I later attended at Lenny's house and recovered more fish and equipment. The lads put their hands up and admitted everything including where they had taken the salmon.

They were, of course, curious as to how I had got on to them so quickly but I would never reveal my source. They blamed everybody from bailiffs to nosey locals. Not for a second did they guess that it was a partner who just wanted a bit of peace and quiet. The local sheriff obliged and both men spent a few months in jail. Their partners got a well-earned rest.

I must confess that in all my dealings with 'angry spouse syndrome', the criminals never thought that it could have possibly been their wives that had fired them in.

LOTHIAN AND BORDERS

Lothian and Borders Police, with 2600 officers and 1100 support staff, is the second largest in Scotland. By far the largest proportion of the officers police the streets of Edinburgh, the capital of Scotland and the second largest city after Glasgow. With a population not far short of half a million, Edinburgh is the home of the Scottish Parliament, the famous castle and over 4,500 listed buildings. After London, it is the most visited tourist destination in the UK, with an annual 13 million visitors.

Lothian and Borders Police have a highly organised and effective response to wildlife crime. There are two critical factors influencing this, the first being the appointment of Constable Jim McGovern to the full time role in 2005. Jim had formerly been a part-time wildlife crime officer, but as in every force so far which has appointed someone in a full-time position, whether that be as a police officer or in a support staff role, the wildlife incidents reported to the police increase dramatically and begin to reflect something like the true scale of wildlife crime.

The second influencing factor was the agreement of the then chief constable of Lothian and Borders Police, Paddy Tomkins, that he would take over the Environmental and Wildlife Crime portfolio on behalf of ACPOS – the Association of Chief Police Officers in Scotland. Though he only held this portfolio for just over a year, it was sufficient to give a boost to his wildlife crime officers by way of clear support that the investigation of wildlife crime was a statutory police responsibility and very much part of core policing.

From this kick-start in the early part of the twenty-first century, Lothian and Borders began to turn in some first class cases, many relating to the three main wildlife crime issues in their force area: the use of pesticides to kill wildlife; crime committed against badgers, of which there is a considerable population in the southern part of Scotland; and the more unusual offence of finch trapping. In mid 2008 they were the first force in Scotland – and only the second in the UK – to appoint a second full-time wildlife crime officer.

Trapping Songbirds

The trapping of songbirds, mainly finches, was banned under the Protection of Birds Act 1954, and successive legislation has reinforced this. Yet, like many other wildlife crimes, there is still a lucrative black market trade in taking these birds from the wild, and prices of over £100 a pair for some species may be paid by the more unscrupulous collectors. Keeping and showing British songbirds is legal provided they are bred in captivity and they have a closed ring fitted while they are at the small fledgling stage. These rings are supplied by two official bird-interest organisations (the British Bird Council and the International Ornithological Association) and have numbers that are traceable through those organisations. Criminals, of course, are masters at trying to circumvent the law and there are several methods of fitting closed rings to adult birds, all extremely painful to the already-stressed captives.

During 2005 intelligence was received by the Lothian and Borders force that a suspected finch trapper was travelling from an address he had in Newport Pagnall to his Scottish address, where he was taking songbirds from the wild and returning with them to England. The officers worked on this information, in particular Constable Ruaraidh Hamilton, one of the Lothian and Borders team of wildlife crime officers with a particular interest in and an almost encyclopaedic knowledge of birds. I thought that I had a good knowledge of British birds but in October 2007 when we were attending the Police and Customs Wildlife Crime Conference on the Isle of Man, Ruaraidh could identify birds from their autumnal song over the sound of the island's traffic; birds that I couldn't even hear!

Ruaraidh researched the ways of bird trappers, making good use of his ornithological expertise. He knew that in autumn, winter and early spring various species of finches, tits and other small passerines (i.e. perching birds) formed loose flocks to forage communally for food. A flock of birds has the benefit of having many eyes and ears to detect avian predators; also the ability to confuse the hungry predator when the flock of dozens or hundreds fly off in different directions at the approach of a sparrowhawk, goshawk or hen harrier intent on picking off one of their number. Ruaraidh realised from experience that flocks are happy to join an apparently relaxed bird outwith the flock and will assume it is safe to do so. Finch trappers also have this knowledge, and can turn it to their advantage. It is no coincidence that most finch trapping is carried out in cold winter weather.

Further intelligence was gained on the man from Newport Pagnall, who for convenience I'll call Wally. In late December of 2005 information was received that he was coming to Scotland again, this time with an illegally-caught goldfinch that he intended to show at a local cage bird show. This was sufficient intelligence to allow Ruaraidh to get a warrant to search Wally's Scottish address in the Lothians. Warrants granted under the Wildlife and Countryside Act 1981 allow the police officer obtaining the warrant to name other parties to advise the police during the search. In this case Ruaraidh named officials from Scottish Natural Heritage, the Scottish SPCA and RSPB; though he knew a lot about birds, these others had expertise and facilities which would benefit the investigation if it went the way he hoped it would.

About 8.00 am on Sunday 8th January 2006 they all met for a briefing at Dalkeith Police Station. Briefings are ultra-important if a large number of people are involved in an operation, particularly if some are from organisations outside the police. Individuals involved must know the part they have to play, in general terms what others are doing, what the overall objectives are, how to communicate with others involved, who is in overall charge and, most importantly, what powers they are acting under and what these powers allow them to do. For those who have been involved in a number of operations – and for some of us older folks this amounts to hundreds – we know that plans must be fluid enough to be able to be adapted at extremely short notice.

An hour later Ruaraidh and his colleague Constable Mark Rafferty were knocking on Wally's front door. Wally's elderly mother answered and said that her son was out. This does not mean that the police walk away; just that they need to exercise some tact. It is inevitable that an elderly lady will be concerned (or frightened or even angry) in these situations so it was gently explained to her what was happening and what the warrant allowed the police to do. This done, Ruaraidh and Mark went to the aviary in the rear garden, leaving Wally's mum to two of their younger colleagues.

Ruaraidh and Mark were joined by Mike Flynn of the Scottish SPCA and Dave Dick of RSPB, while the remainder of the team went to check nearby woodland on the boundary of an industrial estate. This divergence from the original plan paid off and by 10am Wally was traced in the woodland. Ruaraidh was alerted to this by radio and joined the woodland team, searching Wally's pockets and clothing when he arrived.

All sorts of interesting things are carried about in folks' pockets, and sometimes even a person's occupation or hobby can be accurately guessed when their pockets are turned out. If you were to find in a jacket pocket two cloth bags, a stocking, scissors, four elastic bands, a piece of string, a reel of cotton, a small drinking trough, a small bottle of water and a knife you'd be wondering what kind of weirdo you had encountered. Could it be a magician?

Sorry – I forgot the birdseed. Now you know you have found a bird trapper. To remove any doubts about the intentions of their suspect necessitated a thorough search of the nearby woodland. Not too surprisingly the officers soon discovered a mist net set on poles, with several unfortunate birds entangled in it. This type of net is made of material so fine that birds are unable to see it and consequently fly into it. The birds were being encouraged into the area of the net by the presence of three small cages, one containing a bullfinch and two containing siskins. Remember now the theory of the flocks of birds flying to join an apparently relaxed passerine nearby? It is an unfortunate term, since the birds in the cages have no option other than sit there chirping, but they are usually referred to as Judas birds. They have no intention of leading their fellow songbirds into dangerous territory but that is exactly what happens, and the mist net gradually fills with unsuspecting birds. They are doomed either to a life in captivity or much more likely, a premature end to their life from stress.

In the mist net was a bullfinch, two chaffinches and a siskin, which managed to free itself just as the officers arrived. Wally didn't deny setting the mist net, something that would be difficult to believe in any case considering the incriminatory contents of his pockets.

Meantime back at Wally's house the officers left with Wally's mum had some success as well, finding bird rings and two jars with mist nets inside socks. Putting mist nets inside socks was not a way of hiding them but simply a means of carrying them without their fine mesh snagging on everything possible; the same principle as someone who uses a long net to catch rabbits taking the precaution to cut the buttons off his jacket. The officers had also found four tubes of glue, which although proprietary non-drying glue for catching mice would be ideal also for spreading on twigs to catch song birds. This theory was backed up when five jars of tar were also found. Either there was a rodent infestation – which was not evident – or these were other adaptations of the substances for the catching of wild birds. As a variation of illegal activity, possibly on days when the weather was not suitable for finch trapping, Wally had four jars of paste made from boiling up trout or salmon roe and termed 'putty' by salmon poachers, a gaff and a fishing net complete with floats. He was clearly a man who kept his illegal options open.

The team searching the aviary was also having success. After a short time of observing the birds in the cages it was apparent that at least some of them had been taken from the wild. Their actions in the cage were completely different from that of captive-bred birds: these birds sit quietly on their perches, in contrast to the stressed wild-taken birds which fly around the cage, very often landing on the floor. In total twenty siskins, three bullfinches and a goldfinch were considered to have been taken from the wild and were seized by the aviary squad. In addition to the birds, they took possession of some sticks and bird lime, a further two mist nets and some ringing equipment, which included crimping pliers. The pliers were of particular interest as they could potentially be used to crimp a closed ring more tightly on the leg of an adult bird after it had first been expanded to fit over the bird's foot.

Overall it had been a very successful day, though the recovery of the birds and other items was only the start, and much more work had now to be done. For a start, Ruaraidh had to make contact pretty damn quickly with Thames Valley Police to arrange a search of Wally's English abode. The initial intelligence – and also an admission from Wally during his interview – indicated that he kept birds there, and a delay might mean that phone calls could be made and wild-taken birds released. In addition, the officers had to get the birds they had seized to a purpose-built aviary kept by the Scottish SPCA, where they would have some time to recover before being examined by a recognised and well-respected expert in the field of songbird keeping, Roger Caton. Normally Roger would be present at the search and examine the birds at the suspect's aviary to give an opinion. His opinion on whether the birds had been bred in captivity or taken as wild birds would be based on various factors, often including specific damage to the bird feathers or cere (the soft waxy part above the beak and containing the nostrils). When Roger did make the trip from England to examine the birds that had been seized by the police and Scottish SPCA he complimented them on their increasing experience as the majority were found to have been taken from the wild.

In due course, when Wally appeared at Haddington Sheriff Court, he pled guilty to possessing birds that had been taken from the wild and he was fined £1000. The search of his address in England also came up trumps, with wild-taken birds again being recovered by the police and the RSPCA. When Wally was convicted at Milton Keynes Magistrates' Court, the magistrate was not of the view that a custodial sentence was appropriate and, since the finch trapper had considerable health problems, neither was it appropriate to order a community-based penalty. This left the magistrate with conditional and financial penalties only. He ordered a conditional discharge on each of twenty offences for a period of three years and commented that if Wally had not had limited means he would have ordered him to pay all of the costs. However, as frequently happens both with financial penalties and costs, the magistrate had to restrict a Cost Order to an amount that Wally could afford to pay over a period of two years. This was still a substantial sum, being £11,750. Finally, the magistrate ordered forfeiture of the birds that had been seized.

So the question must be asked as to why people with captive-bred finches feel they must take more birds from the wild. The penalties under the Wildlife and Countryside Act 1981 mean that a person can be fined £5,000 (£10,000 in Scotland) for every bird that can be proved to have been wild-taken and the same for every item of illegal equipment that they possess. In addition to this substantial fine they can also be jailed for six months (in Scotland twelve months). Many of these bird keepers are enthusiasts who show birds and want to keep only the best. Many have a reputation at stake for breeding good quality birds and need to maintain this at bird shows. It was interesting that during Ruaraidh's interview with Wally, the finch trapper was of the view that finch breeders need to get fresh blood into their captive-bred stock or the colours of the birds start to deteriorate. The cheapest way of accomplishing this is to catch wild birds.

The cheapest – unless of course you're caught!

CRIMES AGAINST BADGERS

Scotland has a sizeable population of badgers, though their spread is uneven. Large populations are found in the Borders, Dumfries and Galloway, Lanarkshire, Grampian and in the area to the east of Inverness. They appear to be largely absent from areas of high moorland and (with the exception of the Isle or Arran), the Inner and Outer Hebrides and the Northern Isles. Slightly lower badger numbers occur in most of the rest of Scotland, though there are generally fewer in more mountainous areas because of unsuitable habitat and foraging opportunities. It also seems that the numbers in social groups are lower than in other parts of Great Britain. A three-year Heritage Lottery Funded project under the control of Scottish Badgers to establish the distribution of badgers in Scotland began in late 2007.

There is little concern for them spreading bovine tuberculosis since – at least prior to the 2001 outbreak of foot and mouth disease which in Scotland had the worst impact in the counties of Dumfries and Galloway – there were only ever a handful of cases in Scotland annually. This has unfortunately increased very slightly, possibly due to farmers who had cattle culled in the outbreak replenishing their herds in some cases from areas in England or Wales where bovine TB is much more common. Despite this it seems that badgers in Scotland remain largely free of tuberculosis. Possibly because Scottish badgers are healthy there is comparatively little crime committed against them in Scotland by the agricultural sector in comparison to that committed in England and Wales.

But badgers have other worries. There are some instances of setts being interfered with during building development or during agricultural or forestry operations. There are also a handful of instances where badgers have been snared, though in many cases they have been the unfortunate by-catch of fox snaring operations. By far the most repugnant threat to badgers comes from the few home-grown badger diggers, mainly in southern Scotland, their degenerate and deviant number being augmented from time to time by equally repulsive specimens from the north of England. I consider badger digging to be the worst by far of all the wildlife crimes with which the police have to deal.

It is a crime, unfortunately, to which my colleagues in Lothian and Borders Police are far more accustomed and it was little surprise to Constable Mark Rafferty when on 24th January 2007 he received confidential information that three named individuals were engaged in badger digging and that images of their activities had been published on an internet site. This site was identified by Lothian and Borders Police forensic computer department. It was found to show horrific images of a badger being attacked by lurcher dogs. Unbelievably it also contained photographs of one of the three suspects, whom I have no option but to call Dopey. It also included the information that Dopey's hobbies included the offence (unlawful in Scotland apart from some exemptions) of 'hunting with dogs.'

The intelligence received, together with the corroborative website, meant that Mark set about obtaining search warrants for Dopey's house, and those of his associates, Grumpy, Bashful and Happy. Dopey was 16, Grumpy 18, Bashful 24 and Happy was 40. On 15th February Mark organised an early morning briefing with several other of the Lothian and Borders' wildlife crime officers, together with some Scottish SPCA officers.

Inspectors from the Scottish SPCA are invaluable both for their knowledge of animal handling and, in this case, the fact that if injured dogs had to be taken by the police, the Scottish SPCA could kennel them and arrange for any treatment they might need. It is yet another example of using the best available resources in an investigation to achieve the most favourable outcome. In this particular case a policy decision had been made that in any event dogs that were likely to have been used in badger digging would be taken. It is legitimate for the police to do so as dogs in a case such as this could be considered as 'productions' in Scotland (or 'exhibits' in England, Wales and Northern Ireland) and a court could be asked to forfeit the dogs if a conviction was obtained. Further, a court can be asked to consider making an order to ban anyone convicted of animal welfare offences from keeping any relevant species of animal.

The homes of the suspected badger diggers were visited simultaneously by the joint teams. At Dopey's house two lurcher dogs were seized. Lurchers are often used to chase and catch any badger that might manage to make off and possibly outrun the smaller terriers, these being used in the first instance to go into the sett and locate and corner the badger. Dopey also had a bottle of surgical spirit and a bottle of gentian violet that were of interest to the officers, since injuries to dogs used against badgers are seldom treated by vets and normally get patched up by the dogs' owner. It would simply be too risky to take a dog with injuries inflicted by a badger to the vet as most would recognise the injuries: usually severe bites and tears to the underside of the jaw. Lastly – and it was only established later –

Dopey had downloaded footage on to his computer of two badger baiting incidents.

The team at Grumpy and Happy's house (they were father and son) had a similar find. They took possession of two bull lurcher cross dogs, one having old injuries to its face, and a lurcher which had to be promptly taken to the vet as it had a chronically infected wound on its left hind leg. They also took four terriers, two of which also had to be seen by a vet since one had an untreated injury to its lower jaw, and the other had an infected wound on its cheek. Grumpy claimed all the dogs belonged to his father, Happy. All of these were kennelled in the garden at the back of the house, which I'm sure pleased the neighbours no end!

Bashful's house search also resulted in seven dogs being seized, these being either terriers or lurchers. Again some of these had serious scarring around the face and on the lower jaw from historical injuries. Some medicines, including penicillin, and some syringes seemed to indicate home treatment for injuries, and a chrome bar and a baton, both contaminated with blood tended to indicate that Bashful might not win too many awards for being Mr Nice Guy. This next find of a video tape showing the digging of a fox den and a photograph of one of Bashful's dogs being proudly held up to reveal the scarring under its jaw tended to give some credence to my earlier assessment of him. The finding of a dead hare with injuries consistent with being taken by dogs drove away any remaining doubts about Bashful's personality.

Dopey and Grumpy were worryingly inhuman characters. In interview they admitted using their dogs to take rabbits, hares and foxes – and of course badgers. The badgers involved had an unbelievable fate. When they were dragged from the sett they 'got a kicking then the dogs were let go.' Why the kicking? 'I suppose to stun it. If it hudnae been stunned it would have hurt the dogs.' How long till the dogs killed it? 'About five minutes or something.' Being well accustomed to admissions from suspects I'm sure they erred on the safe side.

Each involved the other and gave three different locations where they had been digging badger setts in the Hawick area. True to his name, at interview Bashful said nothing. Even when asked if he was a dog lover.

Despite the claim that all the dogs at Grumpy's house belonged to his father, Happy, no-one implicated Happy in badger digging. He did, however, agree that the dogs belonged to him and that he allowed Grumpy to take them hunting.

Some retrospective investigation revealed that on 9th October 2006, more than four months before the search of the suspects' houses, a part-time gamekeeper and a friend of his were feeding pheasants in woodland on a farm near Hawick when they came across youths at a badger sett. They heard a dog barking underground and saw a black terrier emerge from the sett biting into a badger. A youth then pulled a brown terrier from the sett and all ran off. One of the youths was identified as Dopey, who was found to have taken his dog to a vet for treatment to an extremely serious injury to its throat. Taking the dog for treatment showed a degree of humanity (or was he just thinking of the cost of a new dog?). It was a good link in the chain of evidence and demonstrated that Dopey had once again lived up to his name.

In total six people were charged with this series of incidents. It was the first case in Scotland that had been taken on indictment, in other words to be tried in front of a sheriff and jury, where penalties that are available to the court are higher. The evidence was strongest against Dopey and Grumpy and their pleas of guilty to digging a badger sett, and Dopey's additional plea of guilty to wilfully killing a badger were accepted by the Crown.

The case was called at Jedburgh Sheriff Court in front of Sheriff Kevin Drummond who complimented the Crown on the decision to bring the case at the higher level. He sentenced Dopey to 200 hours community service, a direct alternative to imprisonment – and his associate in crime, Grumpy, to 160 hours. He also banned them both from keeping dogs for a period of five years. Their age and the fact they were first offenders made imprisonment a difficult option for the court.

The cases against Bashful and Happy and the other two that had been charged were dropped by the procurator fiscal.

This was a case that came virtually out of nothing. No investigation with six suspects is easy and involves particularly good police work if a result is to be achieved. The conviction of two out of the six was no mean feat.

The Case of the Pet Alligator

A number of animals classed as being dangerous require to be licensed by the Local Council under the Dangerous Wild Animals Act 1976. Breaches of the Act are normally dealt with by inspectors employed by the local Council, but there is nothing to prevent these breaches being investigated or reported for prosecution by the police. The Dangerous Wild Animals Act has never been an Act that I have been happy with. I like to see logic in legislation and could never understand why some animals, clearly dangerous, fall outside the licensing requirement. An example we recently encountered in a Dundee housing estate was a report of a six feet long Burmese python. Venomous snakes need a licence but this snake is non-venomous and does not require a licence. The principle seems that it's OK to allow the risk of someone being crushed to death by a snake but not to be poisoned by one.

I'm maybe boring or old fashioned but I can't see anything wrong with dogs, cats or goldfish as pets. I appreciate the legal right for a wide range of creatures to be kept in captivity but I often wonder what makes a person keen to keep as a pet a widow spider or a scorpion. You couldn't put them on your knee and tickle the back of their ears like you can with a guinea pig or a rabbit. So what is the thrill of keeping exotic species? Why would anyone want to keep, for instance, a colobus monkey, a serval, a gila monster or a wallaby. Or an alligator.

Once upon a time, in 2004, a man visited Deep Sea World at North Queensferry, Fife, with his son. Deep Sea World displays an amazing array of wildlife that lives round our coasts; anything from crabs to cuttlefish, sharks to seals. The man, who we'll call Coco, saw what he understood to be an alligator. He decided he wanted to own one, and he subsequently placed an advert on a reptile internet site. To call him impulsive would be a gross understatement.

Luck – of some sort – was with him and after a few weeks he was contacted by a man who just happened to have an alligator for sale. The seller and the prospective buyer chatted and the seller discovered that Coco didn't have a dangerous wild animals licence. That should have sounded the death knell for the transaction but this mere detail did not deter either of them. Though it did make the seller cautious enough not to reveal his real name. He told Coco that he just wanted to be called Bobby Brown and he would only meet him in the car park of Harthill Service Station, halfway between Glasgow and Edinburgh.

The fact that he was buying a dangerous wild animal while he didn't have a licence, and the fact that the transaction was to be made in a public place, an offence under the Pet Animals Act 1951, did not seem to register with the gullible Coco. Not only that, he apparently believed he was buying a six inch long alligator which he thought was a minature sub species.

Even when the meeting took place the complications and risks didn't seem to get through to Coco. Instead of the six inch long mini-alligator he expected he saw that it was four feet long with extremely sharp (and numerous) teeth. End of transaction? Not for Coco the clown. Though, in fairness, he did hesitate. For a minute. He had set his heart on owning an alligator so there was no turning back. A deal was struck and the 'gator changed hands.

Since Coco expected he would be travelling home with a pocket-sized version of an alligator he had nowhere prepared in which to house this substantially larger beast. He didn't fancy giving it the run of the house, as he could have done with a dog or a cat, so the bath was the best option. This was the bath in his council flat. His council flat on the fifteenth floor of a highrise block. Mr Coco's allocation of common sense was sufficient to allow him to realise that this was unsuitable. It would only be temporary as this was no place to keep an alligator. It would only be until he looked in to building a pond and rockery feature with palm trees. In his livingroom. Coco had a tendency to be kind to animals but inconsiderate towards neighbours. Especially downstairs neighbours.

Coco's plans to be the proud owner of a small alligator had not exactly worked out and in time he wondered if he had made the right decision. This decision-making process took almost eight weeks. Of course impulsiveness and decisiveness are totally different virtues.

In the first week of July 2004 Chief Inspector Jim Cormack of the Scottish SPCA became aware of an advert in the 'Pets for Sale' section of a local newspaper from a person who wished to sell an alligator. Without identifying his professional interest, he phoned and spoke to the seller, none other than Coco, about potentially buying his alligator. Jim then made contact with Constable Gavin Ross, one of the divisional wildlife crime officers for Lothian and Borders Police, and made him aware of the situation. Gavin was working in plain clothes at the time and was in a position to assist, so Jim contacted Coco about his 'gator again. Coco arranged to meet with Jim that afternoon in a retail car park on Glasgow Road, Edinburgh and show him the alligator with a view to selling it to him.

Jim and his colleague Scottish SPCA Inspector Steven Gray parked their unmarked car in the Comet car park. Gavin and his colleague Constable Paul Scott were in plain clothes in an unmarked police car and parked within sight of the Scottish SPCA witnesses. The stage was set to await the star turn.

In due course Coco arrived along with a friend and parked next to the unmarked Scottish SPCA vehicle. Jim and Steven, still without identifying themselves, were shown the alligator, which was contained in a box in the boot of the car. A signal was given to Gavin and Paul, and they joined Coco and Co, identifying themselves as police officers.

Further enquiries needed to be made and the officers decided to detain Coco and his friend under Section 14 of the Criminal Procedure (Scotland) Act 1995 on suspicion of having terrified a captive wild animal, contrary to the Protection of Animals (Scotland) Act 1912. They then, with the permission of the two men, made a search of their homes, during which they discovered where Coco had been keeping his alligator for the past eight weeks. And how he came to have bought it in the first place.

Six charges were brought against Coco including having no dangerous wild animals licence, a number of cruelty charges and culpable and reckless conduct, a charge at Common Law. This Common Law charge is in essence the carrying out of an act that is likely to endanger human life, a risk that would have been run by anyone carrying out a quick visit to Coco's loo. He signed over the alligator to the Scottish SPCA who in turn handed it over to a person who was already licenced to hold a number of dangerous wild animals and where it would have a considerably better life than it had up till then.

Once Gavin had submitted the case for prosecution, he and Jim Cormack had a meeting with senior fiscals including the Edinburgh wildlife specialist fiscal Jonathan Barclay. It was clear that the fiscals were taking the report very seriously and Gavin and Jim left with a number of further tasks to complete in order to firm up the case.

Coco subsequently pled guilty to three charges with two being dropped. Those to which guilty pleas were offered were of keeping a dangerous wild animal without a licence to do so, abandonment of a captive animal and culpable and reckless conduct. The abandonment charge was a particularly interesting charge. Under the then Abandonment of Animals Act 1960 it was sufficient for an offence to take place if an animal were to be abandoned, albeit for a short time, in circumstances where it was at risk. In this case the alligator was at risk from electrical wiring and a heater which was giving off a high level of heat. The Sheriff said he was unsure what sentence to impose on Coco for such strange breaches of the law and he deferred sentence so that he could take time to consider a just punishment. In the meantime Coco gave a donation of £500 to the Scottish SPCA, a fact made known to the court and which obviously – and fairly – influenced the sentence.

When Coco next appeared in court the sheriff fined him a total of £140 and banned him from keeping animals (with the exception of two pet birds he already had) for five years. And Coco's alligator? It's now enjoying its new home in an alligator park in Torremolinos. A real case of living happily ever after.

DRESSED TO KILL

Constable Mark Rafferty was probably in one of the busiest areas of the UK for wildlife crime in the Borders region of Scotland. As well as badger-related offences, his investigations regularly covered the abuse of pesticides to kill wildlife. One case in the summer of 2006 started off with the finding of two poisoned ravens and was quickly expanded to include a full scale search of a Borders' farm near Lauder. This was led by Mark and other wildlife crime officers from Lothian and Borders Police, augmented by staff from RSPB Scotland and Scottish SPCA. The suspect on this occasion was a man we'll call Dod, a bus driver and part-time gamekeeper who ran a small shoot on the farm for his employer.

Joining the team on the search was Stephen Magee, cameraman and producer of the BBC Scotland series 'Wildlife Detectives'. Stephen was working with several of the Scottish police forces during 2005 and 2006 in the making of this series, though the bulk of his time was spent with Lothian and Borders Police and my own force in Tayside. During the search the officers had a fairly quick find of a quantity of the pesticide carbosulfan in a compartment of the suspect's quad bike. Stephen filmed the find but at the time did not realise that he and the quad bike would meet again later in the day in slightly different circumstances.

Other chemicals were found on the farm, in particular the recently banned chemical Cymag, which was formerly used for the gassing of rats and rabbits. It is a white powder which, when exposed to moisture, gives of the deadly gas hydrogen cyanide, killing the rabbits and rats in their burrows. Out on the farm lands the officers found a number of poisoned baits, particularly dead pheasants laced with carbosulfan. When I say laced I should really say completely covered. The quantity on one pheasant carcass would probably be enough to kill all the inhabitants of an average sized village. It is frightening to think what would happen to any walker who encountered the bait and handled it, maybe wondering what the blue-green crystals were. This is one of the dangers clearly not given consideration by people who are rash enough to throw down these lethal baits. They intend to kill wildlife that might interfere with their game production but these same chemicals can just as easily kill pets and humans.

Dwelling a moment longer on these abhorrent chemicals and their deadly use, I have from time to time during a pesticide investigation in Tayside found a buzzard on its final few breaths.

Their end is horrific and the manner of their final few moments of their life is sometimes preserved in death for the finder in the way they are found, often having pressed on the ground so hard with their legs in the last muscle spasm that they finish upside down with their tail bent up under their back. The person who sets out the baits must encounter this much more than I do and I often wonder if they ever give any thought to the pain the bird – or whichever other hapless victim has its final feed – suffers. No-one who uses this method of controlling wildlife ever deserves to be considered a 'professional'.

Returning to the search, the officers found two butterfly traps baited in each case with a live pigeon. This is a wire netting trap with the pigeon contained in the lower part of the trap in full view of any predator. The predator enters the trap thinking it has an easy meal, lands on a central spar, which collapses and causes the top part of cage to close, containing it inside. The predator is most likely to be a sparrowhawk, peregrine or goshawk. Once inside its fate is sealed, and it will be killed once the trap operator makes his next check. The pigeon is still safe, contained under wire netting in the bottom compartment, but it doesn't know that. It must be absolutely terrified and I'm sure many must die of stress. The situation with the pigeon and the sparrowhawk could be related to you or I in similar circumstances with a lion or a polar bear within touching distance.

As the search was drawing to a close, Dod asked if he could feed his pheasants, which would mean him using his quad bike to transport feed. He did this under Mark's supervision but when he arrived back at the farm he was on his own for a few seconds with the quad bike. Dod decided to have a bit of fun with Steve Magee, the cameraman, and drove straight at him. He probably just meant to frighten him but he left his swerve to avoid Steve too late and hit him full on. The whole incident was captured on camera – apart from when the camera was pointing at the sky and Steve was upside down. Luckily Steve was none the worse and was probably relieved that Dod was just driving a quad bike and not a bus!

Though he was charged with almost double that number of offences, Dod the bus driver/gamekeeper pleaded guilty to eight offences when he appeared in front of Sheriff Kevin Drummond at Selkirk Sheriff Court in April 2007. These were the possession of the pesticides carbosulfan and sodium cyanide (Cymag), the setting in place of pheasant carcasses laced with carbosulfan, setting traps using live pigeons as baits, cruelly ill-treating pigeons, and the possession of a quantity of illegal cage traps. He was sentenced to carry out 220 hours community service, a direct alternative to being imprisoned and a pretty severe and appropriate sentence for a first offender.

Dod was filmed by news teams as he emerged from the court after sentence dressed in combat-style camouflage clothing and paramilitary style full-face balaclava. The offences and the sentence did the game shooting industry no favours but the manner of Dod's emergence from the court set back the industry's argument of becoming more professional in its approach and conduct by years. Here was a man – a bus driver but a professional gamekeeper so far as the millions of television viewers and newspaper readers were concerned – who had pleaded guilty to eight serious wildlife offences. Full-time gamekeepers, most trying to stay within the law and bring their much criticised occupation kicking and screaming into the twenty-first century, were seething and were scathing in their condemnation of him. He was the worst possible advert they could have had.

Carbofuran and carbosulfan are part of the group of carbamate pesticides. This group of pesticides is similar in mode of action to another group, the organophosphorus insecticides, which includes one of the most deadly of all, the banned pesticide mevinphos, commonly know by the trade name Phosdrin. They kill by causing muscle contractions, with death being extremely quick though painful. Carbamates are usually commercially available as granular formulations which are intended to be incorporated into the soil at drilling or planting. An exception is methiocarb which is formulated on a bran or cereal seed base for use as a molluscicide. Carbofuran formulations are currently the subject of extensive abuse to poison non-target animals, clearly being the poison of choice since the late 1990s. Aldicarb and bendiocarb formulations are also subject to abuse.

All approvals for the use of carbofuran were revoked in December 2001. The last formulation of aldicarb, under the tradename Temik 10G, lost its approval for use on 31 December 2007. The pesticide carbosulfan has rarely been abused in the UK as the chemical additive to baits aimed at poisoning wildlife. Its authorisation was withdrawn in December 2007 with the last legal use date of 13 December 2008.

For some reason aldicarb is much more commonly abused in England and Wales and is seldom encountered in Scotland. Conversely carbofuran is much less common in England and Wales than it is in Scotland. Mevinphos was commonly used until about 1990 but stocks now seem almost exhausted. Alphachloralose, which kills by inducing hypothermia, is still available in Ireland. Until the mid 1990s this was by far the most commonly encountered pesticide in the UK, but has now been overtaken by carbofuran.

In Scotland (though not yet elsewhere), it is an offence under the Wildlife and Countryside Act 1981 to possess certain pesticides without reasonable excuse. These pesticides, referred to as 'prescribed,' are listed under the Possession of Pesticides (Scotland) Order 2005 as Aldicarb; Alphachloralose; Aluminium phosphide; Bendiocarb; Carbofuran; Mevinphos; Sodium cyanide and Strychnine. In 2009 two further pesticides are being assessed with a view to adding them to the prescribed list. The maximum penalty, at £10,000 and/or 12 months imprisonment, reflects how seriously Scottish Government now consider the crime.

THE NEED FOR CROSS COMPLIANCE

The sentencing of Dod was not the end of the matter. Farmers and landowners are paid huge sums in the form of single farm payments out of the public purse in the trust that they are good stewards of our countryside. Thankfully this doling out of public funds is being scrutinised much more closely, and the police work closely with Scottish Government in this respect.

To qualify for the single farm payments, the recipients must agree to 'cross compliance,' in other words that they must not:

a) Intentionally or recklessly kill, injure or take any wild bird; take, damage, destroy or otherwise interfere with any nest habitually used by any wild bird included in Schedule A1 of the Nature Conservation (Scotland) Act 2004, obstruct or prevent any wild bird from using its nest, take or prevent any wild bird from using its nest, possess any live or dead wild bird or anything derived from such a bird, take or keep any egg of a wild bird; or intentionally or recklessy disturb certain birds (listed in schedule 1 to the Wildlife and Countryside Act 1981) while they are nesting (including disturbance of dependant young);

b) Kill or take certain huntable birds during the close season for that bird species. Sell or purchase game birds after 10 days from the end of the open season for the bird in question;

c) Use the prohibited means of killing or taking wild birds as set out in section 5 of the Wildlife and Countryside Act 1981 as amended by the Nature Conservation (Scotland) Act 2004.

It was not surprising that Scottish Government were not best pleased with Dod's employer and docked £7,919 from his single farm payment and beef calf scheme payments. This is a substantial penalty and certainly a very good incentive for land owners to ensure that their employees do not take the law into their own hands. Considering that the maximum fine per wildlife offence is £10,000, and is seldom used to its full extent by the courts, docking single farm payments is a salutary sanction. Considering that employers can be charged with causing or permitting an offence to be committed by their employees *if this can be proved to have been done knowingly,* which is almost impossible to prove, this is a good and sensible alternative. This was the first time that Scottish Government had reclaimed public money in this fashion.

As it turned out the second clawback of single farm payment came in my own area. In 2006 two poisoned baits had been found on Glenogil Estate in Angus. A further search by the police and other agencies found traces of the same pesticides in five estate land rovers. The estate was in receipt of an annual single farm payment from the public purse of £240,000. £107,000 of this was taken back by the Scottish Government. I was sure this would not be the last grant – funded by you and I – to be recovered under cross compliance.

FIFE

You would be correct if you are thinking that dog fighting is hardly wildlife crime, the main theme of this book. Police officers require knowledge of a huge variety of crimes, some being Common Law and some being under statute. Statutes empower the police to deal with contraventions in different ways, therefore it is important that some officers can specialise in order to offer advice to colleagues. Most wildlife crime officers, as well as being specialists in crime committed against wild animals, tend to have better knowledge than most of their colleagues regarding animal welfare offences, and offences committed against or involving dogs. We are accordingly involved either in an investigative role, or in an advisory one, with anything remotely connected with animals.

When the incident related here occurred in the Spring of 1990 there were no wildlife crime officers in Scotland, Wales or Northern Ireland and only a handful in England. I was a detective sergeant in Tayside Police drug squad and Ronnie Morris, who relates this tale, was a constable in neighbouring Fife Constabulary. Pit bull terriers were relatively new on the scene though I had met a number in Dundee when jailing their masters for drug dealing. A few years later we were two of the earlier wildlife crime officers but the close involvement with this dog fighting case gave Ronnie an edge over most police officers, in Scotland if not the UK, on animal cruelty legislation.

Beyond Contemplation – Dog Fight Operation in Fife
by Ronnie Morris

The practice of using dogs for fighting purposes appears to have its origins in ancient Rome, when dogs were pitted against larger animals in spectator sports. In later times this practice found its way to Britain and from at least the twelfth century, dogs were commonly used in spectacles such as bull and bear baiting. There is still much cruelty committed in the name of sport against bulls and bears, though not in Britain. As a nation of animal lovers it is incongruous with our nature that dog fighting still regularly occurs in our midst.

The American pit bull terrier was imported to the United Kingdom from the United States in the late 1970s and its progeny quickly spread throughout the country. Although many of these dogs were merely kept as family pets, it wasn't long before an increase in alleged instances of dog fighting surfaced, with American pit bull terriers cited as one of the main types of dog involved. About the same time a number of publications such as *Pit Bull News* magazine started to appear on the market, covering the historical facts about dog fighting, which undoubtedly helped promote the 'sport'.

Dog fights are usually arranged at clandestine locations such as disused warehouses, empty flats, remote farm steadings, or even at remote places outdoors such as in the middle of a forest. The exact location is known only to a few trusted persons, with a select band of spectators only being told of, or taken to, the location of a fight immediately before it takes place. Because of the risks involved, look-outs are usually posted and strangers are certainly not welcome.

Although American pit bull terriers closely resemble the Staffordshire bull terrier they are often bigger and can weigh anything between 35 lbs and 90 lbs. Like many other dogs they can be of any colour or combination of colours. A pit bull terrier is not in fact a breed but a type, making prosecutions for simply keeping an unregistered pit bull terrier a complex offence to prove. Dogs which have proven themselves worthy in the ring, even after the passing of the Dangerous Dogs Act 1991, will be used for breeding and their owners will be able to command high stud fees.

The fight usually takes place in a pit about 12 feet square. Typically, this is an improvised affair, often utilising some of the walls of a building along with boarding two to three feet high to form a fighting arena, sufficiently secure to contain the weight and movement of the fighting dogs. Normally the pit can be dismantled after a fight and returned to an innocent feature in order to remove signs of its illicit use. The floor of the pit is sometimes lined with carpets which will afford the dogs' feet some traction while fighting. A scratch mark is often drawn across the centre of the pit over which the dogs must cross otherwise they will be disqualified and the other dog elected as victor.

Dog fights are usually organised affairs arranged well in advance and involve pitting dogs of equal weight and fitness against each other. In the weeks leading up to a fight the dogs are intensively trained to ensure their readiness for the fight by way of weight, strength and stamina. They are fed on specific diets, steroids or other drugs to minimise exhaustion and pain during the fight. Treadmills are used to exercise and condition the dogs prior to the fight taking place and the owners of the dogs will have agreed a wager beforehand. Sometimes the ears of dogs are cropped back in order to afford an opponent less area to hold onto, or is done after a fight to 'tidy up' injuries sustained.

The dogs are washed down before the fight to ensure there are no substances on their coats which could affect the fighting performance of the opposing animal and a referee is appointed to pass the dogs as 'clean'. The dogs are then weighed, usually on a suspended scale and if a dog is over the pre-arranged weight, the bet of its owner is forfeit. However, even if this occurs it is rare that a fight will be called off. Those attending the fight will then place their respective bets with a person who has agreed to act as 'bookie'.

During a fight the only people who are allowed in the pit are the two owners or handlers of the dogs, the referee and sometimes a person who has agreed to film the fight. The dogs are taken by their handlers to opposing corners and made to face each other. The referee will then ask the handlers, 'Are you ready?' before signalling the start of the fight by telling them to 'let go!' Outside the pit there are usually helpers holding buckets of water to sponge the dogs down if they part and are returned to their corners, prior to being reintroduced to the fight. The owners or handlers and the crowd who have staked money on the dogs will shout encouragement to the dogs to fight, but the handlers are not allowed to touch their animals during the fight unless one of the dogs turns away from the contest. If this happens the referee will shout something like, 'Turn, pick up your dogs,' which is an instruction to the handlers to return their dogs to their respective corners. After a brief period of sponging, the 'turned' dog must re-enter the fight first and the referee will instruct the handlers to face their dogs towards each other and then tell them to 'let go!' The turned dog then has to cross the scratch mark and attack the other dog. If it fails to do so within a prescribed time period it loses the fight. If a dog shows an unwillingness to fight it is called a 'cur' and normally killed, as its owner will not want to keep a loser. A dog which shows willingness to fight is known as 'game' and even if a dog loses a fight but retains its willingness to combat, it is still admired by the dog fighting fraternity.

The 'fights' and 'turns' are timed using stop watches and the lengths of the bouts are determined by the fitness and strength of the dogs involved. Sometimes fights take place in which there are no breaks. They may last anything from only a few minutes to more than two hours, ending only when one dog is killed or the owner or handler of one of the dogs gives in and retrieves his dog if he feels it is receiving too much punishment.

All dogs receive injuries as a result of the fighting; some of them very serious and in some fights dogs are killed by their opponents. There is always a lot of blood, with most injuries being inflicted about the head, chest and shoulders. Some dogs die either of shock or their injuries in the days following a fight. They never receive proper veterinary care as owners cannot risk having their animals examined by a vet since it would be obvious how the animals had come by their injuries. Their often substantial injuries are simply patched up by the owner. While there is no doubt that dogs will suffer considerably after a fight, when they are fighting it seems as if they are so energised by adrenaline they can't feel pain.

Less organised 'test' fights also take place during which younger dogs are tested regarding their 'gameness' for fighting and if they measure up they are then trained up to take part in proper bouts. It's not surprising that training is given to the dogs by pitting them against animals that they are certain to kill, such as cats, small dogs and softer breeds of dogs such as poodles or labradors.

Numbers attending might vary between ten and fifty, but the secretive world in which dog-fighting now operates means there have been very few prosecutions for offences connected with this barbaric crime. The largest number of people ever arrested for involvement in dog fighting was in 1867 at Southwark, when thirty-two men were arrested by the police.

During the third week in May 1990, officers from the Special Operations and Investigations Department (SOID) of the Royal Society for the Prevention of Cruelty to Animals (RSPCA) received reliable confidential information that a dog fight was to take place on Sunday 20th May, within a barn at a remote farm steading near Kennoway in Fife. A dog fight had apparently taken place in the Durham area in the recent past and the planned fight was to be a Scotland versus England international affair, in which dogs from both countries would be pitted against each other. The RSPCA contacted Fife Constabulary, the small Scottish police force within whose boundaries the proposed dog fight fell, along with their sister animal welfare organisation in Scotland, the Scottish Society for the Prevention of Cruelty to Animals (SSPCA). While the police, the RSPCA and SSPCA can all investigate animal welfare cases, the RSPCA and the SSPCA do not have the power to arrest anyone involved, a power devolved solely to the police. Nevertheless the best wildlife crime – or animal cruelty – cases generally result from an amalgam of expertise, which meant that all three investigative bodies began to plan an operation to deal with the forthcoming incident.

Planning started on Wednesday 16th May, four days before the fight was about to take place. As you would expect, the investigation of dog fighting was a new experience for Fife Constabulary. Although they had received one or two reports of alleged dog fighting occurring in their force area during the preceding years, these had always been made retrospectively and the information was far too sparse to act upon. This did not deter a professional and thorough approach being applied to dealing with this latest intelligence, even if four days to make a comprehensive and effective plan was cutting it extremely fine.

Chief Superintendent Dick Borrer commanded the operation. His deputies were Superintendent Tom McCaig and Chief Inspector Willie Drummond. Although the exact location of the dog fight was not initially known, it was quickly identified as Burnside Farm buildings at Burnside of Letham near Kennoway, which were in a dilapidated condition and no longer used for agricultural purposes. They were now occupied by a hardened criminal who in 1977 had received a twelve year term of imprisonment for armed robbery – we'll call him Mr Hair – and he lived with his wife in a caravan sited on the farm courtyard. Another character, who we'll call Sam the Man also stayed in a caravan at the farm and rented part of the disused buildings from Mr Hair. The farm is located near the end of a farm road more than a quarter of a mile in length, leading south from the A916 road, about two miles north-east from Kennoway. The farm buildings roughly form a square shape with the old farm house located on the south side of the courtyard. Several other houses are located off the farm road leading down to Burnside Farm.

In the planning stage, because it was believed that animal cruelty and illegal gambling offences would be committed at the event, sheriff's warrants were obtained authorising the police to search Burnside Farm buildings along with any vehicles and any people found at the premises under the Criminal Procedure (Scotland) Act 1975 and the Betting, Gaming and Lotteries Act 1963. These warrants authorised the police to seize any dogs, any articles pertaining to dog fighting and any evidence relating to illegal gambling. A further warrant was also obtained from a Justice of the Peace under the Misuse of Drugs Act 1971, authorising the police to search the premises, any vehicles and people there, and to take possession of any evidence found in relation to the misuse of drugs.

It was a known fact that the gangs who involve themselves in this type of activity were usually highly organised and would sometimes take extreme precautions to ensure their clandestine activities remained undetected. Measures such as keeping nearby police stations under surveillance for any signs of unusual police activity before dog fights took place, and posting look-outs to make approaches on foot or by vehicles impossible without raising the alarm, were amongst the known practices. Also guard dogs were sometimes strategically placed at venues to give warning of a police approach and to obstruct their entry. In common with most other organised criminals, some of the gang would be listening in to police radio channels, something that was extremely common in the days before the general encryption of radios. Nowadays all police radios are encrypted as a matter of course and are compatible for use across force boundaries.

The appropriate legislation at the time, the Protection of Animals (Scotland) Act 1912 created the offence of being present (spectating) at a dog fight, which would apply to everyone attending, not just those involved in organising or managing the affair. However, to prove 'attendance' individuals would have to be caught within the confines of the dog fighting area itself and not just nearby in another room, or outside. These factors provided logistical problems for the planners that would be more easily dealt with under the much more recent Animal Health and Welfare (Scotland) Act 2006. This Act gives considerable power to the police to detain or arrest suspects and allows the court to jail a person found guilty for up to three years. The Animal Health and Welfare (Scotland) Act is almost mirrored in England and Wales by the Animal Welfare Act 2006.

Importantly, the details of the operation would have to be kept a closely guarded secret from the police officers who would be involved in order to eliminate any risk of information being leaked out and compromising the whole operation. However, only two days before the intended dog fight, an apparently harmless bird watcher and nature buff who just happened to be a senior police officer visited the area of the dog fight location and noticed that horses predominated in the surrounding fields. Since the Fife Agricultural Show was being held in the neighbourhood on the day before the dog fight, it was considered that the use of an enclosed horse box for the necessary transportation of a large number of police officers would attract no attention, especially when such vehicles would have been a familiar sight in such a rural area. A modern day Trojan Horse had been created.

Fife Constabulary is a small police force, which had an establishment of only about 750 officers at the time of this incident. Sufficient numbers of officers had to be found to effectively deal with potentially fifty or more hardened criminals. This was no easy consideration, especially since the force was already committed to meet other staffing demands on the date of the dog fight. In addition to recalling to duty all officers on rest day, and robbing various departments of their staff, the whole force was put on 12 hour shifts in order to provide the required police strength for the operation. Those detailed to take part were instructed to wear old uniform, stout boots and to carry their wooden batons and handcuffs.

A clandestine operation on this scale quite naturally arouses a huge amount of curiosity and eventually the nature of the event did leak out to the ranks. However, apart from being a poorly-kept secret, the truth of the matter was likewise poorly received. Most of the police officers had imagined it was going to be a huge drugs operation, a large bank robbery or even a terrorist plot involving the IRA. They had never thought for a minute that it was to be a dog fight. None of the police officers in the force had had any previous experience of, or possessed any proper perception of what a dog fight entailed, so it was difficult for them to reconcile the term 'dog fight' with the scale of the operation being planned. For many, the reason 'dog fight' was merely being used as a cover to disguise the true nature of the operation, thus whenever it was mentioned amongst the ranks it was generally met with scepticism and derision.

The day of the dog fight turned out to be a beautiful sunny day and officers detailed for the operation duly reported to their respective police stations at 7.00 am. They were then transported at regular intervals to the police station at Glenrothes for assembly and briefing at 9.00 am. within the main hall. Every precaution was taken to give the impression that it was a normal day's business in the policing of Fife and that movement of personnel not did present as unusual activity.

Meanwhile two discreet observation points, each manned by two CID officers, were set up, Observation Point 1 to overlook the farm road entrance and Observation Point 2 to cover the part of the road leading into the farm itself. Their purpose was to monitor all movements of traffic and people going to and from the farm area and to provide intelligence through radio contact to those leading the operation. More than 140 police and a dozen or so RSPCA and SSPCA officers assembled in the main hall at Glenrothes police station. Soup and rolls with sausage were kindly laid on, a small but welcome gesture which prepared everyone for the day ahead; something often overlooked in other police exercises.

At 9.00 am Chief Superintendent Borrer began the briefing, outlining the nature and plans of the operation. Much to the surprise of many, it did indeed turn out to be a dog fight that rest days had been cancelled for. Suddenly, perceptions of this type of obnoxious event became more enlightened amongst the gathered audience. Up to fifty hardened criminals were expected to arrive shortly at the remote location of Burnside Farm near Kennoway, for the sadistic purpose of watching dogs tear each other apart. Not only would they be deriving pleasure from this spectacle, but they would likely be betting on the outcome of the fight. Such contemptible men did not have a history of quiet submission when approached by the police, therefore violent resistance was expected and had to be prepared for. But firstly the planned approach to the farmyard was revealed to the officers at the briefing, most of whom immediately recognised the similarity to the legendary Trojan Horse. An innocent looking horsebox, of the size and shape of a removal van, and borrowed from a local estate owner, would be filled with as many police officers as could fit into its rear and would then be driven down to the farmyard where two police officers would alight from a small access door at the side of the vehicle. They would then quickly go to the rear of the vehicle and let the tailgate down to unleash the expeditionary force, which was to rapidly encircle the farm buildings and descend upon the assemblage at the dog fight and arrest everyone found there.

Boiler suits and riot helmets were provided for the personnel entering the horsebox, including the RSPCA and SSPCA inspectors. The remainder of the police officers, together with several police dogs and their handlers, were to form an outer cordon to prevent the escape of anyone running away. The mustering point for the operation was within the grounds of a private estate not far from the location of the dog fight. It was well away from any public roads and sheltered by surrounding woodland.

After Chief Superintendent Borrer finished his address it then fell to a senior member of the RSPCA to brief the personnel about the sordid details of what a dog fight entailed and the type of dogs involved. It was believed that American pit bull terriers were the type concerned, and could be particularly vicious animals. Once the dogs had a hold of a subject, it was extremely difficult to coerce them to release their grip. Officers therefore risked being attacked by the dogs. There had been several recent cases of people having been mauled by American pit bull terriers. This warning was given to make the police officers aware of the potential danger from these dogs; dangers already known to many police officers, especially those who have drug squad experience. They were not to deal with the dogs them-selves, but to leave this matter to the SSPCA and RSPCA personnel, several of whom would accompany the police contingent in the horse box. The police officers were to concentrate their efforts solely on apprehending the men attending the dog fight. Horses for courses.

For virtually everyone present, dealing with organised dog fighting was a new experience. Preparations were made for a worst case scenario, taking into account there was considerable potential for the criminals to resist arrest, become violent, and attempt to escape. Chief Superintendent Borrer reminded his officers that the law only permitted the use of what force was necessary to restrain the suspects, however he stated that he clearly expected that his officers would need to use that 'necessary force.' These words of strong support for his officers preparing to venture into a major crime scenario, where there was the prospect of meeting the most violent opposition, instilled a high level of confidence and determination through-out the ranks.

New encrypted radios were first issued to officers to overcome any monitoring of police radio channels. The police, RSPCA and SSPCA personnel were then conveyed to the mustering point at staggered intervals, in personnel carriers via long circuitous routes, avoiding travelling anywhere near to the farm location. On disembarking at a secluded area within the private estate the officers relaxed on the grass under a warm sun whilst awaiting the order to strike.

During the course of the morning a small number of vehicles were seen to arrive at the farm at fairly lengthy intervals. Most of these vehicles were vans carrying passengers in their closed sections, making it impossible for the officers at the observation points to gain a proper estimate of numbers of people arriving. It was later learned that most of those travelling to the dog fight had met up in Edinburgh earlier that morning before continuing the remainder of their journey in as few vehicles as possible. This clearly shows the cautious and secretive way in which these people operate. Although an increasing number of men were seen about the farm courtyard, due to the layout of the farm buildings which partially obscured the view of the detective officers maintaining watch, it was still difficult to make any accurate assessment of numbers.

During the early afternoon information was relayed from Observation Point 1 to the effect that it seemed from the lack of activity in the farm courtyard a dog fight was under way. Superintendent Tom McCaig then gave the order to the mustered officers to move into action. He, and about eighty police officers and four RSPCA and SSPCA personnel squeezed themselves into the rear of the horse box, before the full-size tailgate was drawn up. In the cramped conditions it really was standing room only and none of those inside could see the outside world. Adrenalin began to rush as the officers started to prepare themselves mentally for whatever scene would confront them when they next saw daylight. The Trojan horse box then set off on its mission, followed a few minutes later by a fleet of personnel carriers making their way to pre-arranged strategic points on the surrounding road network to form the outer cordon.

With the unlucky and unpredictable timing that jinxes many police operations, just as the horse box was nearing the farm a large crowd of men suddenly spilled out from the buildings onto the farm courtyard, resulting in the sudden decision to abort the mission. The sudden emergence of this crowd was the last thing that was needed just as the trap was about to be sprung so, instead of turning into the farm road, the horsebox continued along the public road before turning at a discreet distance and travelling back to the mustering point, where it re-grouped with the personnel carriers.

Initially there were deep fears that the operation had failed but it soon became clear that the first dog fight had just ended at the time the police were about to strike and the spectators had gone outside for some fresh air and a tin of beer. A waiting game now ensued to see what happened next.

The wait was short-lived as about forty minutes later the men were seen making their way back into the farm buildings, suggesting a second fight was about to get underway. Information obtained later indicated that as far as the 'international match' was concerned, Scotland was leading 1-0 at this point.

In a repeat of the earlier move the Trojan horse box set off once more, followed by the personnel carriers. However, on this occasion the horse box travelled right down the farm track and into the farm courtyard, apparently without being seen, before coming to a halt. If there were look-outs posted, they had been distracted by other matters or had become complacent. Two officers then swiftly alighted from a small door at the side of the vehicle and let down the ramps at the rear and were almost trampled by the sudden exodus of police officers, RSPCA and SSPCA personnel storming into action. Some rushed round to the back of the steading to cover any escape route whilst most poured into the main entrance at the east side. Two Staffordshire terrier bitches were tethered to makeshift kennels near the doorway but were too far off to obstruct the officers' entry. The police officers poured into an old cattle byre area later known as the 'kennel room' for evidence-gathering purposes, and at its west end descended upon a group of about thirty men gathered in a smaller, separate apartment, later known as the 'pit room'. These men were clearly engrossed in watching an ongoing fight between two dogs in a makeshift pit at the west side of the room. The small size of the pit room meant the police officers leaving the horse box had merely transferred from one closely confined environment to another.

The pit room was divided into two areas, with boards and old doors nailed together to form a makeshift barrier about three feet high to form the 'pit area' against the west and south walls, with a short removable section to permit access. In the pit four men were handling two American pit bull terriers, one red coloured and one black and white, locked in fierce combat and tearing at each other. The floor of the pit was covered with carpets and all four walls of the pit were whitewashed and heavily bloodstained. The pit room was illuminated by two trailing lamps fixed to the rafters above the pit area and a fluorescent lamp over the spectating area, which received power from a generator located in an adjoining room. Moments after the police began to enter the already crowded pit room these lights were suddenly extinguished but thankfully there was sufficient ambient light for officers involved in the operation to continue the job they were determined to carry out.

The spectating area was hardly big enough for those already in attendance never mind the onrush of eighty police officers. In the flurry of activity some of the police officers and spectators ended up inside the ring besides the two fighting dogs which thankfully remained oblivious to the ongoing events so intent were they in fighting with each other. Some of the spectators made frantic attempts to escape through windows at the back of the premises, but soon realised the futility of this when they saw there were also police officers outside.

The element of surprise stunned the men at the dog fight. They were so shocked at the sudden appearance of police officers descending in their midst in overwhelming numbers that they submitted quite passively to the instructions of the police. Some even threw their arms up in surrender fashion. There was no violent resistance although some of the men did protest verbally at being arrested. Superintendent McCaig then broadcast over the radio that it was a 'clean sweep' and instructed the personnel carriers and members of the outer cordon to make their way to the farmyard for further instructions.

Two RSPCA and two SSPCA officers entered the pit and separated the dogs, restraining them with graspers, which are poles with nooses. Despite this, the dogs succeeded in lunging at each other, briefly locking themselves again in vicious combat before finally being pulled apart and temporarily placed in kennels found within the kennel room. Both these dogs bore fresh injuries to their heads and shoulders and were covered in blood.

The police officers formed pairs, with each pair arresting one of the accused, cautioning him and handcuffing him. The accused were then led out one by one by their arresting officers with whom they were then photographed, before being placed in the personnel carriers. This is recognised police procedure at football matches and other events where large numbers of people may be arrested and ensures that the arresting officers are known when it comes to preparing a report for the court. Some of the accused made vain efforts to hide their faces whilst being photographed, which required some of the Chief

Superintendent's 'necessary force' in order to bring about the required pose.

In all, thirty six suspects were arrested at or near to the dog fight. However five of them who were arrested in adjoining parts of the property were later released without charge. No police station within Fife could hold so many detainees, so they were distributed amongst all of the force's major police stations, where they were kept until their appearance at Kirkcaldy Sheriff Court the following day.

Once all the arrested men had been led away from the farm, CID officers prepared to carry out scenes of crime examinations, working in pairs for corroboration purposes. The premises and in particular the pit room and kennel rooms, were photographed and filmed before the gathering of evidence began. In the fighting pit the sum of £1,000 was found to have been discarded, which was in all probability the prize money. Two 'breaking sticks' were also discovered lying in the pit. These were wedge-shaped pieces of wood used by the owners of the dogs for prizing their jaws apart when separating them. Several other 'breaking sticks' were found in other parts of the premises. Three treadmills and harnesses for the dogs were found in the kennel room along with a set of hanging scales and two cage-type kennels, in which the SSPCA officers temporarily placed the two fighting dogs.

Six vehicles – three vans, a pick-up and two cars – were thoroughly searched and kept as productions (*exhibits* in England, Wales and Northern Ireland) in the case. In a collapsible dog carrying cage in the rear of one of the vans a badly injured pit bull terrier was found, lying exhausted and in a state of shock. Another uninjured pit bull terrier was found in the back of one of the other vehicles.

A search of the caravan at the farm, the home of Sam the Man, revealed yet another cage containing an injured pit bull terrier. This dog was also seen to be in a state of exhaustion and shock. Clearly this dog and the injured dog found in the rear of the van had been the combatants from the first fight.

Initially 182 items were seized as evidence. These included the bloodstained removable walls of the pit, the sum of £1000.34p which had been flung into the pit on the arrival of the police, two buckets with sponges, two stop watches, two stained towels, a set of hanging scales, three treadmills and harnesses, several collapsible kennels, a number of breaking sticks, a variety of medicates and medical equipment, two dissembled 12-bore shotguns, a number of shotgun cartridges, two .22 calibre air rifles (one with silencer and one with telescopic sights), a quantity of air rifle ammunition, a 6.35 mm semi-automatic pistol, a captive bolt pistol (a humane killer) with blank ammunition for discharging the device, three motor vans, two motor cars and a pick-up truck.

Small quantities of cannabis resin were found on the floor in the pit room, hurriedly dumped by members of the group, whilst during searches of those arrested five deals of cannabis resin and one LSD tablet was found. The sum of £4,524.33p was also seized from the arrested men, and a large quantity of empty beer cans was found discarded in the vicinity of the dog fight. From the nature of many of the items seized, it was clearly obvious that Burnside Farm was intended to be a regular centre for dog-fighting.

Later that day, the seven dogs were taken to SSPCA Lothian Animal Welfare Centre in Edinburgh where they were examined by veterinary surgeons. There were four male American pit bull terriers, which had been involved in the two dog fights, an American pit bull terrier bitch and two Staffordshire bull terrier bitches. The four dogs involved in the fights had puncture wounds and lacerations to their heads and various parts of their bodies. They were in generally poor condition. Three of them had healed wounds, consistent with having been involved in previous dog fights. The American pit bull terrier bitch was in good condition, but also bore healed punctures and lacerations indicative of its having previous involvement in fighting. The two Staffordshire bitches were also in good condition and had no recent injuries. However, like most of the other dogs both bore healed wounds, showing their past involvement in fighting. They were now both heavily pregnant and quite obviously being used for breeding purposes.

All thirty-one men arrested were charged with offences under the Protection of Animals (Scotland) Act 1912. Nineteen of the men originated from the Midlands and north of England, whilst the remainder came from the central belt of Scotland. The police forces which had jurisdiction over the home addresses of the arrested men were contacted and asked to obtain warrants to search their homes for evidence relating to dog fighting. In a number of the properties searched various items of evidence which connected their owners with an interest in dog fighting were found and seized by the police officers. Amongst the most significant finds were the following discovered at properties in the Northumberland and Durham areas:

At the home of one man in Sunderland, a series of kennels containing five American pit bull terriers, including a bitch with five pups and a treadmill in working order. A quantity of veterinary drugs was also found in a refrigerator in the kitchen.

At the Sunderland home of another man, three American pit bull terriers with cropped ears and scars about their heads, a set of 100lb weighing scales, a quantity of veterinary medical equipment and drugs, a quantity of posters, photographs, magazines and videos, all depicting dog fighting scenes, a number of animal traps, a stuffed eagle, two stuffed owls and a stuffed red squirrel.

At the Sunderland home of a third man, five American pit bull terriers, all with cropped ears and bearing the scars of previous fights, a quantity of veterinary drugs and shotgun cartridges.

At the home of another man in Stanley, Durham, a badger's head along with a breaking stick and various photographs and magazines relating to dog fighting.

All of the dogs along with the other items were taken as evidence, the dogs being first examined by a veterinary surgeon. In addition, items of stolen property and quantities of illegal drugs were found at a number of the houses. At one house the sum of £13,000 was discovered hidden under a carpet and is believed to have been the proceeds from criminal activities such as drug dealing and possibly even dog fighting. One of the men arrested at the farm was a fifteen year old youth found in possession of a small quantity of cannabis resin. No proceedings were taken against him in relation to involvement with the dog fight but he was reported for a possession offence under the Misuse of Drugs Act 1971.

All of the other men had criminal backgrounds, some with fairly extensive records. Most had convictions for theft, burglary (theft by housebreaking in Scotland), assault, causing criminal damage (vandalism), and various crimes involving disorderly conduct, whilst some had been convicted of robbery, serious assault, and various firearms, sexual and misuse of drugs offences. Many had served terms of imprisonment for these crimes.

A number of them had also been convicted of various poaching offences as well as offences under the Protection of Badgers Act 1973 involving the killing, attempting to kill or digging for badgers. None was the type of person you would want as your nextdoor neighbour. In fact it would probably be an unpleasant experience just sitting next to one of them on a bus. Even on a short journey.

The thirty men appeared in small groups at Kirkcaldy Sheriff Court on Monday 21st May, 1990, with the initial charges against them relating to contraventions of the Protection of Animals (Scotland) Act 1912, Section 1 (c), i.e. assisting in the fighting of dogs or assisting in the management of premises for the purpose of fighting dogs, and Section 1 (a) as amended by the Protection of Animals (Amendment) Act 1988, that is being present when dogs were placed together for the purpose of fighting with each other. The occupier of Burnside Farm steadings was also charged with six contraventions of the Firearms Act 1968 in relation to the firearms and ammunition found at the premises. Having previously served a long term of imprisonment he was also a person who was prohibited under the Firearms Act from obtaining firearms and ammunition for firearms, including shotguns, air guns and their ammunition.

Some of the accused were remanded in custody owing to their past criminal history, whilst others were released on bail, pending future court appearances. Later, charges under the Betting, Gaming and Lotteries Act, 1963 (i.e. illegal gambling) were libelled against all the men, whilst some also faced additional charges in relation to their possession of firearms and illegal drugs.

At their respective court appearances over the ensuing months, eight of the men either pled guilty to or were found guilty after trial of contravening section 1(c) of the Protection of Animals (Scotland) Act 1912, whilst the remaining twenty two were convicted of section 1(a) of the Act. Most were also convicted of contravening the Betting, Gaming and Lotteries Act 1963, Section 1(1)(a), that is using, causing or knowingly permitting premises to be used for the purpose of the effecting a betting transaction, or alternatively, Section 1(2), that is resorting to premises for the purpose of effecting a betting transaction on a dog fight.

It fell upon Sheriff William Christie to hear all thirty cases in his court. After listening to the evidence he described the dog fight as an abominable event and praised Fife Constabulary for a 'very good piece of work', commenting that the force deserved great credit for their handling of the incident. For a police force as small as Fife Constabulary to muster the necessary staffing and produce the successful operation that they did was nothing short of remarkable. Similar sentiments were also expressed in relation to the involvement of the RSPCA and SSPCA.

On 22nd June 1990, at the trial of three of the accused, Sheriff Christie strongly advised one of the defence solicitors 'not to go any deeper' when he stated his client thought dog fighting was a 'spectator sport, something akin to foxhunting'. The Sheriff went on:

> 'The least said about this frightful, horrid business the better. It is a foul way to pass your time, based on watching poor animals tearing each other apart. A bloodbath. Disgusting. And people who indulge in it are below contempt. I take a very serious view of these matters. If there were no spectators there would be no dog fights, and if there was no betting there would be no dog fights either. Any dealing with the lives of animals and pitting them against each other is beyond contemplation.'

When the Sheriff dealt with another nine of the accused on 12th October 1990, he handed out the following uncompromising warning in his pre-sentencing address:

> 'The sordid and obnoxious practice of organised dog fighting has to be stamped out. On 20th May of this year, in the small town of Kennoway, there was a dog fight, of that there is no doubt. I have before me nine men, all of whom made the journey from England to Kennoway and were present at the dog fight. It is a rather sinister aspect of the proceedings that word should have gone round the north of England and the Midlands about this event and that is very nasty indeed. This is a very sordid and obnoxious pastime and I don't see how anyone can take gratification from it. People who go to these events are really contemptible and they must be stopped.'

In jailing one of the men – who had given evidence from the witness box in his own defence – for four months, he railed on him:

> 'You are an out-and-out liar and one of the worst witnesses I have ever had the misfortune to come across. Your claim you thought you were going to a dog show was utter nonsense.'

At another hearing, one of the accused from Mansfield was fined £500. Sheriff Christie told him:

> 'Your record is pretty deplorable and it's sad to see many convictions under the Badgers Act – that's pretty disgusting stuff!'

Ultimately, ten of the accused were sentenced to terms of imprisonment ranging from three to six months. Nineteen received fines ranging from £300 – £700, averaging at £510 and one man received two community service orders for 200 hours to be served concurrently. The youth found in possession of cannabis resin, by this time having attained 16 years of age, was fined £100.

All the money found in the possession of the men at the time of their arrest and the money found discarded in the pit, totalling some £5,524.67p was forfeited by the court. The dogs seized in Scotland were ordered to be destroyed as there was no realistic hope that such dogs, bred and trained for fighting, could ever be safely rehabilitated in a domestic environment as pets. All other items seized as evidence, with the exception of the vehicles, were also ordered to be destroyed.

In particular three of the men from Sunderland were sentenced to imprisonment for periods ranging between three and six months in jail. Several of the convicted men were banned from keeping animals but it seems remarkable that the owner of the Burnside Farm buildings, a prohibited person under the Firearms Act from holding firearms, originally charged with offences under the Protection of Animals (Scotland) Act, six offences under the Firearms Act and a contravention of the Misuse of Drugs Act, was only convicted of section 1(a) of the Protection of Animals (Scotland) Act and fined £400. Not long after this event he was involved in an armed robbery in the west of Scotland, for which he was convicted along with others on three counts of attempted murder.

This case was the first of its kind recorded in Scotland and the largest in the UK since the Southwark case in 1867. It was a supreme example of inter-agency co-operation and planning between Fife Constabulary and the animal welfare organis- ations, RSPCA and SSPCA, and showed what could be achieved when proper resources are applied to operations founded upon good intelligence.

As previous convictions in this case demonstrated, those involved in the barbaric practice of fighting dogs are often involved in other acts of animal cruelty such as badger baiting, deer poaching and hare coursing. It is also accepted that those involved in animal cruelty are frequently involved in violence towards fellow humans, particularly in a domestic situation. In the years leading up to this event, the majority of suspected badger digging incidents in Fife occurred within a few miles radius of Burnside Farm. Following the police led operation,

After the passing of the Dangerous Dogs Act 1991, the keeping or breeding of pit bull terriers was banned. Dogs already accepted as being pit bull terriers had to be neutered and were not allowed in public places unless muzzled. It was intended that as the existing pit bull terriers died off from old age then the problem would disappear. Alas this poorly thought-out legislation was a hasty knee-jerk reaction to a series of attacks on humans by these dogs, often nicknamed devil-dogs in the media. In effect there was nothing wrong with many of the dogs, simply that they usually had the misfortune to be in the wrong hands and were used for criminal purposes and potential financial gain by masters devoid of any feelings towards either animals or fellow humans.

The fact remains, as was highlighted by the tragic death of a young person in Merseyside in 2006 after an attack by a pit bull terrier kept by a relative, these dogs are still very much with us. This is borne out by intelligence on dog fights still regularly received by police, RSPCA and SSPCA. In Tayside, as in many police force areas, there are regular calls to the police, for a number of reasons, about dogs described as pit bull terriers. Though it is likely that most are Staffordshire terriers or some sort of cross with a Staffordshire terrier, it is entirely possible that some may fit into the general category of a pit bull terrier. Not all police officers will be familiar with dog breeds so it is possible that pit bull terriers may not be recognised as such. Guidance documents under the Dangerous Dogs Act 1991 are available to all officers but this does not necessarily assist them to identify a dog as a pit bull terrier (or one of the other proscribed breeds under that legislation); it simply gives guidance on the law. It is apparent that many – probably most – police forces, need to apply this legislation more vigorously

While the offences under the Act are clear enough, the main difficulty arises in establishing that the dog at issue falls into one of the proscribed categories. Even using the broader test in a stated case (Annan v Parker, 1994 Report Page 675), where a dog is assumed to

[SEE OVER]

reports of such occurrences sharply declined.

This case was largely instrumental in the passing of the Dangerous Dogs Act 1991, which made it an offence to breed American pit bull terriers and several other breeds of fighting dogs. This Act required that any of these prohibited breeds being kept as pets were to be registered. Also, a number of cases had come to light in the UK where people, including young children, had been mauled by American pit bull terriers, earning the breed the infamous label of 'devil dogs'. A major intention behind the passing of the act was to provide circumstances in which certain types of dogs such as American pit bull terriers, which had been specifically bred for fighting, would eventually die out in this country.

be a pit bull terrier unless its owner can show differently, most vets would not be confident they would be able to satisfy a court beyond reasonable doubt that a dog is of the conformation of a pit bull terrier.

In the Merseyside incident, evidence that the dog was a pit bull terrier came from Merseyside Police dog section officers who had attended a two-week dangerous dogs training course run by an accredited police officer in the Metropolitan Police. The Met officer had been trained by one of two vets in London who are experts on the characteristics of pit bull terriers. Merseyside dog section officers are not aware of another vet outside London that would have sufficient knowledge of pit bull terriers to be able to satisfy a court.

Apart from more police officers attending the Metropolitan Police training course, there appears no other satisfactory option in dealing effectively with the ownership of pit bull terriers, though the position is helped slightly by the wording of the Act. This makes a presumption that the dog is one to which Section 1 (a proscribed dog) applies **'unless the contrary is shown by the accused by such evidence as the court considers sufficient; and the accused shall not be permitted to adduce such evidence unless he has given the prosecution notice of his intention to do so not later than the fourteenth day before that on which the evidence is to be adduced.'**

Should we therefore be looking at a change in the law? There would be an obvious benefit in this since the scope of the present Act could be broadened. Despite the narrow range of dogs catered for within the 1991 Act (and the 1994 Act which included two further breeds) there are many serious attacks on humans by other breeds of dogs. Examples are rottweilers, German shepherds, dobermanns, bull mastiffs and Rhodesian ridgebacks. All these breeds and several more, plus many crosses with these breeds, have the potential to cause serious or fatal injuries. All police officers have seen these breeds of dogs in completely the wrong hands, being kept as guard dogs or status symbols either by criminals or totally inept and irresponsible people. Even in the hands of a responsible owner, most would not be trusted on their own with children.

There is little doubt that much of the legislation pertaining to dogs is out of date and unsuitable for purpose. The death of the child in Merseyside could have happened anywhere in the UK with any of the dogs listed above. With remarkable coincidence, as I write this, a year-old child has just been killed by a rottweiler in West Yorkshire.

There is no doubt that all legislation pertaining to dogs needs modernised. It may be difficult to balance the right of individuals to keep dogs against the expectation of the public to be protected against either personal attack or an attack on their livestock by a dangerous dog or a dog out of control, but the issue is surely deeper than simply targeting pit pull terriers.

Before I am deluged by letters from dog owners, there is no question that the majority of dogs that are large enough to have the potential to kill a person are in responsible hands, and consequently are generally well adjusted dogs that are unlikely to attack a person. Of much more risk are large dogs that are in the wrong hands, sometimes directly involved with criminality. If this situation can be eliminated or minimised through legislation then that would be a major success.

Grampian

Grampian Police serves over 530,000 people in a very diverse area of 3373 square miles, stretching from the Cairngorm Mountains (part of the National Park) to the west, to the Moray and Aberdeenshire coasts to the north and east. The region comprises the city of Aberdeen, the oil capital of the UK, many towns and villages and a large rural area; industries include oil and gas, agriculture, fishing and tourism.

The Cairngorm National Park is well integrated within the Grampian region and as the 'jewel in the crown' of Scotland's national parks is the home to the rarest species, including red deer, golden eagle, Scottish wildcat, pine marten, capercaillie and osprey.

A large number of upland and low ground sporting estates are managed for the shooting of red grouse, pheasant and partridge. Conflict of interest between birds of prey and other protected predators can result in breaches of the law, particularly with illegal shooting, poisoning, trapping and snaring. The North East Scotland Raptorwatch Project has brought twenty-three of these estates plus other partner agencies together in an attempt to address these issues.

The coastline of Grampian is home to many species including seals, whales, porpoises and the bottlenose dolphin population in the Moray Firth. Conflict can arise with seals and fishermen, particularly at salmon nets, along with disturbance issues of our cetaceans. Wildlife watching boat trips along the Moray coast is an expanding market and important to the local economy.

The area also features some of the best rivers in the country, especially for salmon and sea trout, most notably the rivers Dee, Don, Deveron, Findhorn and Spey. Grampian Police are therefore not immune to issues with poaching and the disturbance and taking of fresh water pearl mussels in these fast flowing clean rivers.

As one of the more recent full-time wildlife crime officers in Scotland, Constable Dave Mackinnon says, 'I am biased but I often tell people that the Grampian area is second to none in terms of the wildlife and habitat we have on our doorstep. It must be protected and that is part of my job.'

A Plague of Crayfish

In investigating wildlife crime, a relatively new specialist area of police work, it is difficult enough gathering sufficient evidence to charge offenders without the added difficulty of testing out new legislation. The first impacts on the second: if there have been few or no similar cases tested through the courts, the police – and indeed the CPS lawyer or procurator fiscal – has had no chance to gain the experience that builds up with each legal argument.

Constable Dave MacKinnon of Grampian Police has risen to these challenges. In the years since 1998 as a wildlife crime officer he has twice had cases go to court which were potentially groundbreaking. They concerned crayfish and dolphins – an unlikely combination.

It was May 2003 while stationed at Laurencekirk in the Mearns, Kincardineshire that the crayfish enquiry started. At that time Dave was a divisional uniformed officer with a part-time wildlife crime remit. Information comes to the police in many ways and on this occasion Dave learned that a local fishery manager had moved North American signal crayfish from a pond near Edzell in Tayside, which is on the Grampian border, and had released a number of these crayfish into a trout pond on the Drumtochty Estate near Auchenblae, Grampian.

The person passing on the information wished to remain anonymous. Police officers always respect this and can fully understand the varying reasons why people wish to remain so. 'Unofficial' information, even totally anonymous information, is often of value and helps many a police investigation reach a satisfactory conclusion. However, this can also be frustrating as witnesses are a scarce commodity, particularly in wildlife cases.

In the first stages of any police enquiry it has to be established that there is indeed a crime to investigate. Investigation of wildlife and environmental crimes are often complex and whilst wildlife crime officers have a basic level of understanding, the expertise of outside agencies is frequently required to help get a steer on how to go about investigating a particular incident. On this occasion Dave's research led him to the Fisheries Research Services (FRS), a government agency based at Faskally, near Pitlochry in Perthshire. An FRS scientist, Peter Collen, who has studied and amassed considerable knowledge about North American signal crayfish, was to become heavily involved in the case and formed a good working relationship with Grampian Police over the following months.

North American signal crayfish, as their name suggests, are not native to the UK. They were brought to this country from North America in the 1970s to be farmed in commercial fisheries for the restaurant trade. The crayfish look like little lobsters and grow to around six inches in length and, it's worth noting, it has been said that 'crayfish are the masters of escapology'.

Owing to escapes, accidental or otherwise, this non-native species has colonised many of the water systems, particularly in England. Whilst Scotland does not have the same scale of problem, concerns are growing. This crustacean has now colonised parts of the rivers Clyde, Earn and Annan to name a few.

North American signal crayfish are classed as invasive; they are aggressive and can breed at an alarming rate. They will eat almost anything from the larva of other aquatic species to fish eggs and any vegetation. In addition there is evidence to suggest they will exclude juvenile fish from places of shelter on the riverbed, thus making young salmon and trout more prone to predation. They also burrow into river banks causing erosion and other associated problems. Basically they are a river owner's or fisherman's nightmare and once established in a river they are impossible to eradicate.

If these weren't enough reasons for not having signal crayfish released into the wild there is yet another negative aspect. In Britain we have a smaller native crayfish called the white-clawed crayfish, which is found in chalk-rich streams in England and Wales, though there are no records of this native crayfish in Scottish waters. Unfortunately the signal crayfish, like so many other non-native species, carries a disease called crayfish plague which is lethal to our native species and has been linked to their drastic decline.

The intentional or reckless release of these alien species can be likened to the release of the grey squirrel and mink, other American cousins, or Japanese knotweed, all of which have caused untold damage to British biodiversity. Regrettably both the grey squirrel and the mink are here to stay and, sadly, the same can now be said about our little lobster pests that are now widely established across the country.

The Wildlife and Countryside Act 1981 section 14 makes it an offence if any person intentionally or recklessly releases or allows any wild animal not ordinarily resident in Britain to escape into the wild, or releases or allows any animal to escape from captivity if it is listed on Schedule 9 of that Act. The

American signal crayfish is one of the species listed on this Schedule.

So Dave MacKinnon had information that these alien creatures had allegedly been released into a trout pond at Drumtochty Estate and, from local knowledge, he knew the location of the trout pond. How would he proceed from here? Police Officers have certain powers under section 19 of the Wildlife and Countryside Act 1981 to enter land without warrant to search for or gather evidence in relation to wildlife crimes. Unfortunately it wasn't just as simple as visiting the pond, looking in and confirming that the crayfish were there. As you can imagine, as crustaceans, they are generally bottom-feeding creatures and it wasn't even an option to go and have look in the one-acre pond.

Having discussed the matter with Peter Collen, Dave considered placing traps in the pond in an attempt to catch some signal crayfish, that way proving that they were at least present on the estate. To do this, however, was going beyond the powers he had under section 19 and he consulted the area procurator fiscal to seek guidance on the possibility of obtaining a warrant to carry out such an operation. Having relayed the basics of the case to Ernest Barbour, the procurator fiscal based at Stonehaven, Dave was advised that a warrant would not be granted on the information that he had to date – basically an anonymous informant saying that the fishery manager had released these alien creatures into a trout pond on the Drumtochty Estate. There was no chance of a warrant unless further information came to hand, leaving Dave no choice but to approach his suspect and interview him about the allegation.

Dave and his colleague, Neil Thomson, went to the suspect's house on Drumtochty Estate and told him of the reason for their visit. He was quite surprised at the arrival of two uniformed officers at his door but was not forthcoming with any information or admissions about the release of crayfish. It is never easy interviewing a suspect on his own turf; much better if the suspect is under just a bit more pressure and at a police station. There is nothing intrinsically unfair to the suspect in this though it may put him at a disadvantage. The suspect agreed to accompany the officers to nearby Laurencekirk police station to allow an interview to take place.

The interview at Laurencekirk resulted in the suspect admitting that he had released 'around 120-ish' signal crayfish into three different ponds on the estate. He said that he had brought them up from Cleary Wood pond, a flooded gravel pit, where he had previously worked while in employment near Edzell. His reason for transferring the crayfish was that he believed the juvenile crayfish would be a good food source for rainbow and brown trout which he was rearing on Drumtochty Estate. Dave now had an admission that signal crayfish had been released but he still needed hard evidence to back up this admission. This evidence would be found in establishing that the crayfish actually existed in the places named by the suspect.

With the permission of the estate owner and approval from the fishery manager it was agreed that various traps could be set at the three ponds on the estate in an effort to catch some of the crustaceans. Dave contacted Peter Collen and a date was arranged for the pair to attend on the estate and set the crayfish traps. These traps took the form of miniature lobster pots or creels which were temptingly baited with cat food.

Dave says, 'I had to laugh when Peter and I were baiting up the traps with the cat food. Peter said the best results were obtained if it was fish-based. I think it was tuna flavoured cat food but I can't remember if it was Whiskas or Felix. At times like this you have to laugh and appreciate where wildlife crime enquiries sometimes take you but, joking apart, it was all a very necessary part of the enquiry. Without a capture of crayfish we were unlikely to establish a crime. The traps were set and it was now a case of waiting until the following day. I have always enjoyed fishing but this was even more exciting and for the first time I experienced what lobster fisherman must go through each time they lift their creels.'

The following day Dave met with Peter and full of hope and anticipation they returned to Drumtochty Estate to check the traps. The first pond had been covered by twenty traps and to their delight and relief they caught nine crayfish. Peter quickly examined the creatures and confirmed they were North American signal crayfish.

The checking of the ponds continued and resulted in another two crayfish being caught on one of the smaller ponds upstream at another location on the estate. Finally, at Cleary Wood pond, even Peter was amazed by the numbers caught in the traps – one hundred and fifty one from ten traps. This was probably a new catch record by Peter's reckoning as in one trap alone there were thirty crayfish, indicating the vast population of these creatures at this location. All of the crayfish were humanely killed using neat alcohol and a representative sample of males and females were kept as productions for the case.

At this stage Dave believed he had a very strong case: information that North American signal crayfish had been released, admission by the suspect that he had released them, their recovery at each location specified in the admission and expert identification of the species. A statement was noted from Peter Collen and production labels were signed. Even Peter, as a scientist, appeared very hopeful that they had a good case and the possibility of a first in terms of a conviction. They clearly wanted a positive result in this case so that a firm message was delivered across the country that these are extremely damaging non-native species and it was a crime to release them or to allow them to escape into the wild. This concern is reflected in the penalty available to the courts for this crime. The general penalty for offences under the Wildlife and Countryside Act in Scotland is twelve months imprisonment, a fine of £10,000 per offence, or both. For release of non-native species the penalty in a summary court is twelve months imprisonment and/or a fine of up to £40,000. If the case is taken on indictment the court may imprison the accused person for up to two years, impose an unlimited fine, or both.

Peter Collen's statement was long and detailed. One important point that has already been alluded to is that crayfish are masters of escapology. Very young and juvenile crayfish can easily be carried through outflow pipes and washed downstream, especially in times of flood. They can also walk up the side of earth banks and can travel across land for several hundred metres to allow them to enter other ditches or watercourses. Once in ditches these generally lead into burns or streams, which in due course lead to rivers. In next to no time they have colonised considerable stretches of water.

Dave compiled his report and sent it to the procurator fiscal. Fiscal Depute Laura Crockett took on the case with a great degree of optimism about securing a positive result for the prosecution. Possibly the interest that Laura derived from this case later led to her becoming one of the eleven regional (in Scotland) wildlife specialist fiscals. Laura instructed Dave to find an additional expert witness who could speak to the fact that the crayfish that had been recovered from the traps were of the North American signal variety. This involved a trip, armed with two jars of alcohol-preserved specimens, to Aberdeen University to see Dr Christopher Gibbons based at the Geography Department. Dave also noted a statement from the owner of Drumtochty Estate who, as it turned out, knew that the suspect (now the accused since he had been charged) had put crayfish in the pond, albeit not at his request.

The case went to trial at Stonehaven Sheriff Court and finally concluded on 16th September 2004 after all of the witnesses gave evidence. For some reason (still not known to Dave) the additional expert witness was not cited to give evidence. The defence agent did not disagree that the accused had released the crayfish into the ponds at Drumtochty, but argued that in his opinion the ponds were private and would have kept the crayfish contained.

Sheriff Patrick Davis found the accused not guilty. In his summing up he said that he accepted the evidence of the prosecution witnesses including that of the fisheries expert, but felt that the prosecution should have led evidence from an additional expert witness to corroborate the evidence. More importantly, the Sheriff believed that the ponds were indeed a private concern and did not constitute the wild, a vital point to prove to gain a conviction.

Dave and his colleagues were disappointed by the Sheriff's decision – they genuinely believed this was a very strong case – but it was one which they had to respectfully accept.

Some months after the trial, research work took place in the drainage ditch downstream from the main trout pond at Drumtochty in an attempt to establish if these crayfish had escaped from the pond. To the horror of the conservation bodies and scientists involved they found juvenile crayfish in the ditch. Remember the offence: *releases or allows any wild animal not ordinarily resident in Britain to escape into the wild, or releases or allows any animal to escape from captivity if it is listed on Schedule 9 of that Act*. The crayfish had undoubtedly been allowed to escape into the wild, even if they had been placed in what was considered at the trial to be a private concern. Lessons are learned from every case and the lesson here would have been to trap waterways in the vicinity of the ponds as part of the investigation. It is easy to be wise in retrospect.

In this case the drainage ditch feeds into the Luther Water which in turn feeds the River North Esk, a very productive and prestigious salmon river. This has caused an environmental headache on which, by early 2008, Scottish Natural Heritage had spent at least £40,000 trying to eradicate these crayfish from the ponds at Drumtochty and Cleary Wood. There is still much work to be done, though as Dave recalls, 'Peter told me at an early stage in the investigation that if these crayfish get into a river system it only takes one male and one female then they are impossible to eradicate. You have to accept that you have them.'

Skiing with Dolphins

The Moray Firth is a triangular-shaped inlet – termed a firth in Scots – of the North Sea. It is the largest firth in Scotland and is situated north-east of Inverness. The firth has approximately 500 miles of coastline, much of which is cliff. It is one of the most important places on the UK coast for watching whales and dolphins, regularly hosting bottlenose dolphins and harbour porpoises but with frequent visits from common dolphins and minke whales. The inner Moray Firth is designated a Special Protection Area for wildlife conservation purposes. Part of the Moray Firth is policed by Grampian Police and part by Northern Constabulary.

It was a late sunny afternoon in July 2006 when three employees from the MacDuff Marine Aquarium on the north coast of the Moray Firth had closed up for the day and were heading for their cars when they became aware of a school of dolphins in the bay heading east along the coast. Dolphins are always a joy to watch but this particular experience soon turned sour. As they watched the school of around fifteen bottlenose dolphins – which included two young calves – the tranquil scene was broken by a man on a jet ski who came out from the nearby harbour at top speed.

John Smith, a retired North Sea fisherman of thirty years, was at the helm of his now-converted fishing boat called the *Puffin* operating a wildlife watching experience for tourists to the area, and was about half a mile from shore on the far side of the dolphins. John had half a dozen or so passengers from England and Germany who were all very excited to be seeing the school of dolphins but not so happy to see the jet skier.

The jet skier was seen to speed out towards the dolphins and right into the middle of the school, which were spread out and continuing to travel east. The jet skier carried out a series of rapid accelerations over a ten minute period while he was in the centre of the school and obviously trying to get closer to the dolphins. He also executed a series of rapid turns which made the witnesses on both land and sea form the view that the jet skier shouldn't have been doing what he was doing so close to the dolphins. Meanwhile John Smith, armed with his digital camera, was able to capture some images of the jet skier in action with a dolphin surfacing in the background – not an easy shot to take.

The population of bottlenose dolphins that inhabit the Moray Firth are the most northerly population of these cetaceans (whales, dolphins and porpoises) in the world. There are around 130 dolphins, classed as vulnerable, which travel the east coast of Scotland between Fife, up the Tayside coast and as far as the Moray Firth in the north-east. Protection since early 2007 is afforded to these animals under the Conservation (Natural Habitats etc) Regulations 1994, one of the offences being to intentionally or recklessly disturb or harass them. In 2006 there was a similar offence under the Wildlife and Countryside Act 1981 as amended by the Nature Conservation (Scotland) Act 2004. At that time bottlenose dolphins were included on Schedule 5 of that Act, but along with several other mammals, were removed and given their protection under the Habitats Regulations.

Wildlife tourism is a growing market in Scotland and a huge economic value is placed on the population of dolphins that live on the east coast, especially when they are in and around the Moray Firth. Many thousands of visitors to the area, in addition to the locals, derive great enjoyment from watching these endearing creatures in their natural environment and will make special trips to the Moray Firth area to see them. This brings in welcome revenue and can be the highlight of a visitor's holiday.

By 2006 the Wildlife Crime Unit in Grampian Police had developed and in March of that year Dave was appointed as a full-time wildlife crime officer. He was on duty at his base in Stonehaven Police Station when he learned of the dolphin incident. Meanwhile one of the MacDuff witnesses had the foresight to drive round to the harbour and note a car registration number that he believed was linked to the jet skiers. A jet ski trailer and the presence of two men in wet suits was the clue but without this vital piece of information the case may have failed through lack of identification. The witness then phoned Grampian Police to relate the details of the incident. A local police officer from Banff along with a special constable attended the call and noted some details to get the ball rolling.

Having read the incident on the Grampian Police computer system and after discussing it with the enquiry officer at Banff, Dave decided it was best for him to take the enquiry on. This is not uncommon and it is generally preferable that something as unusual and protracted as this should be dealt with by a wildlife crime officer. In addition to this Dave, being full time, could commit time and effort into dealing with the enquiry.

From past experience Dave was aware that there had been two similar cases of disturbance that had gone to trial. Both involved dolphins and both involved people on boats causing the alleged offence. One man accused was found not guilty while the other was not proven, a court disposal unique to Scotland. Though Not Proven as a verdict is still an acquittal, it is a verdict that always appears to leave an element of doubt hanging over the actions of the accused. In the present case Dave thought there would be a reasonable chance of a conviction.

Dave arranged a visit to see John Smith, who was going to be a valuable witness. John was a busy man working as a skipper and guide on his boat, conducting tours every day of the week. It was fortunate that he didn't mind Dave tagging along on one of his tours to note his statement as John steered and they both drank coffee. The hardest part of the whole bucking and rolling operation was trying to keep the coffee in the cup.

Dave reports, 'It was a beautiful sunny day and despite the swell it really made me appreciate why people visit the area and pay to go on these wildlife watching trips albeit we didn't see any dolphins on this occasion but plenty of other bird and sea life. With my statement noted and having taken possession of the photo showing the suspect on the jet ski it was off to the marine aquarium to note more statements from the witnesses there.'

Dave ended up with a total of four witness statements describing the jet skier's actions in and around the dolphins and was quite confident of submitting a reasonable case to the procurator fiscal. Having carried out a Police National Computer check on the registration number, Dave was able to check with the owner of that vehicle. He found out that the car was in fact being used by a friend of the suspect and that indeed they had been jet skiing on that day. He then very politely invited both jet skiers to Banff Police Station and they both equally graciously accepted his invitation.

The owner of the car was interviewed first and admitted that his friend had been out on the jet ski and had returned to the harbour during the afternoon, relaying the information that there were dolphins out in the bay. They swapped over and the car owner then took the jet ski out into the bay to have a closer look at the dolphins. As it turned out the first jet skier was to be used as a prosecution witness against his friend. The car owner was charged and appeared quite bemused by the whole experience. In his view he was doing nothing wrong and said that if the dolphins didn't like what he was doing they would have gone away – or words to that effect. At the end of the interviews (and the inevitable cautioning and charging of the car owner) police, star witness and car owner parted on good terms.

Dave had good witness statements but without the opinion of expert witnesses on how the actions of the jet skier may have disturbed or harassed the dolphins a conviction could definitely not be secured. His first expert was Dr Deborah Benham who is the project officer for the Dolphin Space Programme, a scheme set up to ensure that the wildlife tourist operators acted in a responsible and appropriate manner when engaged in wildlife watching trips. Deborah had an extensive background in research work surrounding dolphin behaviour in different countries across the world. She was given access to the four witness statements and based on this compiled her own expert witness statement indicating that the dolphins were likely to have been disturbed by the actions of the jet skier.

The second expert witness, after some detailed enquiry by Dave in trying to find the right people, was Professor Phil Hammond based at the Sea Mammal Research Unit at the University of St Andrews. Again Phil was afforded the opportunity to view the statements and make comment. He too believed the actions of the jet skier were reckless and were likely to have disturbed or harassed the dolphins.

The police are merely a reporting agency to the procurator fiscal, who has the ultimate say as to the disposal of a case be that no proceedings, a warning or a prosecution based on certain criteria. The case was submitted and it was a now a waiting game. Fiscal David Barclay was very supportive and as wildlife prosecution specialist understood the complexities.

The trial was heard at Banff Sheriff Court and presided over by Sheriff Patrick Davis, the same sheriff who heard the crayfish trial. Two witnesses gave evidence before the accused decided to change his plea to guilty to a slightly amended charge, in that the word *intentional* was dropped. He was accepting that his actions had been *reckless* but not intentional though had disturbed or harassed the dolphins. He was fined £500 and left court after a few strong words from the sheriff stating that this behaviour might not be dealt with in the same way in the future. That completed the first ever conviction in the UK for reckless disturbance to dolphins.

As with most wildlife crime cases the media interest was strong; coverage included BBC Reporting Scotland, local and national radio and local and national press. The BBC Scotland News website registered 107,000 hits online, underlining yet again the public interest in crime committed against wildlife.

NORTHERN

Northern Constabulary has policing responsibility for a huge and relatively unpopulated land mass comprising the Scottish Highlands, the hundreds of islands making up the Outer Hebrides, some of the isles of the Inner Hebrides, and the Northern Isles, comprising the islands of Orkney and Shetland. In an area covering 10,000 square miles – a geographic area the size of Belgium – there are only 300,000 people, a quarter of them in the city of Inverness. It is remarkable that from the southern end of the Northern Constabulary area at its boundary with Tayside, to the most northerly of the isles of Shetland, the distance is almost equivalent to the distance between London and Edinburgh.

The 700 police officers cover some of the last wilderness areas of the UK, an area that attracts many egg thieves from the south. Though there are a dozen part-time wildlife crime officers, the force has not yet gone down the road of having a full-time wildlife crime officer, a somewhat surprising decision considering that the area depends to a high degree on tourism.

Constable Martin Macrae is one of the part-time wildlife crime officers and until 2006 was one of the officers responsible for policing Lewis and Harris in the Outer Hebrides. Lewis is steeped in history, with many restored 'black houses' giving an indication of how our ancestors lived, and going much further back, ancient stone circles, the most famous being the standing stones of Callanish. The main town of Stornoway has a population of 8000, out of a population of 26,000 in the whole of the Western Isles. The islands of the Outer Hebrides are simply teeming with bird life and of course have more than their share of visiting wild bird egg thieves. Not surprisingly in remote communities the most commonly committed wildlife crimes by the resident population are salmon and deer poaching. In some cases this is to get a salmon or some venison 'for the pot', but it also takes place on a commercial scale, with salmon in particular shipped to the mainland for sale.

THE POISONED GOLDEN EAGLE AND THE MAN FROM LEWIS

The Outer Hebrides, possibly because of the absence of commercial game management, is almost free from the scourge of poisoning wildlife that affects much of mainland UK. In October 2005 Martin Macrae was stationed at the village of Balallan, (Gaelic *Baile Ailein* meaning Allan's town) which has the distinction of being the longest village in northern Scotland. It is four miles from end to end along the head of a sea loch and developed due to a mixture of crofting and fishing. As the wildlife crime officer for the Outer Isles, Martin was made aware of the tragic poisoning of a golden eagle at Coduinn on Morsquil Estate on the Isle of Lewis. Tests at the Scottish Agriculture Science Agency in Edinburgh confirmed that the bird had died from eating the pesticide carbofuran, the main pesticide of abuse in Scotland. The scientists at the lab were also able to state that the contaminated bait that had been eaten was a rabbit.

Martin suspected that the culprit had been a crofter trying to (illegally) control the raven population to protect his sheep flock. As would happen on any mainland poisoning investigation he called in some help, this taking the form of staff from the then Scottish Executive Environment and Rural Affairs Department (SEERAD), now the Scottish Government Rural Payment Inspections Department (SGRPID). He also called in some help from Scottish Natural Heritage and RSPB Scotland. The estate was searched, as were some crofts, but after all this Martin was no further forward.

The following month Martin and a colleague were carrying out a completely unconnected enquiry on Lewis in relation to a firearm certificate renewal. Part of this process entails a check of the firearms held by the applicant, and also the security of the place they are kept. In this case this gentleman – we'll call him the Man from Lewis – wished to renew his certificate to possess a .222 rifle. The rifle was examined by the officers and he was asked the reason he required it. 'For deer control,' was the answer. Only roe deer in Scotland can legally be shot with a .222 rifle, and even then under the Deer (Firearms etc) (Scotland) Order 1885 the bullet needs to be of an expanding type of not less than 50 grains, with muzzle velocity of not less than 2450 feet per second and muzzle energy not less than 1000 foot pounds. Worse, there are no roe deer on the Outer Isles, with the only species being the biggest, the red deer. This was the first of the Man from Lewis's problems. This was explained to him, and he changed his mind. 'It's for shooting vermin. Ravens,' he said. Ravens are one of the two members of the corvidae family that are completely protected, the other being the chough. He now had a second problem.

Martin and his colleague continued their questioning and asked the red-faced islander if he had shot any red deer with the rifle but the answer, not surprisingly, was in the negative. The same answer was given when he was asked if he had shot any ravens. The question then had to be asked as to why he needed authority to have a .222 rifle.

If there was some doubt beginning to emerge that the firearm certificate was close to being revoked and the rifle seized by the police, the next find sealed its fate. On a shelf at the back of the gun cabinet Martin spotted a jar that was half-full of dark blue granules, innocently labelled 'celery.' In the recoveries made by the police of illegally-held pesticides they are invariably decanted into a container such as a coffee jar, a juice bottle or a smaller receptacle such as a 35mm film tub. In many cases the label of the original product remains and in one case in Tayside in 1995, while still a police officer, I recovered the most deadly of all pesticides, the liquid pesticide mevinphos, in a Lea and Perrins sauce bottle, two products of a similar colour. In that case there was a real risk of death to anyone who ventured to open the bottle and I charged the person concerned with the common law offence of culpable and reckless conduct.

Because of the infamy of carbofuran as a killer of wildlife it is well-known to all wildlife crime officers. Martin asked the Man from Lewis what the substance in the jar was, but he said he couldn't remember the name. Maybe, maybe not, but Martin knew that he would be aware of its illegal use. He asked him what he had the granules for. 'It was for the turnips,' was the answer. It was the stock answer, sometimes varied to 'It's for the carrots.' He elaborated. 'You spread it on the turnips.' Wrong! 'You hand-spread it on the turnips when the stem is about four inches tall.' Worse! Whatever you would do with carbofuran you wouldn't want to handle it. Whatever other outcome there may be he could now safely say goodbye to his firearms certificate.

There have been countless instances throughout the UK where the police have recovered pesticides in circumstances where they are perfectly well aware that they were held for an illegal purpose. The main legislative difficulty was that until recently this was not an offence in itself. It was an offence to use the pesticide in circumstances outwith its government approval, or to store it outwith the terms of approval on the container, most usually violated by transferring it into another container. Even so, these offences were under the Food and Environment

Protection Act 1985 and only incurred a moderate monetary penalty. It was not until 2005 – and only in Scotland – that possession of the most commonly abused pesticide became an offence in its own right, though there was an exception if the person could show that he had a good reason for possessing it. Carbofuran is top of the list of 'prescribed' pesticides, as they are termed, because of its widespread abuse.

So Martin had a coincidental recovery of carbofuran while investigating the poisoning of a golden eagle, the very bird many visitors go to the Western Isles to see. Whether or not the Man from Lewis had played any part in this crime his excuse that the carbofuran was for nurturing turnips was a lie. Though the approved use for the chemical was as an insecticide on root crops, including of course turnips, it requires to be drilled into the ground by machinery to place it in a position to kill earth-borne pests.

The charge of possession of a banned pesticide then carried a penalty of £5000 and/or 6 months imprisonment. The Man from Lewis was fined £50.

Had there been evidence he was involved in the killing of the golden eagle this penalty would have been considerably increased, though in fairness to him he may not have been in any way involved and his possession of carbofuran purely coincidental. And unfortunate! At least ravens and red deer would be safeguarded against being shot by a .222 rifle!

EGG THIEVES AT LARGE:
THE COLOURFUL TRIO AND THE BUMBLING BROTHERS

Given the variety of nesting bird species there is little wonder that egg thieves are attracted to the Western and Northern Isles. As I write, early May 2008, my wife and I are holidaying in the Outer Isles of North and South Uist, Benbecula, Berneray and Eriskay. I am not a 'twitcher' but I'm able to recognise most of the birds that I see. On each visit I regularly clock up fifty-plus varieties of birds a week, including many rarities such as red-necked phalarope, corncrake, whimbrel, garganey and corn bunting, plus a myriad of waders and sea birds.

Many of the reports made towards the successful Operation Easter [4] originated from the islands, which is not surprising as the locals appreciate and value their wildlife and detest those who might prefer to plunder the eggs and put the shells in a case to gloat over during winter months. All of the isles to the west, and Orkney and Shetland to the north, have an army of people protecting their natural heritage as they go about their daily work. The local people know, despite the distances and remoteness involved, that officers of Northern Constabulary will respond to a call about suspected egg thieves and that whether or not they are wildlife crime officers they will know the appropriate action to take.

Merseyside is as infamous for egg thieves as it is famous for good musicians. Several of those are targets of Operation Easter and in conjunction with Merseyside Police I monitor their movements as closely as possible. I was highly suspicious when on 5th June 2002 I learned that a car from Merseyside was spotted at the Forvie Sands Nature Reserve about ten miles north of Aberdeen. This is exactly the place that would interest egg thieves, having, amongst other interesting birds, a colony of nesting terns. I was slightly more surprised to learn that a camouflage net and two poles belonging to one of the reserve wardens had been stolen and that the occupants of the suspect car were believed responsible. Unknown to me at that time, their next destination, two days later, was Orkney

Orkney – or the Orkney Islands – is an archipelago ten miles north of Caithness on mainland Scotland. It comprises seventy islands, around twenty of which are inhabited. Humans have settled there for at least 5,500 years, originally Neolithic tribes, followed by the Picts. As well as multitudinous birdlife Orkney

---

[4] The author has coordinated Operation Easter which combats egg thieves since 1997 – see Note 3.

contains some of the oldest and best-preserved Neolithic sites in Europe. Its natural and historic jewels make it a favourite with tourists. But not all tourists are welcome.

On 7th June 2002 the three occupants of the same vehicle that had left Forvie Sands were on mainland Orkney and were watched quartering ground on the Birsay Moors as if they were searching for nests. Birsay Moors are well-known for nesting birds, which include oyster catchers, hen harrier and, on Lowrie's Water, red-throated diver. Though the registered keeper of the vehicle was not known to Operation Easter, the area of Merseyside in which the registered keeper resided held several known or suspected egg collectors. Whether or not this turned out to be a coincidence it was sufficient for the police to take the sighting and its suspicious circumstances seriously. The wildlife crime officer for the Orkney Isles at that time was Constable David Dawson, and he took a special interest in this investigation.

David and other officers made a search of the Birsay Moors for the vehicle, but were unable to find it. They established from the ferry company when it was due to return to the mainland and intended to search the car and its occupants before it boarded. Events, however, overtook them.

The following afternoon another sighting of the vehicle was reported by an RSPB warden. It was back in the same area as the previous day and the men were seen walking away from the car over the moorland. The police attended and, through binoculars, watched the men taking photographs of birds at their nests using camouflaged netting as a form of hide. The men were watched until two of them returned to their car, at which point the police approached them. When they were asked their names and addresses one name was familiar to the officers as of interest to Operation Easter (and appearing in a part of the North Wales chapter as a Mr Black.) The men said they had been on the hill photographing great skuas, accompanied by their friend who was still on the hill. When this man returned and the trio were re-united his name was also recognised through Operation Easter. (He also appears in the North Wales chapter, being Mr Brown).

The men had an assortment of maps of the area, bird books, binoculars and expensive camera equipment in their possession; perfectly normal equipment for bird watchers. Less normal was a tractor inner tube, climbing ropes, harnesses, and an incredible thirty 35mm films. The officers were by no means convinced that they were genuine bird watchers and their suspicions were confirmed after they spotted a small white plastic marker pole in the heather about twenty-five metres away. Naturally they investigated and saw that it was a marker for a small plastic food container. This contained six eggs wrapped in toilet paper. The eggs had not been blown, making it likely that they had very recently been removed from the nests. The men were asked about the eggs and one of the three, Mr Black, admitted having taken them, telling the officers they were great skua, common tern and herring gull.

In 2002 there was no power for the police to arrest wildlife criminals, though one of the trio, the man accompanying Mr Brown and Mr Black, made it slightly easier for the police to deal with him by giving a false name and address. To keep life colourful we'll call him Mr Green. This enabled the police to arrest him, but Brown and Black had to be released after their car was thoroughly searched.

At this point I, in my role within Operation Easter, had not been updated by Northern Constabulary officers as to their progress with the suspects so was unable to pass on to them the likelihood that the camouflaged hide and poles were likely to have been those stolen at Forvie Sands in the Grampian Police area. This would have given grounds either to detain or arrest all three men, which would have made the investigation much easier and would have ensured that they could not make contact with their homes and have anything that may have been incriminating spirited away before the local police came knocking at their door with a search warrant.

On 11th June searches made by RSPB wardens in moorland areas where the three men's car had been seen revealed four eggs concealed in heather at the base of a protruding stone, clearly identified as a marker to re-claim the eggs in due course. The police were called and photographed and took possession of the eggs, now making a total of ten recovered.

In the meantime Dave Dick, the then senior investigations officer with RSPB Scotland, was called in to help the police officers dealing with the case. On 17th June Dave travelled to Orkney from Edinburgh and firstly identified the eggs from the plastic box as being three great skua and three Arctic tern. The four most recently recovery were those of snipe. However more evidence was needed to positively link the ten eggs to the suspects. It was important to get the films developed to see what evidence, if any, they revealed.

From the 750 individual photographs on the films it was quite obvious that birds were being disturbed for photography purposes. This is not an offence unless the birds are included on Schedule 1 of the Wildlife and Countryside Act 1981. However some of the photographs were of Schedule 1 birds, particularly red-throated divers. This is where the tractor tube, once inflated, would have come into its own since these birds often nest on small islands on lochans and this would enable them to be accessed in relative safety, if not in comfort.

Dave Dick and Constable David Dawson were appalled at what they found in the photographs. David told me, 'Some of the red-throated diver photographs were sequential, depicting the parent bird approaching the nest from the water then settling on the eggs. Photographs next in sequence clearly showed by the bird's head and neck attitude that it was disturbed; probably at the presence of the photographer under the camouflage netting. In one case a sequence of prints actually showed her rapidly leaving the nest'. This was good photographic evidence indicating, though not necessarily proving, that the crime of intentional disturbance had been caused to the bird.

All of the eggs recovered appeared on the films and it was suspected that many more, probably most or even all of the eggs, had been taken after being photographed on the nest. The men had been seen with large Thermos flasks that were never recovered; probably receptacles for the eggs. The photos also confirmed that Messrs Black, Brown and Green had been at Forvie and also at Dunnet Head, a famous seabird nesting site in the north-east of mainland Scotland.

Now that the photographs had been developed Dave Dick was able to carry out a particularly good piece of detective work. He studied the photos of the great skua, snipe and Arctic tern nests with eggs, then placed the recovered eggs alongside so that the markings on the eggs were exactly the same as those in the nests, and photographed them for comparison. This identification was as good, if not better, than fingerprint identification and was the best possible link in the chain of evidence to convict. The skua eggs and Arctic tern eggs appeared in photos in a roll of film taken from Mr Green, while the snipe eggs appeared in photos in a roll of film taken from Mr Green and Mr Brown.

The men had obviously been travelling much more widely than just the north of Scotland. Photographs showing a nesting peregrine indicated from the vegetation that it was on an inland crag. Orkney peregrines are sea cliff nesters and the type of plants shown would eliminate the location as being Orkney. Other photographs with more background suggested that the location was much more likely to be North Wales or Cumbria.

David Dawson commented, 'The photographs showed all three men in situations which, although not always illegal, were indicative of a cavalier attitude and wanton disregard for the wildlife they claimed to be so enthusiastic about. These ranged from a photograph of a puffin chick just days old to the men holding adult puffins. The only method by which they could have caught them was by removing them from their breeding burrows on cliff tops, an act which was very likely to make them desert their nest. Other photographs showed the men handling an otter cub, with the adult otter a short distance away in the background of one of the photos. From the background this was believed to have taken place on the foreshore either at Waulkmill or Hobbister, Orkney. This was reckless in the extreme, given the possibility that after being handled by humans the mother might have abandoned the cub.'

One site where the disturbance of the red-throated divers had taken place was identified as Loch Burifa, near Dunnet Head, Caithness. An empty nest scrape and two adult birds on the loch minus any brood tended to confirm this. There was a large rock on the loch's shore that appeared in some of the photographs, and tufts of freshly uprooted heather near to it suggested that a hide had recently been erected. Additional evidence in the form of a statement from a Highland Council countryside ranger who had watched the birds was that their actions around 6th June was indicative of birds that had just lost their eggs. Worryingly, it was discovered that this pair of divers had consistently failed during the previous few years and egg collecting was believed to have been the cause.

The three were due to appear at Kirkwall Sheriff Court, Orkney, in December of 2002, but attempted to plea-bargain by letter, an attempt rightly rejected by the temporary procurator fiscal. Pleas were altered and in January 2003 Mr Brown was fined £500 for the theft of the camouflage net. Mr Green was fined £750 for possession of equipment capable of being used to commit an offence against the Wildlife and Countryside Act (cameras, binoculars and films), plus £500 for intentional disturbance of a nesting red-throated diver and £750 for possession of a camera capable of being used in the disturbance. Mr Black was fined £500 for taking the ten eggs that had been recovered, £750 for possession of items capable of being used to commit an offence, £500 for intentional disturbance of a nesting red-throated diver and £750 for being in possession of a camera for that purpose. In addition all of the items recovered – several thousand pounds worth – were forfeit by the court. After passing sentence the sheriff indicated that he would have seriously considered a jail sentence had it been available to him, but a year had yet to pass before the enacting of the Criminal Justice (Scotland) Act 2003 which introduced powers to enable courts to jail wildlife criminals.

Some years earlier, in 1997, the point was much more forcibly made by a sheriff that he was frustrated by the absence of a power under which he could send a wildlife criminal to jail. David Dawson relates the tale of two men I called at the time the Bumbling Brothers, and of their conviction that was a major boost to the embryonic Operation Easter:

'During the afternoon of Monday 26th May 1997 I received a telephone call from Keith Fairclough, RSPB Reserves Manager in Orkney. Keith voiced his suspicions about two men seen acting suspiciously on the Birsay Moors reserve. So as not to draw undue attention to himself, Keith, a canny Liverpudlian, had the presence of mind to take a spade from his van and began digging close to the site of a peat bank, all the time observing the behaviour of the men.

'Initially wary of the presence of a third party on the remote hillside, the men soon returned to their activity, comfortable in the thought that the man with the spade was merely a crofter cutting his winter fuel. The pair was seen to effectively quarter certain areas of the moor, clearly in search of something at ground level. Given the locality's importance as a breeding site for a number of important species such as hen harrier and whimbrel, it was fairly evident that the men were seeking nests.

'When the men disappeared from view over a ridge, Keith returned to his van and drove along the road for a short distance where he found a rather battered old Ford Escort car, parked and unattended. Noting the registration number and having his suspicions further raised by the clear presence of ropes, maps and outdoor gear in the back of the car, Keith returned to his office and contacted me. A PNC check on the vehicle aroused no immediate concerns other than the fact that the somewhat rickety car was registered to a Portsmouth address.

'Some rapid investigative work between Keith and myself soon established that two men of the same surname as the registered keeper had taken up a week's residence in a static caravan adjacent to the village shop in Evie, the community near to the RSPB reserve. Accompanied by Sergeant Nigel Stafford, I drove over to the village of Evie and paid a visit to the caravan. With no vehicle present and the caravan locked it was apparent that the men had not yet returned. A glance through the window drew my attention to a scrap of paper lying on top of the television set. On it was written the words '7.30 – BBC2 Snowdonia programme'.

'In itself such a note was unremarkable. However, it had also been my intention to record that same programme as it was actually a documentary about the work of the RSPB in North Wales and in particular the conflict with egg collectors.

'Although we possessed little in the way of any firm evidence, other than a potential disturbance offence at the hen harrier breeding site, it was decided to obtain a search warrant with which to arm ourselves when we visited the caravan later that evening. Taking a completed warrant to a local JP (a farmer noted for his conservation credentials) it was duly granted with the words, 'We can't have thieves like these robbing Orkney of its heritage!'

'Later that evening, accompanied by Nigel Stafford and Keith Fairclough we made a second visit to the caravan. The door was opened by a seemingly bemused young man, who I'll simply refer to as Lee. Also present was a second man who, it transpired, was Lee's younger brother, Jamie. The reason for our visit was explained and I read the contents of the warrant to them. After a few minutes of fruitless searching, Keith pointed to the bench upon which Jamie was sitting and asked if there was a compartment beneath.

'Oh n. . . no. . . no.' stammered Jamie, 'there's nothing under here. . .'

'I then moved over and asked Jamie if he could stand up to allow us to fully inspect the seating area. Of course, like most caravans, there was a substantial compartment beneath the cushioned seats which contained three cardboard boxes. Carefully opening one I revealed a cotton wool and paper nest containing a clutch of white, very round eggs that looked suspiciously like a clutch of (blown) hen harrier eggs. The brothers stood with what could only be described as a look of horror etched on their faces, and I was met with a 'what can one say?' shrug from Jamie.

'This first box contained two complete clutches of hen harrier eggs. The remaining boxes were found to hold single clutches of merlin and red-throated diver eggs, together with an assortment of single eggs including dunlin, starling, fulmar and curlew.

'As we had now to confirm their identity and address status, together with a closer inspection of their vehicle, it was decided to detain them and return to Kirkwall Police Station. There, a search of the car uncovered ropes, binoculars, and a range of OS maps – one of which (interestingly enough) pertained to Snowdonia and had pen marks indicating the site of peregrine eyries.

'While Hampshire Police set about the task of checking addresses and ultimately searching the addresses for further egg collections, we attempted an interview with the hapless 'oologists'. Lee remained tight-lipped with a series of 'no comment' responses to any questions. Jamie, by contrast, felt the need to get things off his chest and after describing how they had never collected eggs in the past but had done so merely on a whim during their trip to Orkney, did finally admit that his brother 'might have some more [eggs] hidden in a wall cupboard behind his bed!'

'After some initial delay in obtaining search warrants in Portsmouth the pair were released in the early hours of the following morning, by which time the Hampshire wildlife crime officer had recovered a substantial egg collection at Lee's address.

'Unfortunately for the brothers, they had made the mistake of recording their Scottish trip on a camcorder, the tape of which depicted them climbing a cliff and removing a fulmar's egg, not to mention Lee, at one point, looking around warily and suggesting, 'I think we'd better go. This looks like an RSPB place.' For two who claimed to be merely keen 'birders' they seemed to demonstrate an unhealthy phobia of the RSPB.

'At the end of the investigation the brothers were finally charged with over seventy offences under the Wildlife and Countryside Act 1981. Their vehicle and assorted equipment were also retained as productions.

'Next day the duo attended Kirkwall Sheriff Court where they faced Honorary Sheriff Bill Wright. Both pleaded guilty to all charges with the exception of one that related to the use of their car, which was accepted by the Crown. (The truth being that the fiscal did not wish to deny them a means by which to leave Orkney!)

'I did not attend court as I had been struck down with a most vicious viral infection that thankfully only took hold after I had submitted the crime report. Late that afternoon, I received a telephone call at home from Keith Adam, the then Procurator Fiscal. 'Have I got news for you!' Keith chuckled down the line, 'The brothers have been hit for six! Go on – guess how much they've been fined.'

'Scottish courts, at that time, were not well-known for levelling hefty penalties for wildlife crime offences, hence my response of '£1,000 each?'

'Oh, higher than that!' laughed Keith.

'After a guessing game which left me gasping at a £10,000 'guesstimate', Keith finally said, 'Multiply that by nine and you have the total fine – and that applies equally to both.'

'£180,000 in total. It was music to my ears. If that didn't send out a message to eggers planning an Orkney trip, I failed to see what could. It was widely accepted that the sheriff was making the point that he should have the opportunity in law to impose a prison sentence on wildlife criminals, a legislative change that was still six years distant.

'Naturally, after the excitement wore off it became reasonable to assume that such penalties would not be sustained. That proved correct as a subsequent appeal reduced the fines to £6,000 and £4,000 respectively. Nevertheless, there is little doubt that Orkney proved, in years to come, less attractive to eggers than it previously had been.

'The brothers, whilst virtual amateurs in the egg collecting field (with no known connections to other, better known, collectors and employing very rudimentary means by which to blow eggs taken etc.) did, however, cause Orkney's natural environment some degree of damage. At that time, we had a breeding population of approximately twenty pairs of merlin – a species already facing massive threats from other factors, not to mention a most fragile hen harrier population.

'Had the brothers been successful in evading detection and had stayed their planned week (they had actually only been on the island less than 48 hours) the damage they might have wrought could have been devastating.

'This was a great result and an astonishing penalty and one that sent out shockwaves amongst the egg thieves we had begun to target seriously and in an organised, proactive way. I am sure it was also the catalyst that made the more sensible of our many targets give up egg thieving.'

And, not surprisingly, I never heard of the Bumbling Brothers again.

THE THIN GREEN LINE

As I finish putting pen to paper in the early Spring of 2009 I reflect on where we are with the fight against wildlife crime in the countries that make up the United Kingdom. In general terms policing resources devoted to the investigation of crimes committed against wildlife have always been minimal. Even fewer resources are in place to reduce the incidence of wildlife crime. How do we compare with a decade earlier, say 1998? What was the state of the thin green line then?

England was streets ahead of the rest of the UK, which was natural since they were the instigators and developers of the then police wildlife liaison officer post. From memory there was a full-time wildlife crime officer in Avon and Somerset, Cheshire, Lancashire, Metropolitan Police, Northumbria, Thames Valley, Warwickshire and West Yorkshire. From these eight full-time posts there were further developments and several more forces continued down the route of a full-time commitment, including in due course Lincolnshire and Merseyside.

This welcome progress was not to continue and from about 2005 chief constables in many of the English forces had to tighten their financial belts. Decisions had to be made and in many cases their full-time wildlife crime officer was returned to normal policing duties, with their wildlife remit carried out as an adjunct. Forces that had a long-time wildlife crime officer, such as Avon and Somerset, Northumbria and Warwickshire were included in these resource-saving measures. The rest of us were stunned and wondered if the fight against wildlife crime had effectively come to the end of the road.

It may not always be easy for a chief constable to ratify a decision to get rid of a full-time wildlife crime officer. It certainly means one more police officer back to general rather than specialised police work, but these officers were great value for money. Without exception they would work far more hours than was reflected in their remuneration and their experience built up over the years made them much more likely to solve a case. The very fact that their knowledge and operational efficiency would be well-known to those who might be tempted to carry out a crime against wildlife may even in some cases have been effective as a deterrent: no-one commits a crime if they figure they are very likely to be caught.

In 2007 Nigel Lound of Lincolnshire was awarded the WWF

Wildlife Enforcer of the Year trophy. Traditionally, the following February, the winner of this award gives a twenty-minute presentation at the annual PAW Open Seminar in London. This has always covered interesting cases in which he or she has been involved during the year assessed for the award. Nigel unexpectedly changed the format in February 2008 in a heartfelt presentation drawing everyone's attention to the rapid decline in many English forces' commitment to wildlife crime investigation and including an impassioned plea for this retrograde step to become known in the right places so that it might be reversed. The applause was thunderous.

Though disappointment continued, one positive outcome in early 2008 was the placement of a part-time wildlife crime officer – Inspector Nevin Hunter of Devon and Cornwall – in a full-time secondment as chief wildlife inspector with the Animal Health sector of Defra. Simultaneously another part-time wildlife crime officer, Sergeant Mark Rasbeary of North Yorkshire Police was seconded full-time to work with Natural England, mirroring the posts in the Countryside Council for Wales to which Sergeant Ian Guildford of South Wales and the now retired Sergeant Pete Charleston had been seconded for some time. Despite these secondments, the wildlife crime fighting capability in England remains bleak.

In Wales, being a much smaller country, the situation is different. Though neither Ian Guildford nor Pete Charleston was full-time a decade ago in 1998, their work alongside the Countryside Council for Wales has been ground-breaking. Their full-time positions (since 2000 in Pete's case and 2003 in the case of Ian) have made a noticeable and positive impact on the way CCW deals with wildlife and environmental crime issues, and their statistics have demonstrated just how under-recorded wildlife crime is in most other areas of the UK. The police and CCW really have a symbiotic relationship.

The Royal Ulster Constabulary – now the Police Service of Northern Ireland (PSNI) – were under great pressure during the Troubles, a term that diminishes the true extent of the political unrest and horrific atrocities that took place. Nevertheless they had a police officer, Sergeant Mark Mason, who spent a good proportion of his time specialising in the investigation of wildlife crime. This continued during the time he was an inspector and up to his retiral as chief inspector. Mark has now been replaced in a full-time capacity by Emma Meredith, a member of PSNI support staff, who hopes to persuade senior management to appoint a part-time wildlife liaison officer (they still prefer this term in Northern Ireland) in each of the eight sections of the force. The PSNI are still slightly behind the rest of the UK but, importantly, they are making progress.

A decade ago in Scotland I was still the only full-time wildlife crime officer, but by 2006 I was joined by another three (Strathclyde, Lothian and Borders and Grampian). 2007 was a landmark year and as I see it there were three catalysts of change.

First was the former chief constable of Lothian and Borders Police, Paddy Tomkins, in his new role of HM Chief Inspector of Constabulary (HMCIC) in Scotland. Paddy is a great supporter of the wildlife crime officer network and when still with the Lothian and Borders force in 2006 took over as the Association of Chief Police Officers in Scotland (ACPOS) lead on wildlife crime, continuing the good work of his predecessors in that role, the former ACC Bob McMillan and former DCC Ian Gordon, both of Tayside Police.

The second catalyst was the then Minister for the Environment, Mike Russell MSP. Scotland has always been lucky with supportive environment ministers but Mike Russell took the Scottish Government's interest in wildlife crime to a new level; his genuine interest and enthusiasm (not forgetting his political acumen) simply made things happen. He began to make progress – innovative progress – at an unprecedented pace.

The third – and most unexpected factor – was a golden eagle – a dead golden eagle; in fact a poisoned golden eagle which was half of the only pair in the Scottish Borders. This bird was found dead in August 2007 and the fact that it had been poisoned sparked off a real fury, as the majority of the public thought that would be an end for many years of breeding golden eagles in the Borders hills. (As it turned out there was an immature female golden eagle waiting in the wings but this was not realised for the best part of a year).

This unlikely human/avian combination was just what was required to set the wheels in motion for a joint thematic inspection of the arrangements in Scotland for preventing, investigating and prosecuting wildlife crime. It followed a parliamentary debate led by Mike Russell, during which there was broad cross-party support. A team headed by Paddy Tomkins and Joe O'Donnell, HM Chief Inspector of Prosecution in Scotland began interviewing relevant people from the eight Scottish police forces, the Crown Office and Procurator Fiscal

Service (COPFS) and from other organisations that had a view on wildlife crime issues. The team leaders were Chief Superintendent David McCracken of HMCIC and Maura Lynch of the Inspectorate of Prosecutions in Scotland, along with Inspector Scott Jones of Strathclyde Police and myself. [5]

Twenty four recommendations emanated from the review, in particular that each police force in Scotland should have a full-time wildlife crime officer. In March 2009 Central Scotland Police appointed Constable Paul Barr in a full-time role as police officer for the Loch Lomond National Park and incorporated in his duties those of wildlife crime officer. This was a major – and innovative – step forward. To fulfil some of the recommend-ations the Scottish Government has pledged £220,000 available over the three years since their receipt of the review to be used in the investigation of wildlife crime. This is indeed welcome support and the wildlife crime officers in the eight Scottish police forces (and other PAW partners) can now carry out actions, particularly in relation to surveillance and forensic work, which hitherto would have been cost-prohibitive.

Steady progress has been made in the enactment of new wildlife crime legislation enacted by the different countries forming the UK. England took the lead and has since been overtaken. In the same manner as the legislation, I would hope that the Scottish thematic inspection will be mirrored elsewhere and improvements made from which the other UK countries can benefit. In addition to the recommended full-time posts, six sub-groups of the Partnership for Action against Wildlife Crime were recommended and have been formed. They are:

1. Scottish Wildlife Crime Tactical and Co-ordinating Group

2. Media (Scotland) Group

3. Legislation, Regulation and Guidance Group

4. Intelligence and Information-Sharing Group

5. Training and Awareness Group

6. Funding Group

This is a major milestone, and I am sure that under the guidance and cajoling of Richard Brunstrom, chief constable of North Wales Police and ACPO representative on wildlife crime

---

[5] The results (available at www.scotland.gov.uk/Publications/2008/04/03143616) were passed to the Scottish Government in March 2008 and published shortly thereafter.

issues this will soon be replicated in Wales. Richard is a man of vision and (thankfully) impatience: he wants worthwhile actions carried out immediately. This is both rare and invaluable and I am sure that before he retires he will be putting as much pressure as he possibly can on fellow chief constables in England and Wales to follow Scotland's lead.

Richard, along with DCC Iain Macleod of Central Scotland Police, has had a huge input to bringing our National Wildlife Crime Unit to where it is at the present time. Even if England is lagging well behind, and Wales and Northern Ireland are playing catch-up, the National Wildlife Crime Unit is a professional and energetic body well placed to serve all wildlife crime officers in the UK in the collation and allocation of intelligence packages. Because of lack of funding it would by now have gone under if Richard had not given it a home in North Wales, which, courtesy of Paddy Tomkins, then transferred to North Berwick in Lothian and Borders, where it is situated now.

The Republic of Ireland was of particular interest to me since, for a start, I had never visited the country until 2008. When I did so I realised its wildlife crime investigation methods were intriguingly different to those in the UK. What really fascinated me was that there was an untapped source of intelligence-sharing required between the UK and Ireland. Even in the first few months we have shared intelligence leading to a success in a finch-trapping investigation and are working on deer poaching issues with links 'o'er the water'. We intend to build on this and it will hopefully be the first of many shared successes.

So there is good news and bad, but this is nothing new in the police service. Many of us who have been in policing for more years than we care to remember have seen this type of problem come and go. There is no doubt that Scotland is ahead of the wildlife crime field in early 2009 and England, once the leader is probably a poor third. But the police are there to serve the public. I doubt very much if the public want wildlife crime largely ignored and are unlikely to simply sit on their hands if the police pay barely more than lip service to reports of this type of crime. The Scottish Government has demonstrated that if there is political will changes can be made for the better. Let's hope that this political will spreads and before too long Scotland's lead is replicated and indeed bettered elsewhere either in Britain or Ireland.

POSTSCRIPT: THE SEALS OF EAST LINGA

And finally, a landmark case that has just concluded as the text for the book is going to the publisher. For this case we need to travel about as far north in the British Isles as is possible; in fact to the island of East Linga, part of the Shetland Isles. East Linga is about half way up the east side of the group of islands and lies between Whalsay to the west and Grif Skerry to the east. The smaller Calf of Linga lies to the north and is connected to East Linga at low tide. A high proportion – about 3,500 – of the UK seal population live in and around the Shetland Isles and around thirty grey seal pups are born each year on East Linga. (It is interesting that the UK has about 40% of the world population of grey seals – about 120,000 animals – and 90% of those breed in Scotland.) Unlike the common seal breeding time, June to July, grey seal pups are usually born in October or November. Legal protection is given to the seals during their breeding time with grey seals being protected against shooting between 1st September and 31st December unless directly threatening to damage the nets of coastal fishermen.

It has long been suspected that seals are shot during the time they are protected and at a time that they are causing no immediate threat to nets. According to the Seals Protection Action Group the number killed either legally or illegally is around 5000 annually in Scottish waters alone. Evidence of illegal practice is extremely hard to gather since the seals often haul out in remote places and very often the evidence in the form of a dead seal sinks to the bottom of the sea or, if shot on the coastline, is washed out to sea. Occasionally, however, the police have a lucky break and the killing of seals in unlawful circumstances is witnessed. This was the position on East Linga on 29th November 2008.

On that Saturday members of staff from Scottish Natural Heritage were carrying out a seal survey by boat when they saw two men acting suspiciously on the shoreline and suspected they were killing seal pups. One of the men was raising a fence post above his head and bringing it down with some force. The witnesses alerted the police, and Constable Bob Veighey, the wildlife crime officer for the Shetland Isles, chartered a boat and went to the island along with a local Scottish SPCA inspector. They were shocked to find the beach littered with dead seal pups, twenty-one in total. The pups had severe head injuries and it appeared that they had been clubbed to death.

As a result of the police investigations two men from Whalsay were charged. One of the men, who appeared to have instigated the cull, alleged that he had killed the seal pups because they had been abandoned by their mothers. He did not want them to die of starvation and his sole reason for killing them was concern and compassion for their suffering. That they had been abandoned was easily refuted by the evidence of a veterinary pathologist, who examined each dead seal in turn to establish its injuries and found them to be in very good condition, with a thick layer of blubber under the skin.

There was much discussion about the most relevant charges, the reason for this being the poor maximum penalty available under the Conservation of Seals Act 1970. Even with a recent update to the penalties the maximum remains Level 4, which is currently £2,500, and with no option to the courts of imprisonment. Unusually there is nothing in the Conservation of Seals Act that relates to clubbing seals to death. The Act specifies that they may not be poisoned nor shot with the wrong type of firearm but the legislators have not taken into consideration man's ingenuity to devise other means of culling seals. Some legislation – for instance the legislation governing the killing of deer or fishing for salmon – lays down the legal methods and anything outside these methods is considered an offence. Not so the Conservation of Seals Act. The more I see of this Act the more I am convinced of its inability to deal effectively with illegal acts committed against pinnipeds.

Since there was veterinary evidence in relation to each one of the twenty-one dead seals, this allowed the men to be charged under the Wild Mammals (Protection) Act 1996 with twenty-one counts of cruelly killing them by clubbing. This Act was passed to give some protection against cruel treatment meted out to wild animals, in particular prompted by the frequency that hedgehogs were being abused. It covers a variety of methods of cruelly killing or injuring wild mammals, in particular that of beating them. In relation to any mammal that is killed, it would be necessary to prove that there was unnecessary suffering.

As is the right of the procurator fiscal, in this case he decided to combine the twenty-one separate charges of cruelly killing a seal into one single charge of killing twenty-one seals. He dropped twenty-one charges under the Conservation of Seals Act 1970, probably having as little faith in its provisions as I do.

If post mortem examinations showed that in each case the first blow had killed the seal then it would be extremely unlikely that a conviction under the Wild Mammals (Protection) Act 1996

THE LAW ON SEALS: THE ORKNEY AND SHETLAND EXPERIENCE
DAVID DAWSON, WILDLIFE CRIME OFFICER ORKNEY AND SHETLAND

Serving as a Wildlife Crime Officer between 1988 and 2007 in the Northern Isles did not, in the opinion of some mainland based colleagues, offer much in the way of a particularly challenging role. Given the low numbers of grouse and pheasant, there is no commercial interest in game shooting; the fox is unknown; the nearest badger inhabits a sett in Caithness and the only deer are semi-domesticated and confined to a farm on Orkney.

The absence of poaching, unlawful fox hunts, badger baiting, even raptor persecution could create the impression that the Orkney or Shetland Wildlife Crime Officer's lot is indeed a happy one. And in many ways it is – until one raises the subject of seals and fisheries.

Whilst our islands lack any significant land mammal interest – the notable exceptions being the otter and Orkney vole – the wild animal that one readily associates with both Orkney and Shetland is undoubtedly the grey seal. Although adored by tourists and many local islanders, this heavyweight marine predator is considered a menace by the sea-fishing industry and coastal fish farmers alike.

On an almost annual basis, usually coinciding with the pupping season in November, reports would be received of what would amount to an unlawful cull of pups and nursing mothers at one of Orkney's colonies. Besides that, occasional 'mass slaughtering' of adult animals come to attention when carcases, clearly having sustained fatal large calibre bullet wounds, are washed ashore. Given healthy population figures, the impact of this on the grey seal population is negligible. Early winter storms will account for pup losses far and away in excess of actions of this nature. However, the media interest (not, one might add, in pup deaths due to storms) following any illegal 'cull' is intense.

Even murder and other serious crime (thankfully rare in these parts) fail to grab as many headlines as those that depict the lurid and sad images of blood-soaked seal pups. Animal rights groups and a public that may rarely take an interest in wildlife issues suddenly spring to vocal action. The latter, armed with the perception that seals are fully protected by law, demand justice whilst the former, knowing full well that the legislation governing seal conservation is manifestly weak, demand a change in the law.

Arguably, the sad fact is that almost all the protagonists in the debate – including the individuals who shoot seals – have a

[SEE OVER]

287

valid point: the Conservation of Seals Act 1970 offers what amounts to a token protection of both grey and common seals in UK waters. Due to exceptions in the Act that effectively permit fishermen and fish farmers to kill 'rogue' animals in the vicinity (never defined in law) of nets and gear, it remains – thanks to the isolated location of such sites – nigh impossible to prove that a carcass washed ashore had been anything other than lawfully killed.

Certainly, mass shootings of pups at breeding 'rookeries' miles from any fisheries gear, animals shot with a prohibited calibre of weapon (e.g. .22 rifle), are wholly illegal acts. The only problem, again, is that of evidence. Following one illegal pup cull (all shot with a .22 calibre weapon) Northern Constabulary test fired all rifles of that type within the district – all to no avail. Even an illegally held rifle, found in the possession of a leading suspect, proved not to be the weapon used.

As the Orkney wildlife crime officer, the media always beat a path to my door. The tightrope walk would then begin. Responses to emotive questions were carefully measured so as not to be seen as anything but impartial in the debate. Once, however, whilst speaking at one of the annual wildlife crime officers' conferences, I did describe the Conservation of Seals Act 1970 as 'not worth the paper it is printed on'.

Hailed as a 'hero' by the animal rights lobby (an uncomfortable plaudit in light of the sometimes extreme views of one or two within that field of activity) and as inspiration to the fishing industry (not that they were not already aware!), my simple, yet truthful, comment hit the headlines. Despite that, I remained impartial to the continuing dispute, engaging in consultation with fish farmers and lobster fishermen besides local conservation groups.

It was, I must confess, not the easiest of lines to tread. Yet, irrespective of one's personal opinions, which, as wildlife enthusiasts we all possess, the task of the police wildlife crime officer is to work within the parameters of whatever the pertinent legislation might be. The major problem is how to convincingly communicate the inadequacies of some laws to those who cannot rise beyond the emotional impact of seal killings.

When it came to illegal egg collecting (or the removal of fossils, a major attraction in Orkney) things were much simpler.

could follow, since the Act relates to specified acts committed against wild mammals *with intent to inflict unnecessary suffering*. These are detailed in the Act as *mutilate, kick, beat, nail or otherwise impale, stab, burn, stone, crush, drown, drag or asphyxiate*. In this case the seal pups were beaten with a fence post. There was evidence from the post mortem examinations that the heads of the seals had been struck with great force, several blows eventually shattering their skulls and pulping their brains. Importantly the post mortem examinations also showed that some of the animals had ingested and inhaled blood, indicating they had not been killed instantly. Killing cleanly is not cruel treatment, though the killing of the animal may be an offence in itself under other legislation – in this case the Conservation of Seals Act 1970. Police officers, and in due course, prosecutors, have to weight up the options available under a variety of legislation and decide on the charge which best fits the circumstances of the crime. It is also possible to libel two or more charges, as was the case here, though if two different charges arise virtually out of the same circumstances the court may consider this to be double jeopardy.

The charge under the Wild Mammals (Protection) Act is much stronger, and has a penalty of imprisonment available to the court. Under this Act penalties are more in keeping with modern legislation. A maximum fine of £5,000 is available, as is imprisonment of up to six months. If the men were convicted the court now had a much better choice of penalties.

On 25th February 2009 the two men again appeared at Lerwick Sheriff Court. One, James Stewart – the man considered to be the instigator – pled guilty to the single charge under the Wild Mammals (Protection) Act 1996. The other man pled not guilty and his plea was accepted by the procurator fiscal on behalf of the Crown. Of the man pleading guilty, he was unwilling to offer any explanation to the court as to why he clubbed the seals to death, a bizarre situation and one that no doubt raised questions in the sheriff's mind.

The sheriff, Graeme Napier, deferred sentence for a month, warning Mr Stewart that when he returned to court a sentence of imprisonment would be a possibility. On 25th March 2009 Stewart returned to court to be sentenced. The sheriff told him,

'As you are aware you have pled guilty to a very serious offence. It is an unusual offence for the courts to deal with which perhaps, if nothing else does, makes clear the general acceptance by law-abiding members of the community of how unacceptable this behaviour is. I am not here to sentence you on the basis that your actions have caused heightened emotions in certain parts of the community; nor for the fact that your actions will be associated in the public mind with Shetland and more particularly Whalsay. My responsibility is to sentence you in accordance with the law. This is a process that requires an unemotional response to the facts of the case, taking into account the various mitigatory factors identified by your agent and drawn out in the social enquiry report. There are of course many mitigatory factors, not least of which is that you are of previous good character, have no previous convictions and, according to the references I have seen have contributed to the community in Whalsay.

'However I must balance that against the seriousness of the offending and a need to make clear that society in general and the courts will not tolerate the infliction of such unnecessary suffering not just on one but on twenty-one seals.

'Although the social work department has looked at the various alternatives to custody in their report, and I have considered these, in all the circumstances but particularly because of the seriousness and as a discouragement to others who may be tempted to engage in this type of activity, I consider that there is no alternative but a custodial sentence. Parliament in enacting this legislation set the maximum sentence at six months imprisonment. It is difficult to envisage a much more serious case of such offending but given your previous good character and making allowance for the possibility that someone could breach this section in a more serious manner I consider that my starting point for sentence should be one of four months. I will then discount that by one-third to result in a sentence of 80 days from today.'

Like many other investigations, this was a case where evidence was drawn from a number of experts and where the provisions of more than one statute were considered to ensure that the public was given the best chance of seeing justice done. The green line of police wildlife crime officers will always be thin but it is now making a significant impact on those who commit the varieties of crime against wildlife that this book has described. This specialist police work must be encouraged, supported and improved. I am reticent to suggest it be better rewarded; that might just be too much to ask!

Caged finches recovered during a search in Ireland by NPWS staff – see Ireland chapter (Photo: Dr Maurice Eakin, NPWS)

Using glass-bottomed buckets to look for freshwater pearl mussels in an Irish river (Photo Padraigh Comerford, NPWS)

Wild-taken redpoll with ring and brace – see Ireland chapter (Photo: Dr Maurice Eakin, NPWS)

Poisoned immature peregrine that eventually died (Photo: Northern Ireland Raptor Study Group)

Recovery of Irish hares after a coursing incident. Two had been predated. (Photo: Dr Maurice Eakin, NPWS)

Salmon leaping at falls, one of the many obstacles, including poachers, they need to surmount before spawning – see Strathclyde chapter (Photo: Neil Macdonald)

The alligator in the bath! – see Lothian & Borders chapter
(Photo: Jim Cormack, Scottish SPCA)

A dead pheasant laced with an incredible amount of deadly pesticide
(Photo: Lothian and Borders Police)

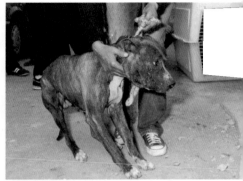

Kennels for the unfortunate pit bull terriers – see Fife chapter

Whether a loser or winner, the dogs sustain serious injuries (Photos: Fife Constabulary)

The jet skier in the process of corralling dolphins – see Grampian chapter (Photo: John Smith)

About to collect evidence in the form of live American signal crayfish, attracted to baited cages in the pond – see Grampian chapter (Photo: Peter Collen)

Now you see them; now you don't. Black-throated diver eggs photographed by the thieves before removing them – see Northern chapter

Common gull eggs, collectable by egg thieves, come in a variety of colours – see Northern chapter

A vet begins a post mortem examination of a seal, with notes being taken by Constable Bob Veighey – see chapter on The Seals of East Linga

Measuring the depth of blubber to prove the seal's health

The dead seals on the beaches were marked by numbered no waiting cones. Incongruous items on an island with no vehicles!
(Photos: Snr Insp Ron Patterson, Scottish SPCA)

Blood samples are frequnetly taken from birds to prove or disprove parentage in police investigations. No bird is more dangerous to handle for this purpose than the golden eagle

Notes

1. CITES: Convention on International Trade in Endangered Species
The international trade in wildlife is a highly profitable business worth billions of pounds and involves a wide variety of species, both dead and alive. Millions of animals and plants are traded every year as pets, ornamental plants, furs and timber.

The over-exploitation for trade gave such concern for the survival of species that in 1973 an international treaty was drawn up to protect wildlife against over-exploitation. The treaty, known as CITES, the Convention on International Trade in Endangered Species of Wild Fauna and Flora, came into force on 1st July, 1975. Although originally only signed by twenty-one countries, the global commitment to wildlife is such that it now has a membership of over 160 countries.

Roughly 5000 species of animals and 28000 species of plants are protected by CITES against over-exploitation through international trade. They are listed in three CITES Appendices. The species are grouped in the Appendices according to how threatened they are by international trade. They include some whole groups, such as primates, cetaceans, sea turtles, parrots, corals, cacti and orchids. In some cases only a subspecies or geographically separate population of a species is listed, for example the population of just one country.

The protection offered by CITES is dependent on the listing a species has been assigned. Species are listed on three Appendices:

> APPENDIX I (approx 800 species) Includes species threatened with extinction and international commercial trade is prohibited. Trade is only authorised in exceptional circumstances;

> APPENDIX II (approx 32,000 species) Includes species not necessarily now threatened with extinction but may become so unless trade is regulated. International commercial trade is allowed so long as the necessary permits have been obtained;

> APPENDIX III (approx 300 species) Contains species that are subject to regulation within the jurisdiction of a member country and for which co-operation of other parties to CITES is needed to prevent or restrict their exploitation.

The Convention is implemented throughout the European Union by Council Regulations, one of which assigns the species to four categories, replacing the word Appendices with Annexes:

Annex A – All CITES App I species and some CITES App II species for which the EU has adopted stricter domestic measures, as well as 'look alike' species;

Annex B – All other CITES App II species and some CITES App III species and non-CITES species for which the EU has adopted strict domestic measures, as well as 'look alike' species. In addition, species known to pose an ecological threat to indigenous species in the EU are included in Annex B.

Annex C – All other CITES App III species.

Annex D – (No CITES equivalent) Includes non-CITES species that are imported into the EU in such numbers as to warrant monitoring.

2. COTES: Control of Trade in Endangered Species (Enforcement) Regulations

At points of entry to the UK the illegal trade in CITES-listed species is enforced by the UK Border Agency, using their considerable powers under the Customs and Excise Management Act 1979 at points of entry to the UK. However once the species have entered the UK the enforcement responsibility passes to the police under the Control of Trade in Endangered Species (Enforcement) Regulations 1997

3. Operation Easter

Operation Easter is a nationwide operation initiated by Tayside Police in 1997 and co-ordinated by the author since that time. Its aim is convicting or deterring the main collectors of rare wild birds' eggs in the UK. Because of the success of the operation, the number of known egg thieves who are believed still active has reduced from somewhere around 130 to no more than 40. Important factors in this dramatic reduction are now the real risk of being caught by the police and the likelihood of being imprisoned if convicted.

Operation Easter is one of very few operations that involves every single police force in the UK and has links with the National Wildlife Crime Unit, HM Revenue and Customs and RSPB.

Because of these risks many egg collectors have given up their 'hobby', though may still retain their egg collections. Some now go abroad to collect eggs, where the police may not treat this crime so seriously.

4. JNCC: The Joint Nature Conservation Committee and Conservation Priorities

The JNCC, based in Peterborough, is a Government body and oversees the statutory nature conservation organisations (SNCOs) in England, Wales, Scotland and Northern Ireland.

The JNCC chair an annual high-level meeting of statutory organisations, including police, HM Revenue and Customs and SNCOs, together with non-government organisations including representatives from Kew Gardens and RSPB. Conservation priorities are agreed, and through the National Wildlife Crime Unit, a process is put in place for the police to take forward an appropriate response to investigate alleged crime committed against species that are of conservation concern. Though investigations into crime committed against these species don't necessarily form the preponderance of a police wildlife crime officer's work, they are aware that when a crime is committed against a conservation priority species it can push the species even closer to the brink in terms of rarity or even extinction. In 2009, conservation priorities are particularly vulnerable birds of prey (hen harrier, goshawk, golden eagle, white-tailed eagle and red kite,) all species of bats, illegal trade in CITES Annex A species and freshwater pearl mussels.

5. DEFRA – Department for Environment Food and Rural Affairs

The Wildlife Species Conservation (WSC) Division of Defra develops UK policies for the global conservation and sustainable human use of wild animals and plants, particularly through CITES and the EU Wildlife Trade Regulations. WSC also has policy responsibility for species conservation in England; it administers the Partnership for Action against Wildlife Crime (PAW) and supports the UK National Wildlife Crime Unit. The Wildlife Licensing and Registration Service (WLRS) in Animal Health (an Executive Agency of Defra) administers the controls on trade in CITES species within the UK. Both Defra and Animal Health work closely with the Police, the UK Border Agency and the National Wildlife Crime Unit in combating illegal global and domestic wildlife trade.

Coincidentally Inspector Nevin Hunter of Devon and Cornwall Constabulary was seconded to the Animal Health Division of Defra in early 2008 for a period of three years. He will assume the role of chief wildlife inspector, supervising the work of 85 wildlife inspectors operating throughout the UK.

6. SSSIs: Sites of Special Scientific Interest

A Site of Special Scientific Interest is an area of land designated by the Statutory Nature Conservation Organisation (SNCO) for the flora, fauna or geology to be found there. The SNCOs are:
England – Natural England (NE);
Wales – Countryside Council for Wales (CCW);
Scotland – Scottish Natural Heritage (SNH);
Northern Ireland – the Environment and Heritage Service (EHS), though in the case of Northern Ireland the protected site is referred to as an *Area* of Special Scientific Interest (ASSI.)

Sites first came to be designated in the 1960s and at that time were little more than a notification of interest to owners and planning authorities. Legislation evolved and a list of potentially damaging operations was supplied to the owner, who was required to notify the SNCO before carrying out any operation that may have a negative impact on the species or geology of interest and for which the site was designated. This has changed yet again and now if the owner wants to carry out work listed as a Potentially Damaging Operation he or she must request permission from the SNCO to do so before the operation is begun. The operations can include ditching, cutting and removal of trees and hedges, changes in a grazing regime and many more. Failure to request permission may well result in an investigation being carried out and the person responsible appearing in court.

In England and Wales these offences can only be reported for prosecution by Natural England or the Countryside Council for Wales and not through the more usual route by the police reporting the case to the Crown Prosecution Service. In Northern Ireland offences against ASSIs are investigated by the Environment and Heritage Service, though a file prepared by them is passed by them to the Public Prosecution Service. This differs from the situation in Scotland where the offences are investigated by the police and passed to the procurator fiscal for prosecution. Since the enactment of the Nature Conservation (Scotland) Act 2004 police in Scotland have been given specific powers to investigate these offences, including power to enter land to do so. These offences are invariably investigated by wildlife crime officers working alongside staff from Scottish Natural Heritage. This is a good use of police expertise, since as investigators they are well versed in preparing reports for submission to the procurator fiscal, while SNH staff has records of the land in question and the species for which it has received the protected status, plus expertise in the ecology and use of the protected site.

A second type of offence that can take place is what is described as a 'third party offence', where a person who is not the owner or occupier of the land causes damage or disturbance to a notified feature of the site. This could include disturbing nesting birds which are included in the notification or digging up plants on the land. Until the introduction of an amended offence under the Natural Environment and Rural Communities Act 2006, it was necessary not only prove that the person had intentionally or recklessly damaged a feature of the site but that he also knew that the site was a protected site. This latter element was often extremely difficult to prove.

All means are used to try to prevent damage taking place in the first instance, and in many instances where the protected area has been damaged, the SNCO, often with the assistance of the police, tries to encourage reinstatement of the damage without the need for a criminal investigation, which is seen as a last resort. Generally the suspect agrees to reinstate any damage done since the offence of intentionally or recklessly damaging a feature of the site can result in an unlimited fine, over and above any reinstatement order made by the court!

7. PAW – The Partnership for Action against Wildlife Crime

This is a multi-agency body comprising representatives of the organisations involved in wildlife law enforcement in the UK. It provides opportunities for statutory and non-Government organisations to work together to combat wildlife crime. Its main objective is to promote the enforcement of wildlife conservation legislation, particularly through supporting the networks of police wildlife crime officers and HM Revenue and Customs officers.

The PAW High Level Group is, by its name, the overseeing body of PAW that can ratify decisions made by lower echelons of the partnership, in this case the PAW Steering Group, in turn advised by the National Wildlife Crime Unit. It seems a complicated process but is a means of ensuring that the police, so far as wildlife crime is concerned, concentrate their main efforts on wildlife criminality affecting not only a considerable proportion of the public, as is the case with poaching and hare coursing offences, but also the criminality that has the most serious effect on species and habitat conservation. PAW has a number of working groups to concentrate on issues such as publicity, legislation, training and development of forensics targeted at aiding the investigation of wildlife crime.

Pete Charleston joined North Wales Police in 1978 and spent 23 years policing on the Isle of Anglesey. Promoted to Sergeant in 1985, in 2000 was appointed as the first fulltime wildlife crime officer in Wales policing the six counties covered by the force. Uniquely on appointment Pete was seconded to work with the Countryside Council for Wales, the Welsh Assembly Government's statutory conservation agency, the first police officer ever to be seconded to work with a conservation agency.

Over the next eight years Pete along with his team of divisional wildlife crime officers were responsible for the effective investigation of over 2000 wildlife crimes. He retired from the police service in February 2008 and is now employed in the dual role of wildlife crime advisor to the ACPO lead on wildlife crime and wildlife crime co-ordinator for Derbyshire Constabulary.

Joe Connelly graduated from Glasgow University with a degree in geology and has also studied marine science. He worked for six years as a geologist, including a spell off-shore, before changing career. This saw him employed for over eight years by Strathclyde Police as a welfare rights officer, a support staff role. A further career change within Strathclyde Police in 2001 made him a welcome second full-time wildlife crime officer in Scotland. He is a member of a number of PAW working groups.

Nick Crampton has been a Crown Prosecutor in Norfolk since 1988, with particular interest in the crimes that occur within the rural community and in wildlife conservation, especially in a European context, and the contribution that law enforcement can make He has provided specialist advice on wildlife crime cases and conducted a variety of such prosecutions since 1990. He has also given talks at wildlife crime training conferences regionally, nationally and in Hungary and Poland on the role of prosecutors and aspects of court presentation in wildlife crime cases. He is a member of BASC, RSPB, Birdlife Cyprus and Birdlife Malta.

Finlay Christine started off his career in the Gorbals, which he paradoxically describes as a tranquil hamlet in the south of Glasgow. In 1991 he was transferred to Mull for what was to be a three to five year secondment, taking on the mantle of wildlife crime officer after catching his first egg thief on the island in 1995. He then set up Mull Eagle Watch the following year to protect the nesting white-tailed and golden eagles and has been co-ordinating it ever since. He is due to retire from policing – still on the Isle of Mull – in 2009.

David Dawson has twenty nine years service with Northern Constabulary. During this period he has served on the Isle of Skye, Lochaber, the Isle of Lewis, and Shetland and is presently based at Kirkwall in Orkney where he is the local community safety officer. He previously worked as a gamekeeper and forest ranger before joining the police.

In 1987 he was appointed a wildlife liaison officer, then being only one of two in the entire Northern Constabulary area. He relinquished the role in 2006 owing to increased responsibilities within the wider field of community safety. Given his background, he maintains a keen interest in all rural affairs and particularly the relationship between field sports and conservation.

Andy Fisher is Head of the Metropolitan Police Wildlife Crime Unit and is responsible for the enforcement of laws protecting wildlife in London. He joined the Metropolitan Police in 1991 and was appointed as the Met's Wildlife Liaison Officer in 1993, launching Operation Charm in 1995. He now heads a police unit covering the whole of London and co-ordinating a network of local Wildlife Crime Officers in all of the London boroughs. He has taken part in many television and radio programmes and has represented the UK by hosting visiting government delegations, including several from China. He has also represented the UK in initiatives to assist other countries, including China and India, in protecting endangered species in their own countries. He has won a number of awards for his work.

Ian Guildford joined the South Wales Police in March 1989. He has had a life long interest in natural history and when time allows is a keen bird watcher. In 1997, Ian became the joint winner of the inaugural Wildlife Enforcer of the Year Award. In 2003 he was seconded to work with the Countryside Council for Wales as a full time wildlife and environmental crime officer. He currently sits on the three PAW groups, those of Training, Enforcers and Welsh working group.

Ruaraidh Hamilton has been with Lothian and Borders Police since 1982, being part-time wildlife crime officer in East Lothian for ten years before being given a full-time wildlife crime role in the Scottish Borders. His specialist interest in wild birds has taken him as far afield as South America.

Neil Hughes joined Leicestershire Constabulary in 1970 and was promoted to sergeant after eight year's service, a relatively short time in comparison to most promotions to that rank and was an inspector by 1987. He volunteered for the post of wildlife crime officer in 1990, a part-time post he held till his retiral in 2000. Most unusually, and to his great credit, he has since carried out this role for Leicestershire Constabulary as a special constable; unpaid apart from expenses but with the same police powers as a regular constable.

Nigel Lound has been with Lincolnshire Police since 1978. His wildlife crime officer role was made full-time in 2003. The fact that in the months of September to March in 2002, 2003 and 2004 he dealt with 1600 calls relating to hare coursing alone seems to more than justify his full-time position. In the first of his many badger-digging cases three men received substantial fines at court and one was imprisoned. Wildlife crime statistics made available in June 2008 to the PAW High Level Group show that Lincolnshire records a higher rate of reported wildlife crime and submissions of intelligence on wildlife crime than any other UK force.

Dave MacKinnon who really went to Aberdeen to study agriculture, finished up joining Grampian Police. Almost ten years of his police service included carrying the additional part-time responsibility, along with a handful of other Grampian officers, for the investigation of wildlife crime. He has now taken up the challenge as the first full-time wildlife crime officer in

Grampian Police, and the fourth in a full-time position amongst all eight Scottish police forces.

Andy McWilliam was the full-time wildlife crime officer for Merseyside Police from 1999 until he retired in 2006. He is now re-employed as an investigative support officer with the National Wildlife Crime Unit. His contribution to tackling wildlife crimes was fully recognised in 2002, when he won the prestigious WWF Enforcer of the Year Award and in addition won a National Certificate of Merit from the RSPCA for an outstanding level of dedication and commitment displayed in tackling wildlife crime. He was one of the best police officers in the country at eliciting intelligence about active wildlife criminals. Once he had the information the subject may have as well walked into the police station with his hands up, since Andy was methodical, innovative and thorough. Most importantly he never gave up.

Emma Meredith is the first full-time wildlife liaison officer with the Police Service of Northern Ireland and has been in the post since 2007. Her role is to act as a central point of contact within the PSNI, providing advice and support to police officers and police staff when animal crime and welfare issues require police investigation.

She has a keen interest in wildlife and animals. After completing her BSc Hons degree in 2003 from the University of Ulster in Jordanstown she worked as a learning manager/volunteer coordinator for a conservation organisation. She continues to develop her skills through training and has been successful in obtaining a scholarship to study wildlife crime and animal welfare internationally.

Ronnie Morris, from 1996 to his retiral in 2001, was Fife Constabulary's Force Wildlife Crime Co-ordinator. He was involved in the investigation of a variety of crimes against wildlife, including the shooting of cormorants and a great-crested grebe, badger-related crime, poisoning of birds of prey and poaching offences. He describes his involvement in the dog fighting case as a small pawn in a very extensive operation for which the senior officers in charge deserve considerable credit. Ronnie has written several short books about the wildlife and history of some of the islands in the Firth of Forth.

Enda Mullen like many of the contributors, has had a deep interest in wildlife from childhood, and while working as an educator she sought to pass this on to the children in her care. After completing an MSc in Protected Area Management at Birkbeck College in 1999 she joined the National Parks and Wildlife Service as a Conservation Ranger. She is now District Conservation Officer responsible for the Wicklow District.

Mark Rafferty was an officer in the Metropolitan Police before transferring to Lothian and Borders Police, where he had a part-time wildlife crime role for ten years. After twenty two years policing he took the unusual step of resigning and joining the Scottish SPCA, where he is now one of four investigations officers. His commitment and passion for animal welfare issues are unquestionable and he continues to be involved in many joint investigations with the police.

Alan Roberts served twenty years with Greater Manchester police and ten as a sergeant in Norfolk. Most of his time in

Norfolk was as wildlife crime officer, becoming the force co-ordinator for the last few years. He retired in 2007 and was re-employed by the National Wildlife Crime Unit as an investigative support officer carrying out preliminary investigations in order to gain evidence in the form of intelligence packages to be passed to wildlife crime officers. It seems an ideal way in which talent, enthusiasm and vast experience can be harnessed and utilised after the official retrial from frontline policing duties.

Gavin Ross has been interested in wildlife since childhood thanks to a rural upbringing in the Scottish Borders. He first became an outdoor pursuits instructor on the west coast of Scotland, then a game ranger on a private game reserve in South Africa. He has been with Lothian and Borders Police for ten years, during eight of which he has been a wildlife crime officer, conducting wildlife investigations, talks and events alongside his normal duties as a uniformed response officer.

Val Swan was an avid hunting and shooting enthusiast before becoming preoccupied with nature conservation issues. In 1979 he was successful in being included in the first batch of wildlife rangers recruited into the Wildlife Service to implement and enforce the provisions of the Wildlife Act 1976. He now has thirty years service with the National Parks and Wildlife Service, currently serving as Deputy Regional Manager for the North East Region, which comprises the counties of Louth, Meath, Dublin, Kildare, Laois and Offaly.

Bob Veighey joined Northern Constabulary in 1984. He began his career in Shetland, then worked in Badenoch and Strathspey, back north again to the northern-most mainland county, Caithness, then Ross-shire, and finally back to Shetland, where he has been for the last seven years. He has been wildlife crime officer for the Shetland Isles for the last five years.

INDEX